Hugo's Simplified System

German
in Three Months

Sigrid-B. Martin

Hugo's Language Books

This new and enlarged edition published in Great Britain
in 1997 by Hugo's Language Books,
an imprint of Dorling Kindersley Limited,
9 Henrietta Street, London WC2E 8PS

Visit us on the World Wide Web at http://www.dk.com

Copyright 1997 © Dorling Kindersley Ltd

A CIP catalogue record is available from the British Library.

ISBN 0 85285 160 X

'German in Three Months' is also available in a
pack with four 4 audio cassettes, ISBN 0 85285

Written by

Sigrid-B. Martin
Lecturer in German
University of Kent at Canterbury

set in 10/12pt Palatino by
Alastair Wardle
Reproduced, printed and bound in Italy by
L.E.G.O., Vicenza

Preface

'German in Three Months' has been written for us by Sigrid Martin, whose experience in teaching her native tongue ranges from beginners to post-graduate level. She has drawn on this expertise to produce a simple yet complete course for students aiming to acquire a good working knowledge of the language in a short time, and who will probably be studying alone at home.

The book begins with an explanation of German pronunciation, as far as this is possible without going too deeply into all the nuances and varying sounds involved. If you are working without a teacher, you should find that our system of 'imitated pronunciation' simplifies matters considerably. Using the book together with our cassette recordings (allowing you to hear the German text at the same time that you read it) is an ideal combination, giving another dimension to the course.

It has always been a principle of the Hugo method to teach only what is really essential. We assume that the student wants to learn German from a practical angle; the chapters contain those rules of grammar that will be of most use in this respect. Constructions are clearly explained, and the order in which everything is presented takes into consideration the need for rapid progress. Chapter 1 concentrates on pronunciation. Chapters 2–13 include exercises and conversations; later in the course you will move on to the use of idiom and colloquialisms, so necessary for a thorough grasp of conversational German. The reading passages following Chapter 13 provide an introduction to written German, to prepare you for reading German books and magazines. Answers to the exercises, and a full vocabulary list, appear at the back of the book.

Ideally you should spend about an hour a day on your work (slightly less, maybe, if you do not use the cassette recordings), although there is no hard and fast rule on this. Do as much as you feel capable of doing; if you have no special aptitude for language-learning, there is no point in forcing yourself beyond your daily capacity to assimilate new material. It is much better to learn a little at a time, and to learn that thoroughly. However, ideally you should try to complete one chapter each week.

In studying the chapters, first read each rule or numbered section carefully and re-read it to ensure that you have fully understood the grammar, then work through any following exercise(s) as they occur by writing down the answers. Check these by referring to the key at the back of the book; if you have made too many mistakes, go back over the instruction before attempting the same questions again. The conversational exercises and conversations should be read aloud and their constructions carefully noted. If you have the cassette recordings, you should listen to these at the same time as you read. Listen also to the spoken German of each exercise, both before you complete the written work and again as you check the answers. After you have listened to the conversations and read them aloud, see how closely you can imitate the voices on the recording. It is best to keep at all times your own running list of new words; this way, you will remember them better.

When you think you have completed a section satisfactorily (alternatively, just before your daily study period is over) go back over what you have recently done, to ensure that it is firmly committed to memory. When the course is completed, you should have a very good understanding of the language—more than sufficient for general holiday or business purposes, and enough to lead quickly into an examination syllabus if this is your eventual aim.

If time allows, you can experiment with what you have learned – and consolidate your learning – by tackling the passages in the Reading Practice section, most of which are typical examples of popular journalism. Each passage focuses on the new material covered by two chapters and should only be attempted after these have been completed. Do not make a written English translation but, at most, take a few notes and from these attempt to re-tell the contents (to yourself, to a teacher, or to someone learning with you) to check that you have grasped and can convey the sense of the passage. Any vocabulary not found in the German–English Mini-dictionary, which covers only the chapters themselves, is given below the passage concerned.

We hope you will enjoy 'German in Three Months', and we wish you success with your studies.

ACKNOWLEDGEMENTS

The author would like to thank especially her husband John Martin, for many years Director of the Institute of Languages & Linguistics in the University of Kent at Canterbury, without whose help she could never have written 'German in Three Months'. Thanks also to Naomi Laredo whose expert editing and calming influence in times of stress ensured that the text remained 'on course', and to those others who gave their encouragement and made comments on various drafts of this book.

Picture credits

Jacket: model photography Hanya Chala; ROBERT HARDING PICTURE LIBRARY: Bildagnetur Schuster/Gluck bottom right above; Hans Peter Merten centre right; Adam Woolfitt bottom left above; IMAGES COLOUR LIBRARY: top left; NEIL SETCHFIELD: top centre, centre left, bottom left below, bottom right below, spine bottom; ZEFA: top right, /Rossenbach bottom centre.

Contents

Chapter 1

Chapter 1 gives an explanation of German pronunciation and its relation to the written language. We deliberately avoid anything but passing references to meaning, and ask you – hard as it may seem – to resist the temptation to worry about meaning, just for this chapter, so that you can concentrate on the sounds of the words.

1 Speaking German

Although there are a few sounds in German which will be unfamiliar to you as a native speaker of English, on the whole English speakers find German easier to pronounce than French. Since the main thing is to be understood, don't worry if your pronunciation is less than perfect; to correct it, keep listening and practising, particularly with the cassettes which are an optional extra to this course.

Some concepts introduced here will seem strange at first, but as you work through the course they will become familiar. You will find it worthwhile to refer back to Chapter 1 at frequent intervals for practice and revision.

2 The alphabet and spelling

(a) The German alphabet contains all the 26 letters, small and capital, of the English alphabet. In addition, three of the vowel letters – **a/A, o/O, u/U** – also appear in the forms **ä/Ä, ö/Ö, ü/Ü**, which represent entirely different

9

sounds from the same letters without the 'Umlaut' symbol (¨) above.

(b) Note that double **ss** is always written **ß** (which never starts a word and occurs only as a small letter) *except* when the following two conditions hold good at the same time:

(i) the preceding vowel in the word is pronounced *short* (see Section 3);

(ii) another vowel follows *immediately* in the same word.

Even if these two conditions are fulfilled, the form **ß** is still used if the double **ss** ends either a prefix or a word that is part of a compound word. The following examples and comments show the principles involved:

blaß **mußte**	Preceding vowels are short but no vowel follows.
Füße	Vowel follows but preceding vowel is pronounced long.
Eßapfel **mißachten**	Preceding vowels are short, and vowels follow immediately, but the **ß** ends a word in a compound word (**Eß | apfel**) or a prefix (**miß | achten**).
Flüsse	Preceding vowel is short and vowel follows immediately.

(c) All nouns, not just names, begin with capital letters. The pronoun **Sie**, the formal word for 'you' (see Section 15), and related words (e.g. **Ihr** 'your') always begin with capitals. In correspondence only, the pronouns **Du** (see Section 31) and **Ihr** (see Section 76), used when addressing intimates, together with related words, begin with capitals. On the other hand, the first person singular pronoun ('I') starts with a small letter (**ich**).

10

(d) Here are the letters of the alphabet with their names given in our imitated pronunciation, which is explained in the following sections. These are the names used when spelling out words.

A	ah	J	yot	S	es
B	beh	K	kah	T	teh
C	tseh	L	el	U	oo
D	deh	M	em	V	fow
E	eh	N	en	W	veh
F	ef	O	oh	X	iks
G	geh	P	peh	Y	uepsilon
H	hah	Q	koo	Z	tset
I	ee	R	eer		

3 Spelling and pronunciation

There is a far greater consistency between spelling and pronunciation in German than exists in English. However, some letters consistently require a pronunciation different from the same letters in English, and some letters appear in combinations unfamiliar in English, so we need to mention these before looking at the sounds of German in detail. Try to say aloud each of the examples in this section and in Sections 4, 5, 6 and 7, preferably with the aid of the cassette or a native speaker of German. No English meanings are given for the examples, which have been chosen for their usefulness as illustrations.

The following letters are pronounced differently from their English counterparts, or are subject to different rules of pronunciation depending on their position:

Imitated pronunciation

b	[b],	[p]	At the start of words *and syllables*
d	[d],	[t]	pronounced as in English. At the end
g	[g],	[k],	of words *and syllables* (standing either
	[*h*],	[*k*]	alone or in a cluster of consonants of

which they may not be the last) these letters MUST be pronounced as **p, t** and **k** (or **ch**) respectively: this means that **habt** rhymes with **klappt**, that **wird** sounds exactly the same as **Wirt, Rad** like **Rat**, that **Erdöl** is spoken **Ert-öl**, and that **folg** could sound like **Volk, Krieg** like **kriech**. (All these words actually exist and some are therefore 'homophones': words spelt differently but sounding alike.)

c   Is used constantly in the combinations **ch** and **ck** but is rarely found on its own except in foreign words.

j   [y]   Is almost always spoken as English *y* at the start of a word (*yet, yonder*), thus **Junge, Jammer.**

q   Is always, as in English, in combination with **u**, but the combination is spoken differently, like English *k* + *v* in rapid succession, thus **quer, Quatsch, Qualität.**

s   [s],   [z]   Like English *s* (compare *s* in *sit, busy, its, is*) it is pronounced in two different ways: like the *s* in *sits* and *its*, and like the *z* sound in *busy* and *is*. However, distribution of the two types of **s** in German is exactly opposite to that in English. Whereas in English the *s*-sounding *s* occurs at the start of words (and syllables) and the *z*-sounding *s* is found (though not universally) at the end, German **s** (except in **sp** and **st**) is *always* pronounced z-sounding at the start and s-sounding at the end of words *and syllables*:

z-sounding: **sein, Symbol, Absicht (Ab I sicht), Fürsorge (Für I sorge), Rose (Ro I se), Riese (Rie I se)**

s-sounding: **Gast, längst, Wespe (Wes I pe), Muster (Mus I ter), meins, meines (mei I nes)**

Words containing both sounds: **süß, seins, seines (sei I nes), dieses (die I ses)**

	[sh]	*s* in the combinations **sp** and **st** at the start of words and syllables is spoken like English *sh*: **Speck, spät, spülen, gespannt (ge I spannt), Stamm, sterben, Strecke, steigen, erstaunt (er I staunt), verstimmt (ver I stimmt), Anstand (An I stand)**
th	[t]	Is never like *th* in *this* or *thing*, but pronounced simply as *t*/**t**. Found only in words of foreign origin, thus **Apotheke, Hypothek, Thymian, These.**
tion	[tsiohn]	Found only in the many 'imported' words ending in -**tion**, thus **Station, Aktion, Funktion, Tradition**
v	[f]	Is almost always like English *f* in *from, first*, thus **Vater, von, Verlag, bevor.**
w	[v]	Is like English *v* in *very*, thus **was, Wein, Weg, Wirt.**
y	[ue]	Is not like the English *y* in either *yet* or

13

very, but is pronounced like the German (short) vowel **ü** (see Section 4), thus **System, sympatisch.**

z	[ts]	Is NEVER like the English *z* as in *hazard,* but like *t* + *s* spoken in rapid succession, almost simultaneously, often with no more than a trace of the *t*. Something similar is found in the usual English pronunciation of the name *Mozart,* though **z** can also start a word, where it seems very odd to speakers of English: **Zeit, zu, Zinsen, Zange, Zorn, zusammen, beizeiten, inzwischen (in ǀ zwischen), Weizen (wei ǀ zen), Schnauze (Schnau ǀ ze), Konzert, Winzer, Geiz, Sitz, Franz, Holz, Harz, Lenz.**

The appearance of consonants in unfamiliar groups, or in unfamiliar places in words, can make a written foreign language difficult for the eye to grasp. The following combinations contain only sounds that the English speaker can easily pronounce, so it is well worthwhile getting used to *seeing* the combinations as 'blocks' for which the right pronunciation is ready to hand.

dsch	[dj]	Like the *j* in *jump.* Quite rare and only used for some foreign words: **Dschungel, Dschihad, Dschunke.**
gd	[kt]	Pronounced *kt,* like the end of *flicked.* Rare, but the first example given is much used: **Jagd, Magd.**
hd, hl(t), hm(t), hn(t), hr(t), ht		Ignore the **h**, which merely shows that the preceding vowel is pronounced *long* (see Section 4). Similarly ignore **h** between vowels, except in compounds: **Fehde, Mehl, wählt, lahm, rahmt, kühn, wohnt, wahr, lehrt, weht; sehen,**

ruhen BUT **Seehafen (See I hafen),
bleihaltig (blei I haltig).**

ng   There is no *g* sound in this combination
when it occurs between vowels, so care
is needed with words like **Anger,
Finger, Hunger.**

pf   This can come at the beginning or end
of words and syllables. *p* + *f* are spoken
in rapid succession, almost simultane-
ously, often with no more than a trace
of the *p*: **Pfeil, Pferd, Pfund, Dampfer,
impfen, Kupfer, Sumpf, Krampf,
glimpflich.**

sch, schl, schm,   **sch** is like *sh* in *shut, wish*. While **sch**
schn, schr, schw   can start or end words and syllables,
combinations with the further conso-
nant letter can only start them:
**Schande, Rausch, Schlampe,
schmelzen, Schnauze, Schraube,
schwitzen.**

tsch [ch]   This is like *(t)ch* in *chap, much, match*. It
is found less at the start than in the
middle or at the end of words: **tschüs,
Tscheche, Matsch, futsch,
Deutschland, Rutsch.**

tz   [ts]   This only occurs in the middle or at the
end of words. It is like the *ts* in *gets*, or
like German **z**: **plötzlich, platzen,
sitzen, Fritz, Gesetz.**

zw   [tsv]   This is like *t* + *s* + *v* spoken in rapid
succession and occurs only at the start
of words and syllables: **Zwang,
bezwingen (be I zwingen), Zwerg,
zwei, inzwischen (in I zwischen),
Zweck.**

4 Vowels and vowel combinations

Though there are only 8 vowel letters in German (the five of
the English alphabet, plus **ä, ö, ü**), there are potentially 16, in
practice 15, vowel sounds, because each vowel letter has two
pronunciations, a long and a short one. It is vital to note and
produce this distinction, as the long-short contrast is accompanied by a difference in the *nature* of the sound.

The spelling is sometimes an aid to knowing whether a
vowel is long or short:

A vowel is *long* if
- the vowel letter is doubled: **Beet, Saat, Boot**
- the vowel letter is followed by **h: Bahn, Huhn, Lohn**
- the vowel **i** is followed by **e: fies, mies, Grieß**
- the vowel letter is followed by **ß**, which is in turn
  immediately followed by a vowel letter in the same
  word (see Section 2(b)): **Füße, Blöße, Maße.**

A vowel is *short* if
- the vowel letter is followed by a doubled consonant
  letter or by **ck: Hütte, Affe, Zweck**
- the vowel letter is followed by **ss**, which is in turn
  immediately followed by a vowel letter in the same
  word (see Section 2(b)): **Flüsse, wissen, Masse**
- the vowel letter is followed by **ng: Rang, jung, ging**.

All the following vowel descriptions in terms of English
sounds are, of course, only approximations and no substitute for genuine models of pronunciation. One general,
though impressionistic, guideline to help you to know what
to aim at in the vowels and vowel combinations is a greater
tenseness and energy than with those of English. Avoid at all
costs substituting English vowel glides, where the nature of
the vowel sound changes progressively (as in standard
southern English *lane* and *home*, the vowel-glide sounds of
which do not exist in German), for any of the German
single-sound vowels. It is for this reason that we use northern English vowels as benchmarks, especially for the

German long vowels. Northern English vowels tend to have more of a single-sound quality than do those of standard southern English.

(a) *Vowels*

long **a** [ah] Long **a** as the vowel in northern English *father, barn.*

short a [ah] Short **a** as in northern English *fat, track.*
Bahn/Bann, Kahn/kann, Wahn/wann, kam/Kamm, mahn/Mann, Saat/satt

long **e** [eh] Long **e** as the vowel in northern English *lane, drape.*

short **e** [e] Short **e** as in standard southern English *get, crept.*
Beet/Bett, wen/wenn, den/denn, hehl/hell, fehl/Fell, gehl/gell

long **i(e)** [ee] Long **i(e)** as the vowel in northern English *keen, lean.*

short **i** [i] Short **i** as in standard southern English *fit, clip.*
ihm/im, schief/Schiff, Stil/still, rief/Riff, siech/sich, mies/miß

long **o** [oh] Long **o** as the vowel in northern English *home, bone.*

short **o** [o] Short o as in standard southern English *shot, crop.*
Hof/hoff, Ofen/offen, wohne/Wonne, Wohle/Wolle

long **u** [oo] Long **u** as the vowel in northern English *moon, doom.*

short **u** [oo] Short **u** as the vowel in standard southern English *put, foot.*
Pute/Putte, Ruhm/Rum, Kruke/Krucke, Mus/muß

long **ä** [e] Long **ä** similar to northern English

17

		vowel in *lane,* but more open in the direction of the vowel in standard southern English *leg.*
short ä	[e]	Short ä exactly like short German **e**. **käme/Kämme, stähle/Ställe, Pfähle/Fälle, wähle/Wälle**
long ö	[oe]	Neither has any parallel in English. For long ö say German long **e** while rounding and protruding the lips.
short ö	[oe]	For short ö say German short **e** while rounding and protruding the lips. Both are similar to the tight, pursed vowel of French *oeuf.* **Höhle/Hölle, Flöße/flösse**
long ü	[ue]	Neither has any parallel in English. For long ü say German long **i(e)** while rounding and protruding the lips.
short ü	[ue]	For short ü say German short **i** while rounding and protruding the lips. Both are similar to the tight, pursed vowel in French *tu, une.* **Wüste/wüßte, Hüte/Hütte, fühlen/füllen, führst/Fürst**

(b) *Vowel combinations or glides*

Vowel combinations are always pronounced *long.* All three glides somewhat resemble sounds from standard southern English, but they can be made to sound much more German if you make a special effort to move the tongue (and jaw) more dramatically than for the matching English sounds.

| **ai/ei** [y] | Similar to the standard southern English glide in *bribe, guide*: **Hain, Mai, Kai, weiß, Kleid, weich.** |
| **au** [ow] | Similar to the standard southern English glide in *cow, mouth*: **Raum, Zaun, Maul, Haus, Haut, Raub.** |

äu/eu	[oy]	Similar to the standard southern English glide in *void, annoy*: **häuft, läuft, Säume, deutet, freut, neun.**

(c) *Unstressed syllables containing* **e** *or* **er**

[e] Unstressed (unaccented) syllables containing the vowel letter **e** require a sound similar to that indicated in English *property, relative, anemone, Saturday*, but with a trace more of the short **c** described in (a) above: **Befund, Gericht, waagerecht, Hilferuf.**

The same sound is required if the **e** ends a word, and the sound ending English *never, weather* is undesirable because the jaw drops further, resulting in a sound closer to unstressed **er: Hilfe, welche, Menge, ihre.**

Essentially the same sound is required if the **e** is followed by a consonant (other than **r**): **Hallenbad, Spiegelei, Dankesbrief, deutet.**

[er] Unstressed syllables containing the letters **er** require a sound similar to that in standard southern English *hut, clutch*, and the **r** is NOT pronounced in this particular context: **Wiederkehr, Kinderwagen, Messerkante, besser, heller, ihrer.**

The same sound, only lengthened, is required if the **er** is followed by **n**. Again the **r** is not pronounced: **gestern, Brüdern, andernfalls, kentern.**

The distinction between **e** and **er**, between **en** and **ern**, is essential, since understanding correctly and being correctly understood depend on it. The following pairs show the contrast: **Ehe/eher, Feste/fester, Silbe/Silber, Güte/Güter, Lehren/Lehrern wischen/Wischern, Wäschen/Wäschern.**

5 Consonants

You saw in Section 3 that most of the consonants present no intrinsic difficulty for the English learner. We need now, therefore, consider only the three that do: **ch**, **l** and **r**.

ch		Although always using the same letters, this has two radically different versions, neither found in English:

(i)　[*h*]　After **e, ei, eu, i, ie, ä, äu, ü,** and after consonants:
The best way to achieve the sound required is to whisper very forcefully words like *Hugo, human,* and then to use the initial sound of the *h* for German **ch: Blech, Reich, Seuche, mich, riechen, Bäche, Bäuche, Küche, Storch, Dolch, durch.**

The same sound is used in three common words of foreign origin, **Chemie, China, Chirurg,** and at the start of the diminutive ending **-chen** ('little ...'), no matter what precedes: **Mädchen, Riemchen, Häuschen, Küßchen, Gläschen, Frauchen.**

It is also a very common pronunciation of the consonant letter **g**, either alone or with other consonants, when at the end of a word or syllable following any of the vowel and vowel-glide sounds listed above. It is thus an alternative to the pronunciation of such **g**s as **ks** (see Section 3): **wichtig, grantig, Predigt, liegst, Zweig, gütig.**

(ii)　[*k*]　After **a, au, o, u:**
This is akin to the Scottish pronunciation of *ch* in *loch, Pitlochry,* and is made by tensing the back of the throat while forcing plenty of breath through it: **auch, Bach, Suche, Loch, brauchen, Sucht, machen.**

The same sound is also a very common pronunciation of the consonant letter **g**, either alone or with other consonants, when at the end of a word or syllable following any of the vowel and vowel-glide sounds listed above. It is thus an alternative to the pronunciation of such **g**s as **k**s (see Section 3): **Zug, wagt, mag, saugt, klug, flog, Sog, fragt.**

l   Each English speaker has a range of pronunciations of *l* according to its position in a word and the sounds that surround it. German **l**, however, whatever its environment, is restricted to one type only. The closest parallels in standard southern English are the *l* sounds in *clean, leek, language* (though even these are not totally right), whereas those in *vault, feel, Oliver, culvert, apple* are very different from the German sound. Consequently it is the German **l** in such positions as these that needs the most care and practice:
lieb, leben, lang, laut, Leute;
Klippe, Klang, Flamme, Klug, Flucht;
goldig, Walzer, älter, albern, ulkig;
belebt, Brille, Rolle, völlig; fällig;
Esel, fühl, voll, wohl, Stahl;
wedelt, wählt, Silber, Felder, Helm.

r   The **r** sound, when it is needed (and in many cases where there is a letter **r** it is not pronounced), is best made at the back of the throat in the same place as **ch** (ii), but with much less breath force. No **r** sound found in standard southern English is really satisfactory.

r must be pronounced as the consonant described above
- alone at the start of a word: **Rand, rund, Rasen, Riese**
- after another consonant at the start of a word: **Frau, grün, Gras, Gruß**

21

- between vowels or vowel glides in the middle of words: **Beere, Fähre, Karre, mürrisch, waren.**

r is not pronounced as a consonant but merely affects the preceding vowel sound, often lengthening it or turning it into a sort of vowel glide
- alone at the end of a word or syllable: **besser, woher, war, klar, Herr, Meer, mehr, fror, gar, wurde, warte, würdig** (**Narr** is an exception and needs the consonant)
- before another consonant at the end of a word or syllable: **Schwert, Wurst, Herz, warnte, horchte.**

6 The hiatus or stop

Whereas in standard southern English the words in a phrase or sentence run into one another, so that a word beginning with a vowel appears to borrow the final consonant of the preceding word as a bridge, German does not allow this. Words beginning with a vowel have to start with the hiatus or 'stop'. This is not difficult to do – simply clear your throat gently in a whisper – but it is difficult to use. It is required even within a word, when the word is a compound of two or more words or contains a prefix before a vowel. The stop is also required to separate a vowel ending from a vowel beginning. For example:

mach * aus, im * Auge, hau * ab, Vor*arbeiter, miß*achten, ge*einigt, im * Ofen, würde * ich * auch

Compare **hau * ab** with, say, *How are you?*, and **Vor*arbeiter** with *for ages*.

7 Stressed (accented, emphasised) syllables

Effective speech depends on applying the speech rhythms and tunes of a language, and the rhythms and tunes of phrases and sentences are best learnt by imitation. However, within the limits of individual words it is useful to note that in German the stress usually falls on the first syllable, though there are many exceptions. One reliable rule is that whereas all English words starting with *un-* are unstressed on that first syllable, such words in German have stress on the **un-**:

únglücklich, únerfahren, únfreundlich, úngeduldig

German creates many conglomerate words out of smaller word-units. In such cases the stress is on the normally stressed syllable of the first word-unit:

kréideweiß, Pláttenspieler, Bríllenetui, Studéntenwohnheim (kreide | weiß, Platten | spieler, Brillen | etui, Studenten | wohn | heim)

Most of the exceptions to first-syllable stress are either words of foreign origin (though they do not necessarily keep the stress of the language of origin) or words containing specifically unstressed first syllables or prefixes, explained in Section 47(b):

Foreign words:
kontrollíeren, telefoníeren, Maschíne, Pakét, offiziéll
unstressed prefixes:
be | spréchen, miß | bráuchen, ver | ráten, ge | língen, er | röten

However, some short words in frequent use are also exceptions, while combinations with **da-** and **wo-** (see Sections 40 and 63(a)) are usually not stressed on the **da-** or **wo:**
jedóch, sogár, damít, dazú, danében, woráuf, inzwíschen

In our imitated pronunciation, the stressed syllable is printed in bold type. Good dictionaries give reliable information about stress and also about the length of vowels.

8 Punctuation

German uses punctuation in a more formal way than English, so that relating commas to speech pauses and meaning as in the following is not possible. Commas are always inserted between such word sequences:

My sister, who hates noise, was sent to a hotel next to a disco.
The girl who rang yesterday was a friend of my sister's.

In German, commas would follow *girl* and *yesterday*.

The punctuation used for quoted speech is different from English usage (see Section 80), and colons are used much more liberally, often to introduce quite short inserts into the middle of sentences. The exclamation mark is also found more frequently than in English.

Chapter 2

In this chapter you will learn some greetings and useful everyday phrases. The chapter also introduces three important features of German:

- *The order of words in a German sentence is often different from English*
- *The German word for 'the' varies according to the gender (masculine, feminine or neuter) of the noun it refers to and whether it is singular or plural*
- *The plurals of nouns are formed by adding various endings, and not generally by adding '-(e)s' as in English.*

9 Word endings and word sequences

There are two surprises in store for the English speaker who is beginning to learn German:

(a) Words that in English never vary, like 'the' and 'a/an', and simple invariable suffixes, like '-(e)s' for the plural (dog → dogs, class → classes) have no single equivalents in German but present us with sets of equivalents to choose from.

(b) The sequence in which the words in a sentence appear in German may and often must be different from the sequence in the English equivalent. 'I can't find the key because it's too dark' would emerge in German as 'I can the key not find because it too dark is' or 'The key can I not find because it too dark is'.

These two features in particular mean that you have to think differently to speak, write and *understand* German. To enable you to achieve this in the most effective way, we separate (a) and (b), first firmly establishing the principles behind (a) and introducing (b) gradually from Chapter 7.

10 Greetings, everyday phrases

However, first note some conversational phrases that you are bound to need – or at least could use – immediately:

All over Germany the commonest greeting during the daytime is **Guten Tag!** (alternatively, in the morning, **Guten Morgen!**). In the evening **Guten Abend!** is required. In southern Germany and Austria **Grüß Gott!** is usual at any time of day. All these are often accompanied by a handshake, even within the family. After the greeting one person will often add **Wie geht's?** or **Wie geht's Ihnen?** ('How are you?'), to which the response is usually **Danke, gut,** or **Gut, danke,** or simply **Danke.**

IMITATED PRONUNCIATION: **goo**-ten tahk; **goo**-ten **moer**-gen; **goo**-ten **ah**-bent; grues got; vee gehts **ee**-nen; **dahng**-ke goot

---

Exercise 1

Practise all the sentences in the dialogue below until you know them by heart.

Two impecunious customers at a refreshment kiosk

Kunde	Guten Tag!
Customer	*Hello!*
Besitzerin	Guten Tag! Bitte schön ...?
Proprietress	*Hello! Yes please ...?*

K	Zwei Coca-Cola und eine Wurst mit Brot, bitte.
	Two Coca-Colas and one sausage with bread, please.
B	Was? Sie wollen zwei Cola aber nur eine Wurst?
	What? You want two Colas but only one sausage?
K	Ja ..., das heißt, ja und nein. Wie teuer ist eine Wurst?
	Yes ..., I mean yes and no. How much is a sausage?
B	Nur zwei Mark.
	Only two marks.
K	Na gut, dann zwei Cola und zweimal Wurst mit Brot.
	All right, then two Colas and twice sausage with bread.
B	Bitte schön ... Sechs Mark zusammen.
	Here you are ... Six marks altogether.
K	Danke schön. Auf Wiedersehen!
	Thank you. Goodbye!
B	Auf Wiedersehen!
	Goodbye!

11 'the' and gender

German has a total of six words for 'the': **der, die, das, den, dem, des,** so it is best to think of the word as **d. .** (like the 'th.' of English 'the') plus a variable ending. The correct choice of ending depends on three factors, one of which is gender.

All German naming words (or nouns) belong to one of three gender groups: masculine (*m*), feminine (*f*) or neuter (*n*). Most – but not all – nouns of male/female beings are masculine/feminine respectively, but this is not very useful as a guide. It is much easier from the start to learn each noun with the appropriate **der, die** or **das** in front of it, as shown in the following sentences:

der Junge (*m*) ist krank (*the boy is ill*), so der Junge
der Preis (*m*) ist hoch (*the price is high*), so der Preis
die Tante (*f*) ist freundlich (*the aunt is kind*), so die Tante
die Farbe (*f*) ist dunkel (*the colour is dark*), so die Farbe
das Kind (*n*) ist nett (*the child is nice*), so das Kind
das Haus (*n*) ist alt (*the house is old*), so das Haus

IMITATED PRONUNCIATION: de*er* **yoong**-*e* ist krahnk;
de*er* prys; h<u>oh</u>*k*; d<u>ee</u> **tahn**-t*e*; **froynt**-li*h*; d<u>ee</u> **fah**-b*e*;
doong-k*e*l; dahs kint; net; dahs hows; ahlt

Exercise 2

*Learn the lists of words in (a) about house and family, saying
each word with* **der, die** *or* **das** *in front of it. Then cover up the
lists and say the jumbled sequence in (b) providing each word
with the correct* **der, die, das,** *checking that you also know the
meaning. Finally cover up (b) as well and say the German words
(preceded by* **der, die, das**) *for the jumbled English list in (c).*

*(Note: We shall not use this type of exercise again, but it is one
that you will need to devise for yourself with each new set of
words, chapter by chapter.)*

(a)

m		*f*		*n*	
Mann	man/ husband	**Frau**	woman/ wife	**Kind**	child
Vater	father	**Mutter**	mother	**Mädchen**	girl
Sohn	son	**Tochter**	daughter	**Haus**	house
Bruder	brother	**Schwester**	sister	**Zimmer**	room
Wirt	landlord	**Wirtin**	landlady	**Fenster**	window
Tisch	table	**Küche**	kitchen	**Bett**	bed
Stuhl	chair	**Tür**	door	**Wasser**	water
Schrank	cupboard	**Zeitung**	newspaper	**Auto**	car
Flur	hall	**Uhr**	clock	**Buch**	book
Hund	dog	**Katze**	cat	**Messer**	knife

(b) **Auto, Fenster, Wirt, Uhr, Tochter, Haus, Flur, Messer, Tür, Hund, Küche, Katze, Bruder, Mann, Kind, Zeitung, Sohn, Schwester, Stuhl, Buch, Wirtin, Schrank, Frau, Bett, Vater, Zimmer, Mutter, Wasser, Mädchen, Tisch**

(c) book, knife, sister, door, newspaper, woman, room, landlord, car, table, water, clock, house, window, child, cupboard, girl, cat, kitchen, father, dog, brother, daughter, hall, mother, chair, son, man, landlady, bed

IMITATED PRONUNCIATION: mahn; **fah**-t*er*; z*ohn*; **broo**-d*er*; vi*ert*; tish; sht*ool*; shrahnk; fl*ooer*; hoont; frow; **moo**-t*er*; to**kt***er*; **shves**-t*er*; **vier**-tin; **kue**-*he*; t*ueer*; **tsy**-toong; *ooer*; **kaht**-s*e*; kint; **m***et-hen*; hows; **tsi**-m*er*; **fens**-t*er*; bet; vah-s*er*; **ow**-t*oh*; b*ook*; **me**-s*er*

12 'the' and singular/plural

When the noun is in the plural (i.e. refers to more than one) the distinction between *m*, *f* and *n* in 'the' disappears and **die** is used for all:

die	**Preise sind hoch** **Farben sind dunkel** **Häuser sind alt**	*the*	*prices are high* *colours are dark* *houses are old*	

Summary:

singular			plural
m	*f*	*n*	*m f n*
der	**die**	**das**	**die**

IMITATED PRONUNCIATION: de*er*; d*ee*; dahs; d*ee*

29

13 Plural of nouns

You will have seen in Section 12 that though the plural **die** is simple, the noun itself has no single way of showing the plural, like the English '-(e)s'. You must therefore learn each noun not only with **der, die, das,** but also with its plural.

There are a few rough guidelines for emergency use:

(a) *f* nouns usually add -**n** or -**en** to the singular:

    Küche →**Küchen**   but   **Mutter** →**Mütter**
    Zeitung →**Zeitungen**   **Tochter** →**Töchter**
    Frau →**Frauen**   **Wirtin** →**Wirtinnen**

(b) *m* and *n* nouns often add
    -**e** (**Hund** →**Hunde**)
    -**en** (**Bett** →**Betten**)
    -**er** (**Kind** →**Kinder**)
and any of these endings may be accompanied by a change in the sound of the following vowels of the singular:
    -**a**- (**Mann** → **Männer**)
    -**o**- (**Sohn** → **Söhne**)
    -**u**- (**Stuhl** → **Stühle**)
    -**au**-(**Haus** → **Häuser**)

(c) Some *m* and *n* nouns do not change at all:
    Zimmer → **Zimmer**
    Messer → **Messer**

(d) With some *m* and *n* nouns the only change is that the vowel sound of the singular is changed (by adding ¨):
    Vater → **Väter**
    Bruder → **Brüder**

(e) Some words taken from other languages add -**s**:
    Auto → **Autos**

Exercise 3

(a) *lists the words you learned in Exercise 2, but they are now shown first with the plural abbreviation generally used in dictionaries etc.† and then in the full plural form. Learn these, then cover up* (a) *and try to say the plurals of all the jumbled singular words in* (b).

(a)

Mann (⸚er)	Männer	Frau (-en)	Frauen
Vater (⸚)	Väter	Mutter (⸚)	Mütter
Sohn (⸚e)	Söhne	Tochter (⸚)	Töchter
Bruder (⸚)	Brüder	Schwester (-n)	Schwestern
Wirt (-e)	Wirte	Wirtin (-nen)	Wirtinnen
Tisch (-e)	Tische	Küche (-n)	Küchen
Stuhl (⸚e)	Stühle	Tür (-en)	Türen
Schrank (⸚e)	Schränke	Zeitung (-en)	Zeitungen
Flur (-e)	Flure	Uhr (-en)	Uhren
Hund (-e)	Hunde	Katze (-n)	Katzen
Kind (-er)	Kinder	Bett (-en)	Betten
Mädchen (-)	Mädchen	Wasser	*No plural*
Haus (⸚er)	Häuser	Auto (-s)	Autos
Zimmer (-)	Zimmer	Buch (⸚er)	Bücher
Fenster (-)	Fenster	Messer (-)	Messer

†*In later word lists and in the Mini-dictionary, the plural of each noun will be indicated by the appropriate abbreviation in brackets.*

(b) Auto, Fenster, Wirt, Uhr, Tochter, Haus, Flur, Messer, Tür, Hund, Küche, Katze, Bruder, Mann, Kind, Zeitung, Sohn, Schwester, Stuhl, Buch, Wirtin, Schrank, Frau, Bett, Vater, Zimmer, Mutter, Mädchen, Tisch

IMITATED PRONUNCIATION: **me**-n*er*; **fe**-t*er*; **zoe**-n*e*; **brue**-d*er*; **vier**-t*e*; **ti**-sh*e*; **shtue**-l*e*; **shreng**-k*e*; **floo**-r*e*; **hoon**-d*e*; **frow**-*en*; **mue**-t*er*; **toeh**-t*er*; **shves**-t*ern*; **vier**-ti-n*en*; **kue**-h*en*; **tue**-ren **tsy**-toong-*en*; **oo**-ren; **kaht**-s*en*; **kin**-d*er*; **met**-h*en*; **hoy**-z*er*; **tsi**-m*er*; **fens**-t*er*; **be**-t*en*; **ow**-t*ohs*; **bue**-h*er*; **me**-s*er*

Chapter 3

Chapter 3 introduces the important concept of 'case' in German. You will also learn:

- *more about the German word for 'the'*
- *the German words for 'I' and 'me', 'we' and 'us', etc.*
- *the present tense of two of the most commonly used German verbs – 'to be' and 'to have'*
- *the present tense of many other verbs, which follow a regular pattern.*

14 'the' and case

You have seen that the choice of **der, die, das,** etc. is affected by:
(i) gender (*m/f/n*)
(ii) number (*singular/plural*)
The third factor determining the choice is case, which means the function of a noun in the idea expressed in the sentence. Compare:

(a) **Der Hund ist harmlos.**   *The dog is harmless.*
(b) **Der Junge liebt den Hund.**   *The boy loves the dog.*

In (a) it is clearly the *dog* that *is* or *does* something (in this particular case *is*), while in (b) it is the *boy* that *is* or *does* something (in this case *does*), and the *dog* has become the thing *affected* by the boy's doing. In order to refer to these roles easily we can say that the *be-er* or *doer* is the *subject* in a sentence, and the thing *directly affected,* like the dog here, is the *direct object.* We shall need to use these terms often, so the abbreviations SU and DO will be useful. Returning to the German sentences, we can now say that in (a) **der Hund**

has the *subject* (SU) function; in (b) **der Junge** has the subject
function and **den Hund** has the direct object (DO) function.
Note the change from **der** to **den**. This particular change,
required when a *m* noun is used as DO instead of SU, does
not apply to singular *f* and *n* nouns or to plural nouns.
Nevertheless, native speakers of German have a strong
sense of case even when there is no visible change, and this
is something you will also get a feel for.

Summary:

	singular			plural
	m	*f*	*n*	*m f n*
SU	**der**			**die**
DO	**den**	**die**	**das**	

15 'I, me, we, us, you ...' (pronouns)

		person						
		1st		2nd	3rd			
		sing.	plural		singular			plural
					m	*f*	*n*	
case	SU	**ich**	**wir**		**er**			
		I	we	**Sie†**	he	**sie**	**es**	**sie**
	DO	**mich**	**uns**	you	**ihn**	she/her	it	they/
		me	us		him			them

†Except when addressing intimates (see Sections 31 and 76)

IMITATED PRONUNCTATION: d<u>eh</u>n; i*h*; mi*h*; v<u>ee</u>*er*; oons;
z<u>ee</u>; e*er*; <u>ee</u>n; z<u>ee</u>; es; z<u>ee</u>

16 Verbs: present tense of 'to be', 'to have' and 'to make'

After naming words (nouns) and their substitutes (pronouns), we need – to make sentences – process words or verbs. Like 'to be' and 'to have', **sein** and **haben** are exceptional but indispensable, while **machen** ('to make') is a model for all standard German verbs, just as 'to work' would be for standard English verbs. Here are the verb forms required to denote present-time processes (e.g. 'I work', 'I am working', 'I do work'). We call this the *present tense*.

(a) to be, **sein**

I	am	**ich**	**bin**
we		**wir**	
you	are	**Sie**	**sind**
they		**sie**	
he		**er**	
she	is	**sie**	**ist**
it		**es**	

(b) to have, **haben**

I	have	**ich**	**habe**
we		**wir**	
you	have	**Sie**	**haben**
they		**sie**	
he		**er**	
she	has	**sie**	**hat**
it		**es**	

(c) to make, **machen**

I	make	**ich**	**mache**
we		**wir**	
you	make	**Sie**	**machen**
they		**sie**	
he		**er**	
she	makes	**sie**	**macht**
it		**es**	

Verbs are found in a dictionary, and in the Mini-dictionary, in the form *stem* + **en**, e.g. **mach** + **en** → **machen.** To make the present tense of most verbs, you simply take the stem and add these endings:

1st person singular	(I ...):	**-e**
1st person plural	(we ...):	
2nd person { singular / plural	(you ...):	**-en**
3rd person plural	(they ...):	
3rd person singular	(he etc. ...):	**-t** **-et** for *stems* ending in **-d** or **-t**

Exercise 4

(a) *Learn the following verbs and then translate the sentences in* (b):

lieben	to love	**rufen**	to call
kaufen	to buy	**kommen**	to come
machen	to make	**bringen**	to bring
holen	to fetch	**trinken**	to drink

(b) *Translate into German:*
1 The father loves the landlady. Der Vater liebt die Wirtin.
2 It is harmless (**harmlos**)! Es ist harmlos.
3 He buys the newspaper. Er kauft die Zeitung.
4 She makes the beds. Sie macht die Betten.
5 The daughter fetches the car. Die Tochter holt das Auto.
6 She calls the cat and the dog. Sie ruft die Katz und den Hund.
7 he cat and the dog come. Die Katz und der Hund kommen.
8 The landlady brings water. Die Wirtin bringt Wasser.
9 Father, landlady, daughter, dog and cat drink the water.
Vater, Wirtin, Tochter, Hund und Katz
trinken das Wasser.

IMITATED PRONUNCIATION: (16) zyn; bin; zint; ist; **hah**-ben; **hah**-be; haht; **mah**-ken; **mah**-ke; mahkt; (Ex. 4) **lee**-ben; **kow**-fen; **mah**-ken; **hoh**-len; **roo**-fen; **ko**-men; **bring**-en; **tring**-ken

Vocabulary

Practise all the sentences in the conversation that follows until you know them by heart. These are new words:

Entschuldigung!	Excuse me!
suchen	to look for
die **Touristeninformation**	tourist information office
liegen	to be (situated)
am	in/on the
der **Theaterplatz**	Theatre Square
wie?	how?
dahin	(to) there
nicht	not
leicht	easy
Moment mal	just a moment
gehen	to go
über	over, across
die **Kreuzung (-en)**	crossroads
zweite	second
die **Straße (-n)**	street
rechts	on the right
der **Marktplatz (¨e)**	marketplace
sehen	to see
dann	then
die **Kirche (-n)**	church
das **Gasthaus (¨er)**	inn
die **Rose (-n)**	rose
nehmen	to take
zwischen	between
eins	one
zwei	two
drei	three
vierte	fourth
immer geradeaus	straight ahead
für	for
etwa	about
fünfhundert	five hundred
der **Meter (-)**	metre
finden	to find

sofort	immediately
furchtbar	terribly
schwierig	difficult
es macht nichts	it doesn't matter
um	at (time of day)
dieser	this
die Zeit (-en)	time
sowieso	anyway
geschlossen	closed

IMITATED PRONUNCIATION: ent-**shool**-di-goonk;
zoo-ken; dee **too**-**ris**-ten*in-foe-mah-tsiohn; **lee**-gen; ahm;
deer teh-**ah**-ter-plahts; vee; dah-**hin**; niht; lyht; **moh**-**ment**
mahl; **geh**-en; **ue**-ber; dee **kroy**-tsung; **tsvy**-te; dee **shtrah**-se,
rehts; deer **mahkt**-plahts; **zeh**-en; dahn; dee **keeer**-he, dahs
gahst-hows; dee **roh**-ze; **neh**-men; **tsvi**-shen; yns; tsvy; dry;
feeer-te; i-mer ge-**rah**-de*ows; **fueer**; et-vah; **fuenf**-hoon-dert;
deer **meh**-ter; **fin**-den; **zoh**-**foert**; **fooerht**-bah; **shvee**-rih; es
mahkt nihts; oom; **dee**-zer; dee tsyt; **zoh**-vee-zoh; ge-**shlo**-sen

---

CONVERSATION

An encounter in the street

Touristin	**Entschuldigung! ... ich suche die** **Touristeninformation.**
Tourist	*Excuse me ... I'm looking for the tourist information office.*
Passant	**Ja ... die liegt am Theaterplatz.**
Passer-by	*Oh ... that's in Theatre Square.*
T	**Und wie komme ich dahin?**
	And how do I get there?
P	**Das ist nicht so leicht ... Moment mal ...** **Sie gehen über die Kreuzung,**
	That's not so easy ... Just a moment ... *You go over the crossroads,*

zweite Straße rechts, über den Marktplatz.
second street on the right, across the marketplace.
Sie sehen dann die Kirche und das
Gasthaus Zur Rose.
You'll then see the church and the Rose Inn.
Sie nehmen die Straße zwischen Gasthaus
You take the street between (the) inn
und Kirche, dann...
and (the) church, then ...
eins ... zwei ... drei ... ja, dann die vierte
one ... two ... three ... yes, then the fourth
Straße rechts, dann immer geradeaus
street on the right, then straight ahead
für etwa fünfhundert Meter.
for about five hundred metres.
Sie finden dann
You'll then find
sofort den Theaterplatz.
(the) Theatre Square immediately.

T **O, das ist furchtbar schwierig!**
Oh, that's terribly difficult!

P **Es macht nichts, die Touristeninformation**
It doesn't matter, the information office
ist um diese Zeit sowieso geschlossen.
is closed at this time anyway.

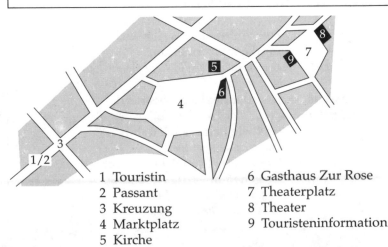

1 Touristin	6 Gasthaus Zur Rose
2 Passant	7 Theaterplatz
3 Kreuzung	8 Theater
4 Marktplatz	9 Touristeninformation
5 Kirche	

Chapter 4

> *In this chapter you will learn:*
>
> * *the German words for 'a/an' and 'not a/an', and how they vary in a similar way to **d**. .*
> * *the numbers from zero to a million, and how to talk about years and prices*
> * *the 'indirect object' case and some verbs which are used with it.*

17 'a/an'

German uses the same word for 'a/an' as it does for 'one': **ein**. When **ein** is used to mean 'a/an' (or 'one' in front of nouns, e.g. 'one cup') it has these endings:

	singular		
	m	*f*	*n*
SU	ein		
DO	einen	eine	ein

Used thus **ein** has of course no plural (its meaning is by definition singular). As in English, sometimes just the plural noun alone is used for the plural, or sometimes the noun is preceded by words like 'some' (German **einige**) or 'several' (**mehrere**) or 'a few' (**ein paar**, always found in this form, without endings).

Wir haben { Freunde / einige Freunde / mehrere Freunde / ein paar Freunde } hier.

ein has a parallel, **kein**, which means 'not a / not an' or
'no ...', and this naturally does have a plural (cf. 'no friends').

	singular			plural
	m	*f*	*n*	*m f n*
SU	**kein**	**keine**	**kein**	**keine**
DO	**keinen**			

Whereas in English we generally say, for example, 'I haven't
any friends', in German the expression is always on the pattern of **Ich habe keine Freunde. kein** is therefore in constant
use, as the following examples show (the phrases in brackets
give the literal meanings):

Wir trinken kein Bier.
We don't drink beer. (We drink no beer.)
Ich habe keine Ahnung.
I haven't a clue. (I have no clue/no idea.)
Kein Mensch glaubt so etwas.
*Nobody would believe anything like that. (No person believes such
a thing.)*
Sie hat Angst, aber er hat keine Angst.
She is afraid but he is not. (She has fear but he has no fear.)
Er hat keinen Beruf.
He isn't trained for anything. (He has no profession/trade.)
Wir sind keine Anfänger.
We aren't beginners. (We are no beginners.)

Finally, stating someone's job does not involve **ein**, while
stating what someone is *not* is usually done with **nicht**
('not'):

Die Mutter ist Lehrerin.
The mother is a teacher.
Er ist nicht Zahnarzt, er ist Kinderarzt.
He's not a dentist, he's a paediatrician.

Exercise 5

Translate the following sentences into German. You will need these new words:

to build	**bauen**
flat	**die Wohnung (-en)**
problem	**das Problem (-e)**
to install	**installieren**
water system	**das Wassersystem (-e)**
electricity	**die Elektrizität**
electrician	**der Elektriker (-)**
catastrophe	**die Katastrophe (-n)**

1 They are buying a house and making flats.
2 One flat hasn't got a kitchen.
3 That's a problem and they are building a kitchen.
4 One flat hasn't any water.
5 That's also a problem but the father is installing a water system.
6 One flat hasn't got electricity.
7 That's no problem. The son is an electrician.
8 One flat has a kitchen, water, electricity, and some cupboards, but no windows.
9 That's not a problem, it's a catastrophe.

IMITATED PRONUNCIATION: **bow**-*e*n; d*ee* **voh**-noong; dahs prob-**lehm**; in-stah-**lee**-r*e*n; dahs **vah**-s*e*r-zues-t**ehm**; d*ee**e-lek-tri-tsi-**tet**; d*eer**e-**lek**-tri-k*e*r, d*ee* kah-tahs-**troh**-f*e*

18 Numerals: cardinal numbers

0	**null**	6	**sechs**
1	**eins**	7	**sieben**
2	**zwei**	8	**acht**
3	**drei**	9	**neun**
4	**vier**	10	**zehn**
5	**fünf**		

First learn to count from 0 to 10. **Null** is needed mainly when citing decimals or reading out single digits (as sometimes in telephone numbers).

11	**elf**
12	**zwölf**
13	**dreizehn**
14	**vierzehn**
15	**fünfzehn**
16	**sechzehn**
17	**siebzehn**
18	**achtzehn**
19	**neunzehn**
20	**zwanzig**

16 **sechzehn** (note that the **-s** of **sechs** disappears!)
17 **siebzehn** (note that the **-en** of **sieben** vanishes!)

Now learn to count from 0 to 20, always stressing the first syllable.

21	**einundzwanzig**
22	**zweiundzwanzig**
23	**dreiundzwanzig**
24	**vierundzwanzig**
25	**fünfundzwanzig**
26	**sechsundzwanzig**
27	**siebenundzwanzig**
28	**achtundzwanzig**
29	**neunundzwanzig**
30	**dreißig**

26 **sechsundzwanzig** (note that because this means six-and-twenty the **-s** of **sechs** has naturally returned!)
27 **siebenundzwanzig** (see above)

Next learn to count from 21 to 30, carefully observing the stress on the first syllable, and noting that the units precede the tens and are joined to them by **und**.

10	**zehn**
20	**zwanzig**
30	**dreißig**
40	**vierzig**
50	**fünfzig**
60	**sechzig**

60 **sechzig** (note that the **-s** is lost again!)

70	siebzig	(the **-en** of **sieben** is again lopped off!)
80	achtzig	
90	neunzig	
100	hundert	

Count from 10 to 100 in tens. Then learn the following examples combining units and tens. Because these are isolated numbers the stress is always on the penultimate syllable, whereas the sequence counting from 21 to 29 (above) required it on the first syllable.

31	**einunddreißig**
42	**zweiundvierzig**
53	**dreiundfünfzig**
64	**vierundsechzig**
66	**sechsundsechzig**
75	**fünfundsiebzig**
77	**siebenundsiebzig**
86	**sechsundachtzig**
97	**siebenundneunzig**

Beyond 100, note that, if written in words, any number below the millions appears as one word. Whereas in English the hundreds are linked to the tens and units by 'and', there is hardly ever an **und** after the hundreds in German (and never in sequence counting). The units and tens continue to appear in the reverse order to English, with **und** in between, and, however long the number, a number in isolation has the stress on the normally stressed syllable of the final component (300 **dreihúndert,** 507 **fünfhundertsíeben,** 629 **sechshundertneunundzwánzig**).

Practise saying these examples:

101	**hunderteins,** (or less usually) **einhunderteins**
212	**zweihundertzwölf**
323	**dreihundertdreiundzwanzig**
434	**vierhundertvierunddreißig**
545	**fünfhundertfünfundvierzig**
656	**sechshundertsechsundfünfzig**
666	**sechshundertsechsundsechzig**

767	siebenhundertsiebenundsechzig
777	siebenhundertsiebenundsiebzig
878	achthundertachtundsiebzig
989	neunhundertneunundachtzig

Now count in hundreds from 100 to 1000 as shown:

100	(ein)hundert
200	zweihundert
300	dreihundert
400	vierhundert
500	fünfhundert
600	sechshundert
700	siebenhundert
800	achthundert
900	neunhundert
1,000	tausend

1,000,000 is **eine Million (-en)**, so the figure 5,723,926 would be spoken: **fünf Millionen siebenhundertdreiundzwanzig-tausendneunhundertsechsundzwanzig**. A number of more than four figures is separated in thousands by thin spaces, not by commas. Note also (Section 19) that a comma is used for the decimal point in German.

Years are designated, as in English, using only hundreds, so 1992 is **neunzehnhundertzweiundneunzig.** 'The 1920s' is **die zwanziger Jahre**, 'the 1980s' **die achtziger Jahre**, with the ending **-er** added on to the cardinal number. Unlike most endings this one *never* changes. All the numbers given here can be used both in sequence counting (1, 2, 3 etc.) and as single items in front of nouns ('fifty pages', **fünfzig Seiten**), without any change. The sole exceptions are any numbers ending in **-eins**, where the **-s** is dropped before a noun and the choice is as follows:

The book has 201 pages.
(i) **Das Buch hat zweihundertundeine Seite.**
(ii) **Das Buch hat zweihundert(und)ein Seiten.**

In (i) the **-ein** is given the *f* singular ending **-e** and the noun is singular; in (ii) the **-ein** is left without ending, the **und** can be dropped as in sequence counting, and the noun is plural.

Cardinal numbers usually require a plural noun to follow, but there are common exceptions like units of currency (see Section 19) and of measurement etc. (see Section 36).

IMITATED PRONUNCIATION: nool, yns, tsvy, dry, fe_ee_r, fuenf, zeks, **z_ee_**-b_e_n, ah_k_t, noyn, ts_ehn_; elf, tsvoelf, **dry**-ts_ehn_, **fe_ee_r**-ts_ehn_, **fuenf**-ts_ehn_, **zeh**-ts_ehn_, **z_ee_p**-ts_ehn_, **ah_k_t**-ts_ehn_, noyn-ts_ehn_, tsvahn-tsi_h_; yn*oont-tsvahn-tsi_h_, tsvy*oont-tsvahn-tsi_h_, ...; **dry**-si_h_, **fe_ee_r**-tsi_h_, **fuenf**-tsi_h_, zeh-tsi_h_, **z_ee_p**-tsi_h_, ah_k_t-tsi_h_, **noyn**-tsi_h_, **hoon**-d_e_rt; hoon-d_e_rt*yns; **tow**-zent; y-n_e_ mi-li-**yohn**

19 Prices

The basic unit of German currency is the **Deutsche Mark** (*f*), which is divided into 100 **Pfennig** (*m*). Though often preceded by cardinal numbers, **Mark** is never and **Pfennig** hardly ever found in the plural. Price tags are usually written, and the sums spoken, as follows:

Written:	Spoken:
DM 0,55 or **55 Pfg.**	**fünfundfünfzig Pfennig**
DM 1,20	**eine Mark zwanzig** ⎱ **eins zwanzig** ⎰ (equally common) **eine Mark und zwanzig Pfennig** (less common)
DM 4,85	**vier Mark fünfundachtzig** **vier fünfundachtzig** **vier Mark und fünfundachtzig Pfennig**

45

Price tags are sometimes more explicit, e.g.

Written: Spoken, and meaning:

Pfd. DM 2,40   **zwei Mark vierzig das Pfund**
DM 2.40 per pound
(the German pound = 500 grams)

Stück   **das Stück drei Mark**
     DM 3,00   or **drei Mark das Stück**
Stck   *DM 3.00 for one item* or *each*

You enquire the cost of goods for sale as follows:

Was kostet das?
Wie teuer ist das? } *How much is that?*
Was kosten die Kartoffeln?
Wie teuer sind die Kartoffeln? } *How much are the potatoes*

IMITATED PRONUNCIATION: **pfe**-ni*h*; **y**-n*e* m<u>a</u>hk; dahs
pfoont; dahs shtuek

Exercise 6

1   Ein Buch kostet DM 12,80 (zwölf Mark achtzig).
    Zwei Bücher kosten DM 25,60 (fünfundzwanzig Mark
    sechzig).
*Now continue the pattern with the following, writing out the
missing sentences and giving the prices in figures and words:*

2   Ein Brot kostet DM 4,80 (vier Mark achtzig).
    Zwei …
3   Eine Wurst kostet DM 3,25 (drei Mark füfundzwanzig).
    Zwei …
4   Eine Uhr kostet DM 85,00 (fünfundachtzig Mark).
    Zwei …
5   Eine Zeitung kostet DM 2,50 (zwei Mark fünfzig).
    Zwei …
6   Ein Bett kostet DM 488,00 (vierhundertachtundachtzig

Mark).
Zwei …
7   Ein Schrank kostet DM 505,00 (fünfhundertfünf Mark).
Zwei …
8   Ein Messer kostet DM 7,50 (sieben Mark fünfzig).
Zwei …
9   Eine Rose kostet DM 3,75 (drei Mark fünfundsiebzig).
Zwei …
10   Ein Auto kostet DM 18000,00 (achtzehntausend Mark).
Zwei …

20 Another case: indirect object (IO)

The English sentence 'I am lending him it' has not *one* but *two* objects: 'it' denotes the item directly affected by the process 'am lending' and is the familiar DO, while 'him' denotes the recipient or beneficiary of the process and so may be called the indirect object (IO). In English we are hardly aware of the IO as a case, since we generally either use words like 'to' or 'for' to indicate a recipient or beneficiary, or indeed just let the noun stand alone and leave the meaning to be understood from the context, with possibly some help from the sequence of the words:

I am lending him it.
I am lending it to my friend.
I am lending the book to my friend.
I am lending my friend the book.

German speakers, as already noted in Section 14, have a strong sense of case, and the indirect object (IO) has a mostly very distinctive set of IO words for 'the', '(not) a/an' and 'no', as well as a separate set of pronouns.

(a) *'(to/for) the, (not) a/an, no'*

	singular			plural
	m	*f*	*n*	*m f n*
IO	**dem**	**der**	**dem**	**den**
	(k)einem	**(k)einer**	**(k)einem**	**keinen**

(b) *IO pronouns*

	person						
	1st		2nd	3rd			
	sing.	plural		singular			plural
				m	*f*	*n*	
IO	**mir**	**uns**	**Ihnen**	**ihm**	**ihr**	**ihm**	**ihnen**
(to/for)	me	us	you	him	her	it	them

Summary of SU, DO and IO cases for 'the', '(not) a/an' and 'no':

	singular			plural
	m	*f*	*n*	
SU	**der**	**die**	**das**	**die**
	(k)ein	**(k)eine**	**(k)ein**	**keine**
DO	**den**	**die**	**das**	**die**
	(k)einen	**(k)eine**	**(k)ein**	**keine**
IO	**dem**	**der**	**dem**	**den**
	(k)einem	**(k)einer**	**(k)einem**	**keinen**

Summary of SU, DO and IO cases for pronouns:

	person						
	1st		2nd	3rd			
	sing.	plural		singular			plural
				m	*f*	*n*	
SU	**ich**	**wir**	**Sie**	**er**	**sie**	**es**	**sie**
DO	**mich**	**uns**	**Sie**	**ihn**	**sie**	**es**	**sie**
IO	**mir**	**uns**	**Ihnen**	**ihm**	**ihr**	**ihm**	**ihnen**

It may be a small aid to memory to note that, with **d. .**, **(k)ein** *and* the pronouns, the *m* and *n* singular IO case *always* ends with the letter **m**, which is unique to this case; that the *f* singular IO case always ends with the letter **r**; and that the plural IO case of **d. .** and **kein** along with the 2nd person and the 3rd person plural pronouns all end with the letters **en**.

IMITATED PRONUNCIATION: d<u>ee</u>r, yn, kyn; d<u>eh</u>n, **y**-n<u>e</u>n, **ky**-n<u>e</u>n; d<u>eh</u>m, **y**-n<u>e</u>m, **ky**-n<u>e</u>m; d<u>ee</u>, **y**-n<u>e</u>, **ky**-n<u>e</u>; d<u>ee</u>r, **y**-n<u>e</u>r, **ky**-n<u>e</u>r; dahs, yn, kyn; ... i<u>h</u>, mi<u>h</u>, m<u>ee</u>er; v<u>ee</u>er, oons; z<u>ee</u>, <u>ee</u>-n<u>e</u>n; <u>ee</u>r, <u>ee</u>n, <u>ee</u>m; z<u>ee</u>, <u>ee</u>er; es, <u>ee</u>m

21 Verbs using the IO case

Apart from verbs like

bringen	to bring (someone something)
geben	to give (someone something)
schenken	to give (someone something) as a present
wünschen	to wish (someone something)

which may obviously, as implied by their *meaning*, relate to two objects, a DO and an IO, German has some verbs which, if they have an object that is *human*, require this to be an IO, e.g.

begegnen	to meet (someone)
helfen	to help (someone)
gefallen	to please (someone)
glauben	to believe (someone)
verzeihen	to forgive (someone)
raten	to advise (someone)

IMITATED PRONUNCIATION: **bring**-*e*n; **<u>geh</u>**-ben; sheng-k*e*n; **vuen**-sh*e*n; be-**<u>gehg</u>**-n*e*n; **hel**-f*e*n; g*e*-**fah**-len; **glow**-ben; f*e*r-**tsy**-*e*n; **<u>rah</u>**-ten

Exercise 7

Rewrite the following, substituting the nouns in brackets for those that precede them and making the other changes required. To help you, the words that have to be changed are underlined.

Ich bringe meiner Mutter (Vater) eine Zeitung (Buch).
Ich gebe sie ihr in der Küche (Flur).
Ich schenke meiner Schwester (Bruder) eine Katze (Hund) und wünsche ihr einen guten Tag.

Vocabulary

Study the conversation that follows until you know all the sentences (and their meaning) by heart. These are new words:

heute abend	this evening
eingeladen	invited (out)
man	one
netten	nice
die Dame (-n)	lady
rote	red
bestimmt	definitely
gut	fine
wieviele?	how many?
sollen	shall, is to, are to
ach!	oh!
verheiratet	married
vielleicht	perhaps
wieso denn?	why is that?
bedeuten	to mean
gelbe	yellow
die Nelke (-n)	carnation
bitte schön!	there you are! you're welcome!
viel Spaß!	(have) a nice time!

IMITATED PRONUNCIATION: **hoy**-*te****ah**-b*e*nt;
yn-g*e*-l<u>ah</u>-d*e*n; mahn; **ne**-t*e*n; d<u>ee</u> **dah**-m*e*; **r<u>oh</u>**-t*e*; b*e*-**shtimt**;
goot; v<u>ee</u>-**f<u>ee</u>**-l*e*; **zo**-l*e*n; ah*k*; f*e*r-**hy**-r<u>ah</u>-t*e*t; f<u>ee</u>-**ly***h*t; n<u>ee</u>;
v<u>ee</u>-**z<u>oh</u>** den; b*e*-**doy**-t*e*n; **gel**-b*e*; d<u>ee</u> **nel**-k*e*; **bi**-*te* sh<u>oe</u>n; f<u>ee</u>l
shp<u>ah</u>s

CONVERSATION

A problem of etiquette at the florist's

Kunde	Ich bin heute abend eingeladen. Was schenkt man einer netten Dame?
Besitzerin	Moment bitte … Ich helfe Ihnen sofort. Rote Rosen gefallen ihr bestimmt.
K	Wie teuer sind rote Rosen?
B	Sie kosten zwei Mark fünfzig das Strück.
K	Gut, ich nehme Rosen.
B	Wieviele sollen es sein? … fünf …, sieben …, neun …?
K	Geben Sie mir fünf Stück bitte? … Ach ja, bringe ich ihrem Mann auch etwas?
B	Was!? Die Dame ist verheiratet!!?? Rote Rosen gefallen ihr vielleicht, aber ihr Mann verzeiht Ihnen nie, glauben Sie mir.
K	Wieso denn?
B	Rote Rosen bedeuten Liebe. Ich rate Ihnen, schenken Sie ihr gelbe Nelken … Bitte schön … Ich wünsche Ihnen viel Spaß heute abend!

TRANSLATION

Customer	I am invited out this evening. What does one give a nice lady?
Proprietress	Just a moment please ... I'll help you straight away. Red roses will definitely please her.
C	How much are red roses?
P	They cost two marks fifty each.
C	Fine, I'll take roses.
P	How many is it to be?... five ..., seven ..., nine?
C	Will you give me five please? ... Oh yes, shall I take something for her husband too?
P	What!? The lady is married!!?? Red roses will perhaps please her, but her husband will never forgive you, believe me!
C	Why is that?
P	Red roses mean love. I advise you, give her yellow carnations ... There you are ... I wish you a pleasant time this evening!

Chapter 5

In Chapter 5 you will find out how to ask questions and give instructions. This chapter covers:

- *question words such as 'who?', 'when?' and 'why?'*
- *the use of **nicht** ('not') to make negative sentences*
- *word order in instructions and requests*
- *some common descriptive words (adjectives and adverbs) and their comparative and superlative forms (e.g. 'old, older, oldest').*

22 Asking questions

(a) *When the answer is expected to be* **ja** *('yes') or* **nein** *('no')*
To ask a question requiring a 'yes' or 'no' answer, simply begin with the verb and follow immediately with the SU. In English this is possible only with a handful of verbs, like 'be', 'have', 'can', 'must', while if none of these is present 'do' is universally used first, with the main verb (if there is one) coming after the SU:

Ist er Elektriker?	<u>Is</u> he an electrician?
Kommt er heute?	<u>Is</u> he <u>coming</u> today?
Kommt er oft?	<u>Does</u> he <u>come</u> often?
Hat sie Geschwister?	<u>Has</u> she (<u>got</u>)(any) brothers and sisters?
Arbeiten sie?	<u>Are</u> they <u>working</u>?

(b) *When the answer is expected to be a piece of information*

To ask a question requiring particular information in the answer, start with the appropriate question-word –

Woher - where from?

was?	what?
wie?	how?
wo?	where?
wer?	who?
wen?	who(m)?
wem?	who(m) to / for?
wann?	when?
warum?	why?

– follow it with the verb (*any* verb, as in (a)), then with the SU, except when the SU is the question-word itself, as is sometimes the case with **wer?** and **was?** (e.g. questions marked † below):

Was kosten die Kartoffeln?	*What do the potatoes cost?*
Was macht das?	*How much is that?*
†Was kommt jetzt?	*What is coming now?*
Wie fahren Sie?	*How are you travelling (i.e. by what means)?*
Wie heißt der Sohn?	*How is the son called (i.e. what is his name)?*
Wo wohnt die Freundin?	*Where does the girlfriend live?*
†Wer wohnt hier?	*Who lives here?*
Wer ist der Besitzer?	*Who is the proprietor?*
Wen kennt der Junge?	*Who(m) does the boy know?*
Wem bringt er die Blumen?	*Who(m) is he taking the flowers to?*
Wann fahren wir?	*When are we travelling (i.e. when do we leave)?*

This list of question-words is not exhaustive.

IMITATED PRONUNCIATION: ist * e*er* * e-**lek**-tri-k*er*; komt * e*er* **hoy**-t*e*; komt * e*er* * oft; haht z*ee* ge-**shvis**-t*er*; <u>ah</u>-by-t*en* z<u>ee</u>; vahs; v<u>ee</u>; v<u>oh</u>; v*eer*; v<u>eh</u>n; v<u>eh</u>m; vahn; vah-**room**; vahs **kos**-t*en* d<u>ee</u> k<u>ah</u>-**to**-f*eln*; vahs mah*k*t dahs; vahs komt yetst; v<u>ee</u> **fah**-r*en* z<u>ee</u>; v<u>ee</u> hyst d*eer* z<u>oh</u>n; v<u>oh</u> v<u>oh</u>nt d<u>ee</u> **froyn**-din; v*eer* v<u>oh</u>nt h<u>ee</u>*er*; v*eer* * ist d*eer* b*e*-**zit**-s*er*; v<u>eh</u>n kent d*eer* **yoong**-*e*; v<u>eh</u>m bringt * e*er* d<u>ee</u> **bloo**-m*en*; vahn **fah**-r*en* v<u>ee</u>*er*

Notes:

(i) If the person asked does not know the answer, a typical response might be:

Ich weiß (es) nicht.   *I don't know.*

The use of **nicht** is explained in Section 23.

(ii) Questions in German are frequently used as a way of making polite requests. They may take the same form as the English 'Would you ...?' (Section 69) or they may be more direct, in a form which would be felt to be rude in English:

Geben Sie mir bitte die Zeitung?
Will you give me the paper, please? (literally: *Are you giving me the paper, please?*)
Reichen Sie bitte den Zucker?
Will you pass the sugar, please?

(iii) The phrase **was für (ein)?** means 'what sort of (a)?':

Was für ein Auto haben Sie?
What sort of (a) car do you have?
Was für Blumen bringt er?
What sort of flowers does he bring?
Was für einen Teppich sucht sie?
What sort of (a) carpet is she looking for?
Was für ein Mensch ist er?
What sort of a person is he?

In **was für ein?** the **ein** has the ending it would be given in the statement presupposing the question:

Sie haben <u>ein</u> Auto. Was für ein Auto haben Sie?
You have a car. What sort of a car do you have?
Sie sucht <u>einen</u> Teppich. Was für einen Teppich sucht sie?
She's looking for a carpet. What sort of a carpet is she looking for?

IMITATED PRONUNCIATION: i*h* vys * es ni*h*t; **geh**-ben z<u>ee</u> m<u>ee</u>e*r* **bi**-t*e* d<u>ee</u> **tsy**-toong; **ry**-*h*en z<u>ee</u> **bi**-t*e* d<u>eh</u>n **tsoo**-k*er*; vahs fue*er* * yn * **ow**-t<u>oh</u> **hah**-ben z<u>ee</u>; vahs fue*er* **bloo**-m*en* bringt * ee*r*; vahs fue*er* * **y**-n*en* **te**-pi*h* z<u>oo</u>kt z<u>ee</u>; vahs fue*er* * yn mensh * ist * ee*r*; z<u>ee</u> **hah**-ben * yn * **ow**-t<u>oh</u>; vahs fue*er* * yn * **ow**-t<u>oh</u> **hah**-ben z<u>ee</u>; z<u>ee</u> z<u>oo</u>kt * **y**-n*en* **te**-pi*h*; vahs fue*er* * **y**-n*en* **te**-pi*h* z<u>oo</u>kt z<u>ee</u>

Exercise 8

Insert the correct question-word from the column on the right in the following questions:

1 ... für ein Auto hat er?	Wen
2 ... kommt er?	Wer
3 ... besucht er?	Was
4 ... wohnt die Freundin?	Wie
5 ... ist sie?	Warum
6 ... heißt sie?	Wann
7 ... liebt er sie?	Wo

---

23 Negative sentences

Section 17 showed the wide use of **kein** to make negative sentences. Where this is not possible (**kein** can only be used before nouns and can only mean 'not a/an' or 'no', but never 'not the') **nicht** ('not') is used. The most usual way of making a negative sentence in English is to attach 'n't' to one of the small number of verbs mentioned in Section 22(a), e.g. 'aren't', 'haven't', 'can't', 'mustn't', or in the absence of one of these, to 'do' ('doesn't/don't'). If there is a main verb in the sentence, it follows either immediately or almost immediately, e.g. 'He doesn't always swim', 'We don't know her yet', 'It isn't working well'.

nicht cannot combine with the verb in the way 'n't' does, and while 'n't' comes early in the sentence, **nicht** comes late and sometimes last. It never comes between the SU and the verb in sentences such as you have met so far, and it has no effect on the verb (from which it is sometimes quite distant), as 'n't' does, requiring 'swims' to become 'doesn't swim':

Er schwimmt nicht immer.	*He doesn't always swim.*
Wir kennen sie noch nicht.	*We don't know her yet.*
Es funktioniert nicht gut.	*It isn't working well.*

The same principle applies to questions, as the following examples derived from Section 22 show:

Ist er nicht Elektriker?	*Isn't he an electrician?*
Kommt er nicht heute?	*Isn't he coming today?*
Kommt er nicht oft?	*Doesn't he come often?*
Warum arbeiten sie nicht?	*Why aren't they working?*
but:	
Hat sie keine Geschwister?	*Has she no brothers or sisters?*
	Hasn't she any brothers or sisters?

24 Instructions and requests

Begin with the verb, with its **-en** ending attached, and follow it immediately with **Sie**:

Kommen Sie sofort!	*Come at once!*

This is generally felt to be nothing like as abrupt as the English equivalent and can be toned down still further by adding **bitte** ('please').

Geben Sie mir bitte die Zeitung!	*Give me the paper please!*

Note the distinction between this sentence and the apparently identical one in Section 22. They look the same but sound different.

The only instruction form which is exceptional is that from 'be' (**sein**): **seien Sie!** So:

Seien Sie so nett und bringen Sie mir die Zeitung!
Be so kind and bring me the paper!

Exercise 9

Translate the following 'scene' into German. Translate only what the speakers say, not the 'stage directions'. You will need these new words:

yes please ...?	**bitte schön ...?**
guide	**der Führer (-)**
town guide	**der Stadtführer (-)**
to ask	**fragen**
boss, manager	**der Chef (-s)**
to look for	**suchen**
such a thing	**so etwas**
certainly	**sicher**
over there	**drüben**
to have a look	**gucken** (pronounced **kucken**)
there	**dort**
crazy	**verrückt**
of	**von**
of course	**natürlich**
to need	**brauchen**
here	**hier**
to know	**kennen**
town	**die Stadt (-̈e)**

IMITATED PRONUNCIATION: **bi**-*te* sh<u>oe</u>n; de*er* **fue**-*rer*; de*er* **shtaht**-fue-*rer*, **frah**-ge*n*; de*er* shef; z<u>oo</u>-*ke*n; z<u>oh</u> * et-vahs; **zi**-*her*, **drue**-ben; **koo**-*ke*n; do*ert*; f*er*-**ruekt**; fon; na-**tueer**-li*h*; **brow**-*ke*n; h<u>ee</u>*er*, **ke**-n*en*; d<u>ee</u> shtaht

After correcting your translation with the help of the Key, learn the dialogue by heart.

A stranger (Fremde) tries to buy a town guide in a book-shop in Bunsenheim

Assistant	Yes please ...?
Stranger	Hello. Have you got a guide?
A	What sort of a guide?
S	A town guide.
A	I don't know. Please ask the boss.
S (to Manager)	Hello. I'm looking for a town guide. Have you got such a thing?
Manager	Yes, certainly. The town guides are over there. Have a look there.

Ten minutes later

S	It's crazy. I find town guides of Frankfurt, Gießen, Marburg and Kassel but I don't find a town guide of Bunsenheim.
M	Of course not. Why do we need town guides of Bunsenheim? We live here and know the town!

25 Descriptive and amplifying words: adjectives and adverbs

You already know something about nouns and verbs in German, and will remember how we called them naming words and process words. Now we introduce *descriptive* and *amplifying* words, otherwise known as *adjectives* and *adverbs*.

Adjectives either precede nouns directly (cf. 'fine weather') or follow them and refer to them by having some form of **sein** ('be') sandwiched in between (cf. 'the weather was fine'). Adverbs are used much more loosely and embellish or amplify the process indicated by the verb (cf. 'he stumbled badly') or indeed the process indicated by the sentence as a whole (cf. 'she thumped the table <u>violently</u>'). In German, unlike English, exactly the same word can generally be used as either adjective or adverb:

Das Wetter ist schlecht. *The weather is bad.*
Das Kind singt schlecht. *The child sings badly.*

We shall not just now consider adjectives when they precede the noun. This is dealt with separately in Section 29.

(a) Adjectives and adverbs share the use of a small set of words to precede them, by which their meaning can be enhanced or reduced or negated:

sehr	very
zu	too
so	so
ziemlich	fairly, rather, pretty
etwas	rather, somewhat
nicht	not
nicht so	not so
gar nicht	not at all

Der Chef ist gar nicht höflich.
The boss isn't at all polite.
Das Kind trinkt die Milch ziemlich schnell.
The child drinks the milk pretty quickly.

IMITATED PRONUNCIATION: z<u>eh</u>er; ts<u>oo</u>; z<u>oh</u>; **tseem**-li*h*; **et**-vahs; ni*h*t; ni*h*t z<u>oh</u>; g<u>ah</u> ni*h*t

(b) Adjectives and adverbs also share the same methods of making comparisons:

(i) *Comparatives (higher degree)*

Das Wetter ist heute <u>schlechter</u> <u>als</u> gestern.
The weather is <u>worse</u> today <u>than</u> yesterday.
Das Kind singt schlecht, aber die Mutter singt <u>schlechter</u>.
The child sings badly, but the mother sings <u>worse</u>.

To make comparatives add **-er** to the basic adjective or adverb and if you need 'than' use **als**. Sometimes – especially in the case of a few much-used adjectives / adverbs – you must also change the sound of the vowel:

alt	old	**älter**	older
arm	poor	**ärmer**	poorer
groß	big	**größer**	bigger
hart	hard	**härter**	harder
jung	young	**jünger**	younger
kalt	cold	**kälter**	colder
klug	clever	**klüger**	cleverer
krank	ill	**kränker**	more ill
kurz	short	**kürzer**	shorter
lang	long	**länger**	longer
oft	often	**öfter**	more often
schwach	weak	**schwächer**	weaker
stark	strong	**stärker**	stronger
warm	warm	**wärmer**	warmer

These vowel changes are carried over into the superlative.

(ii) *Superlatives (highest degree)*

Das Wetter war vorgestern <u>am schlechtesten</u>.
The weather was <u>worst</u> (of all) the day before yesterday.
Der Vater sings <u>am schlechtesten</u>.
The father sings <u>worst</u> (of all).
Das Wetter war vorvorgestern <u>am schönsten</u>.
The weather was <u>nicest</u> (of all) three days ago (lit. the day before the day before yesterday).
Die Kusine singt <u>am schönsten</u>.
The (female) cousin sings <u>the most beautifully</u> (of all).

To make superlatives, precede the adjective / adverb with **am** and add **-(e)sten** to the word itself. The **-(e)** is generally used when the word (i.e. the stem) ends in **-s, -ß** (but not **groß** → **am größten**), **-d** and **-t**.

However, when a superlative adjective precedes the noun (cf. 'the finest weather'), the **am** is not used and the ending may be other than **-en**. This is dealt with in Section 29.

IMITATED PRONUNCIATION: ahlt, **el**-*ter*; a<u>h</u>m, **eer**-m*er*; grohs, **gro<u>e</u>**-*ser*; hah*ert*, **heer**-*ter*; yoong, **yueng**-*er*; ka<u>h</u>lt, **kel**-*ter*; kl<u>oo</u>k, **kl<u>ue</u>**-g*er*; krahnk, **kreng**-k*er*; koo*erts*, **kue***ert*-*ser*; lahng, **leng**-*er*; oft, **oef**-*ter*; shvah*k*, **shve**-*her*; shta<u>h</u>k, **ste***er*-k*er*; v<u>ah</u>m, **veer**-m*er*

(c) Like English, German has one or two such words that are a law unto themselves:

gut	good	**besser**	better	**am besten**	best
viel	much	**mehr**	more	**am meisten**	most
hoch	high	**höher**	higher	**am höchsten**	highest
nahe	near	**näher**	nearer	**am nächsten**	nearest

(d) To convey 'as … as', where the gap may represent an adjective or an adverb, German uses **so … wie:**

Das Haus ist <u>so</u> klein <u>wie</u> ein Schuppen.
The house is as small as a shed.
Ich komme <u>so</u> schnell <u>wie</u> möglich.
I'll come as quickly as possible.

'just as … as' is **ebenso … wie:**

Das Schlafzimmer ist <u>ebenso</u> groß <u>wie</u> das Wohnzimmer.
The bedroom is just as big as the living room.
Der Vetter singt <u>ebenso</u> schön <u>wie</u> die Kusine.
The (male) cousin sings just as beautifully as the (female) cousin.

IMITATED PRONUNCIATION: g<u>oo</u>t, **be**-*ser*, ahm **bes**-*ten*; f<u>ee</u>l, **me**h*er*, ahm **mys**-*ten*; hoh*k*, **hoe**-*er*, ahm **hoe**h*s*-*ten*; **nah**-*e*, **ne**-*er*, ahm **ne**h*s*-*ten*; z<u>oh</u> … v<u>ee</u>; <u>eh</u>-ben-z<u>oh</u> … v<u>ee</u>

Exercise 10

1 Meine Mutter ist alt, aber mein Vater ist älter.

Now continue the pattern, writing the sentences in full:

2 Mein Bruder ist groß, aber meine Schwester ist ...
3 Die Frau ist jung, aber die Wirtin ist ...
4 Der Sohn ist klug, aber die Tochter ist ...
5 Das Zimmer ist warm, aber das Bett ist ...
6 Die gelbe Nelke ist lang, aber die rote Rose ist ...
7 Die Frau ist nett, aber der Mann ist ...

Vocabulary

Translate the 'scene' that follows into English. You will need these words:

die Hausbesitzerin (-nen)	house owner
dies..	this
das Wohnzimmer (-)	living room
das Schlafzimmer (-)	bedroom
der Mieter (-)	tenant
der Flur (-e)	hall
dunk(e)l†	dark
die Straße (-n)	street
laut	noisy
eigentlich	really, actually
oben	upstairs
hell	light, bright
der Raum (¨e)	room, space
bestimmt	definitely
breit	wide
unten	downstairs
die Decke (-n)	ceiling
niedrig	low
winzig	tiny

gegenüber	opposite
die Aussicht (-en)	view
wunderschön	glorious, splendid
der Garten (-)	garden
liegen	to lie
nämlich	you see (in explanation)
hinten	at the back, rear
ruhig	quiet
vorn	at the front
nehmen	to take
übrigens	by the way
derMonat (-e)	month
teu(e)rt	dear, expensive
jetzt	now, at present
zahlen	to pay

† The bracketed letter disappears when another syllable, like **-er**, is added to the adjective / adverb.

IMITATED PRONUNCIATION: d<u>ee</u> **hows**-be-zit-se-rin; d<u>ee</u>s; dahs **vohn**-tsi-m*er*; dahs **shlahf**-tsi-m*er*; de*er* **mee**-t*er*; de*er* fl<u>oo</u>*er*; **doong**-k*el*; d<u>ee</u> **shtrah**-se; lowt; y-gent-li*h*; **oh**-ben; hel; de*er* rowm; be-**shtimt**; bryt; **oon**-ten; d<u>ee</u> **de**-k*e*; n<u>ee</u>-dri*h*; **win**-tsi*h*; g<u>e</u>h-gen*<u>ue</u>-ber; d<u>ee</u> **ows**-ziht; **voon**-d*er*-sh<u>oe</u>n; de*er* **gah**-ten; **lee**-gen; n<u>e</u>m-li*h*; **hin**-ten; **r<u>oo</u>**-i*h*; fo*er*n; **neh**-men; **ueb**-ri-g*en*s; de*er* **moh**-n<u>ah</u>t; **toy**-*er*; yetst; **tsah**-len

CONVERSATION

Scene: A house owner shows three vacant flats to a prospective tenant: one on the ground floor at the front of the house, and two situated opposite each other on the first floor, one at the front and the other at the rear.

(a) In the ground floor flat

Hausbesitzerin   Diese Wohnung ist schön groß, zwei Wohnzimmer, vier Schlafzimmer, zwei Toiletten ...

Mieter   Der Flur ist zu dunkel, und die Straße ist ziemlich laut. Diese Wohnung ist mir eigentlich zu groß. Ich brauche keine vier Schlafzimmer, eigentlich nur zwei ...Sind die Wohnungen oben kleiner?

H   Ja. Sie sind auch etwas heller als diese.

(b) In the first floor flat at the front

H   Diese Räume gefallen Ihnen bestimmt ... nur ein Wohnzimmer, aber breiter und länger als das Wohnzimmer unten.

M   Ja, schön, aber die Decke ist niedriger als unten. Die drei Schlafzimmer sind mir zu winzig, und es ist ebenso laut hier wie unten.

(c) In the first floor flat at the rear

H   Diese Wohnung ist am schönsten. Hier sind nur zwei Schlafzimmer. Sie sind aber etwas größer als die Schlafzimmer gegenüber. Die Aussicht ist wunderschön, der Garten liegt nämlich hinten.

M   Ja, und diese Wohnung ist auch viel ruhiger als die Wohnungen vorn. Ja, ich nehme sie ...Wie hoch ist übrigens die Miete?

H   Neunhundertfünfzig Mark pro Monat.

M   Was!!?? Nein, das ist mir zu teuer. Das ist viel mehr, als ich jetzt zahle.

Now compare your translation with the translation below.
After you have corrected your version, learn the sentences of
the conversation by heart.

TRANSLATION

(a) In the ground floor flat

House owner   This flat is beautifully spacious, two living rooms, four bedrooms, two toilets ...

Tenant   The hall is too dark, and the street is rather noisy. This flat is really too large for me. I don't need four bedrooms, only two really ...
Are the flats upstairs smaller?

H   Yes. They're rather lighter than this one, too.

(b) In the first floor flat at the front

H   You'll definitely like these rooms ... only one living room, but wider and longer than the living room downstairs.

T   Yes, fine, but the ceiling is lower than downstairs. The three bedrooms are too tiny for me, and it's just as noisy here as downstairs.

(c) In the first floor flat at the rear

H   This flat is the nicest of all. Here there are only two bedrooms. But they're somewhat larger than the bedrooms opposite. The view is glorious. The garden's at the back, you see.

T   Yes, and this flat is quieter than the flats at the front, too. Yes, I'll take it ...
By the way, how much is the rent?

H   Nine hundred and fifty marks a month.

T   What!!?? No, that's too dear for me. That's much more than I'm paying now.

Chapter 6

This chapter introduces prepositions ('in', 'by', 'of', etc.) and shows how they affect the case of the following noun or pronoun. You will also learn how to express the idea of existence or availability, using the phrase es gibt ('there is/ there are').

26 Structural words: prepositions

Structural words are the short (often monosyllabic) words which have little 'meaning' in isolation but are used to link together items from the major word-classes of nouns, adjectives and verbs. They thus enable more complex structures to be built up, and this is why we call them *structural* words, or *prepositions*, because they usually precede nouns or pronouns:

going into the house
stolen by a thief
a letter from you
fond of her mother
insist on payment

Whereas in English we can simply place any preposition in front of any noun or in front of the pronouns 'me, us, you, him, her, it' and 'them' without complication, in German each preposition requires the noun or pronoun following to be in a particular case, generally DO or IO. Some prepositions require DO exclusively, some IO exclusively, and some require either DO or IO according to the sense. Here are the bulk of prepositions, grouped according to the cases required. It is impossible to translate prepositions from one language to another out of context. However, the most common English equivalents are given here. You can only learn prepositions by finding them and learning to use them in genuine contexts, noting any particularly idiomatic or (apparently) exceptional usage.

(a) *DO prepositions*

durch	through, by, by means of
für	for
gegen	against, towards
ohne	without
um	round, at (time of day)

Note three contracted forms frequently found when **das** follows:

durchs (= durch das) Fenster	through the window
fürs (= für das) Theater	for the theatre
ums (= um das) Feuer	round the fire

(b) *IO prepositions*

aus	out of, from
bei	with, at (so-and-so's house), near, in (such-and-such conditions or weather), during, in the process/course of
mit	with
nach	to (certain locations, including one's own house: **nach Hause**), after (time), according to
seit	since, for (period of time up to now)
von	from (place and time), by (indicating agency or authorship), of (possession)
zu	to (certain locations), at (e.g. home: **zu Hause**)

Note these contracted forms when **dem** follows:

beim (= bei dem) Gewitter	*in/during the thunderstorm*
vom (= von dem) Dach	*from the roof*
zum (= zu dem) Arzt	*to the doctor*

and when **der** (*f* IO case) follows:
zur (= zu der) Seite   *to the side, aside*

(c) *DO/IO prepositions*

The rule is that if the context indicates or implies a change
of location or of condition, these prepositions have to be
followed by a (pro)noun of DO case; otherwise they are
followed by the IO case. (Senses which are not spatial or
temporal usually need the DO case.)

	DO	IO
an	on to (the side of); up to (the edge of)	at, by, on (the side of) (a non-horizontal surface); on (with days and dates)
auf	on to (the top of) (a horizontal surface)	on (the top of) (a horizontal surface)
hinter	(to) behind	behind
in	into	in (spatial, and temporal, though year numbers need **im Jahre**, e.g. **im Jahre 1992**); inside, within
neben	(to) next to, (to) alongside	next to, alongside, along with
über	across, over (i.e. from one side to the other), via	above, over (i.e. on top of)
unter	(to) underneath, (to) below, under (from one side to the other)	below, underneath, under
vor	(to) in front of, (to) before	in front of, before; (in past time contexts) ago
zwischen	(to) in between	between

Note these contracted forms when **das** follows:

ans (= **an das**) **Feuer**	*up to the fire*
aufs (= **auf das**) **Wasser**	*on to the water*
ins (= **in das**) **Netz**	*into the net*
vors (= **vor das**) **Auto**	*in front of the car*

and when **dem** follows:

am (= **an dem**) **Montag**	*on Monday*
im (= **in dem**) **Schnee**	*in the snow*

The following sentences are designed to illustrate the principle underlying the selection of DO or IO:

(i) **Fritz geht an den Schrank, Liese steht am Schrank.**
Fritz goes to the wardrobe. Liese stands by the wardrobe.

(ii) **Er legt die Zeitung auf den Schrank, sie liegt jetzt auf dem Schrank.**
He puts (lays) the newspaper on the wardrobe. It's now (now lies) on the wardrobe.

(iii) **Fritz springt hinter den Schrank, Liese ist schon hinter dem Schrank.**
Fritz jumps behind the wardrobe. Liese is already behind the wardrobe.

(iv) **Fritz geht jetzt in den Schrank, Liese singt im Schrank.**
Fritz now goes into the wardrobe. Liese is singing in the wardrobe.

(v) **Die Katze geht neben den Stuhl, der Hund liegt schon neben dem Stuhl.**
The cat goes next to the chair. The dog is already lying next to the chair.

(vi) **Die Katze springt über den Tisch, die Uhr hängt über dem Tisch.**
The cat jumps over the table. The clock is hanging above the table.

(vii) **Fritz kriecht unter den Tisch, die Zeitung liegt unter dem Tisch.**
Fritz creeps under the table. The newspaper is (lies) under the table.

(d) *Two odd prepositions:* **bis** *and* **gegenüber**

(i) **bis** can be used in two ways:

* in expressing time / numbers, it means 'until', 'up to',
  'by'. *Note:* DO case follows, e.g. **bis nächstes Jahr**, till
  next year; **bis nächsten Montag**, till next Monday.

* in other expressions, it means 'up to', 'as far as'.
  Note: it cannot stand alone, except before place names. It
  must also be followed by a preposition like **an, auf, in**.
  The case is determined by this second preposition.

The following exemplifies both usages:

**Fritz kommt nur bis Bunsenheim, findet ein Gasthaus,
geht bis an die Tür, wartet bis fünf Uhr, zählt bis
fünfzig, kommt dann bis in die Gaststube, aber:
keiner ist da!**
*Fritz only gets as far as Bunsenheim, finds an inn, goes up to
the door, waits until five o'clock, counts up to fifty, then gets
as far as the lounge, but – no one is there!*

(ii) **gegenüber** means 'opposite', 'towards', 'compared to'.
Note: it usually follows the (pro)noun to which it relates,
and requires the IO case for that preceding (pro)noun.

Thus:

**Die Kirche steht am Marktplatz dem Gasthaus Zur
Rose gegenüber, und Sie finden das Theater am
Theaterplatz der Touristeninformation gegenüber.**
*The church is on the marketplace opposite the Rose Inn, and
you'll find the theatre on Theatre Square opposite the tourist
information office.*

Exercise 11

Complete the story which follows, based on the cartoon, by inserting prepositions in the gaps marked 'P' and putting the right case-endings on **d. .** *and* **ein**. *You will need this information:*

(i) Prepositions, listed
in the order in which
they are required.
**mit, in, vor, auf, auf,
neben, hinter, mit,
auf, für, in**

(ii) *New words, for both meaning
and gender, listed in the order required:*

der Verbrecher (-)	criminal
der Pinsel (-)	paintbrush
die Palette (-n)	palette
die Hand (⁻e)	hand
das Bild (-er)	picture
die Sache (-n)	thing
die Tischdecke (-n)	tablecloth
das Brot (-e)	loaf
das Glas (⁻er)	glass
die Flasche (-n)	bottle
der Korken (-)	cork
das Etikett (-en)	label
wichtig	important
die Feile (-n)	file

Der Verbrecher steht __P__ ein. . Pinsel und ein. . Palette
__P__ d. . Hand __P__ ein. . Bild. __P__ d. . Bild sind mehrere
Sachen. __P__ ein. . Tischdecke liegt ein Brot. __P__ d. . Brot
ist ein Glas, und __P__ d. . Brot ist eine Flasche __P__ ein. .
Korken. __P__ d. . Flasche ist ein Etikett. Was ist aber __P__
d. . Verbrecher am wichtigsten? Die Feile __P__ d. . Brot
natürlich!

Exercise 12

Translate the following sentences, which constitute a mini-'thriller', into German. You will need some new words, which are given below, and the appropriate prepositions are indicated at the end of each English sentence. The English is meant to elicit the best German, so ignore the words in brackets.

burglar/intruder	der	Einbrecher (-)
front door	die	Haustür (-en)
to knock		klopfen
no one		niemand, keiner
to peep		gucken
to find		finden
number plate	das	Nummernschild (-er)
garage	die	Garage (-n)
back		zurück
to put (inside or between)		stecken
frame	der	Rahmen (-)
to open		öffnen
stairs (i.e. staircase)	die	Treppe (-n)
to sit		sitzen
skeleton	das	Skelett (-e)
axe	die	Axt (-̈e)

The intruder goes (right) up to the front door. (**bis an**)
He knocks on the door. (**an**)
No one comes to the door. (**zu**)
He goes round the house and peeps through the windows. (**um, durch**)
He finds a car without (a) number plate between the house and the garage. (**ohne, zwischen**)
He goes back to the front door. (**an**)
He pushes a file between the door and the frame. (**zwischen**)
He opens the door with the file and goes into the hall. (**mit, in**)
Opposite him on the stairs sits a skeleton with an axe in the (its) hand. (**gegenüber, auf, mit, in**)

27 Expressing existence or availability

One of the basic requirements in any language is a means of expressing the idea that something exists or does not exist, is available or not available. This is done in English with 'there is/are' etc. Note how the verb changes, not only according to time but also to match the singular or plural nature of the item(s) referred to:

There's a mouse in the larder.
There are rats by the river.
There was cake for tea.
There were hamburgers for supper.

When (*non-*)*existence* or (*un*)*availability* is the main focus of what is being said (as above), German uses **es gibt** (from **geben**, 'to give'). In this expression **es** is the SU, and the item(s) being talked about must be in the DO case:

Es gibt heute einen Film im Fernsehen.
There's a film on television today.
Gibt es keinen Kuchen mehr?
Is there no more cake?
Es gibt mehrere Fehler in dem Brief.
There are several mistakes in the letter.
Es gibt einige Ausländer im Hotel.
There are some foreigners in the hotel.
Es gibt jetzt Abendbrot!
Now we're going to have supper! (literally: There is supper now.)

You will see from the above examples that **es gibt** does not change for the plural, which is logical since **es** is the real SU, unlike English 'there', which merely stands in for the SU itself. The question **Was gibt es?** (usually spoken **Was gibt's?**) means 'What is there?' (e.g. for a meal, available in a shop, on television, etc.).

Exercise 13

Translate the following short conversation into German.
You will need these words:

hotel guest	**der**	**Hotelgast (¨e)**
television	**das**	**Fernsehen**
on television		**im Fernsehen**
this evening		**heute abend**
waiter	**der**	**Kellner (-)**
TV magazine	**die**	**Fernsehzeitung (-en)**
week	**die**	**Woche (-n)**
this week		**diese Woche**
daily paper	**die**	**Tageszeitung (-en)**
here		**hier**
unfortunately		**leider**
yesterday		**gestern**

In the television lounge of a hotel

Hotel guest	What is there on television this evening?
Waiter	I don't know.
H	Look in the TV magazine please. (**in**+DO)
W	There is no TV magazine this week.
H	Is there a daily paper?
W	Yes, here is a daily paper ... but it is unfortunately from yesterday. (**von**)

Chapter 7

This chapter builds on the foundations laid in earlier
chapters. You will learn:

- a group of words which follow the same pattern as **d. .**,
  including the words for 'this' and 'that'
- a group of words which follow the same pattern as **ein**:
  the possessive words 'my', 'your', etc.
- the endings that are added to adjectives when they precede
  a noun
- how to form ordinal numbers ('first', 'second', etc.)
  and fractions
- the 'familiar' forms used when talking to friends or children
- the order of words in a simple German sentence.

28 Words parallel to d. . and ein

d. . signals that the following noun means a particular speci-
men (or particular specimens) of the class of items mentioned.

ein on the other hand signals that the speaker is not concerned to identify any such particular specimen(s).

There are a further small number of words that are parallel
to **d. .** and **ein** in that they appear in the same position before
the noun and have either the **d. .** endings or the **ein** endings.
As to their meaning, almost all of them indicate like **d. .** that
particular specimens of the classes of items mentioned are in
the speaker's mind. The **ein** endings are exclusive to words
indicating possession ('my, our, your, his, her, its, their'). The
d. . endings are used on six other, non-possessive words
including 'this', 'every', and 'which?'

(a) *Words taking the* **d. .** *endings*

d. . -type word	singular		plural
dies. .	this, (*sometimes*) that		these, (*sometimes*) those
jed. .	each, every, any		—
welch. . ?/!		which? what? what (a)!	
jen. .	that		those
solch. .		such	
manch. .		quite a few, a fair number of	

(i) **jen. .** is little used, except when paired with **dies. .** (**jen. ., dies. .** 'the former, the latter'). The usual way of conveying 'that' is either **d. .** spoken with stress, or **dies. .**

(ii) **solch. .** and **manch. .** in the singular have the alternatives **solch ein** and **manch ein**, where only the **ein** takes endings, and to convey the meaning of **solch ein** there are the further alternatives **ein solch. .** (endings as in Section 29(b)) and the very frequent **so ein**.

(iii) **manch. .** has no one-word equivalent in English. It means more than 'some' and fewer than 'many', and whether singular or plural in form it must be regarded as having a plural meaning.

Summary of **d. .**-type endings, with **dies. .** as model:

	singular			plural
	m	*f*	*n*	*m f n*
SU	**dieser**	**diese**	**dieses†**	**diese**
DO	**diesen**	**diese**	**dieses†**	**diese**
IO	**diesem**	**dieser**	**diesem**	**diesen**

† The **d. .** *n* ending **-as** is replaced by **-es** in all the **d. .**-type words.

Examples:

dies. .	**Kennen Sie dieses Buch aus der Hugo-Reihe?** *Do you know <u>this</u> book from the Hugo series?*
jed. .	**Jedes Kind bekommt ein Ei.** *<u>Each</u> (or <u>Every</u>) child will get an egg.* **Ich bin für jeden Vorschlag offen.** *I am open to <u>any</u> suggestion.*
welch. . ?/!	**Auf welchen Bus warten Sie?** *<u>Which</u> bus are you waiting for?* **Welchen Druck hat der Reifen?** *<u>What</u> pressure does the tyre have?*
jen. .	**Der Film stammt aus jener Zeit vor dem 1. Weltkrieg.** *The film comes from <u>that</u> period before World War I.* **Wir sprechen oft über dieses und jenes.** *We often talk about <u>this</u> and <u>that</u>.*
solch. .	**Er hat solche Schwierigkeiten mit seinem Vater.** *He has <u>such</u> difficulties with his father.* **Wir haben solches Glück mit dem Wetter.** *We're having <u>such</u> luck with the weather.*
manch. .	**Mancher Polizist trinkt selbst zu viel.** *<u>Quite a few</u> policemen drink too much themselves.*

All the **d. .**-type words can be used not only before nouns but on their own, with a noun being clearly understood from the context:

Ich trinke aus diesem Glas. Trinken Sie aus diesem?
I'll drink from this glass. (Indicating) Will you drink from this one?

jeder (DO **jeden**, IO **jedem**) on its own means 'everybody' (just as **keiner** (DO **keinen**, IO **keinem**) on its own means 'no one', 'nobody').

(b) *Words taking the* **ein** *endings*

person						
1st		2nd	3rd			
singular	plural		singular			plural
			m	*f*	*n*	
mein	**unser**	**Ihr**	**sein**	**ihr**	**sein**	**ihr**
my	our	your	his	her	its	their

Summary of **ein**-type endings, with **unser** and **Ihr** as models:

	singular			plural
	m	*f*	*n*	*m f n*
SU	**unser**	**unsere**	**unser**	**unsere**
DO	**unseren**	**unsere**	**unser**	**unsere**
IO	**unserem**	**unserer**	**unserem**	**unseren**

It is important not to mistake **unser**, in which the -er belongs to the stem, for a **d. .**-type word, in which **-er** occurs only as an ending.

	singular			plural
	m	*f*	*n*	*m f n*
SU	**Ihr**	**Ihre**	**Ihr**	**Ihre**
DO	**Ihren**	**Ihre**	**Ihr**	**Ihre**
IO	**Ihrem**	**Ihrer**	**Ihrem**	**Ihren**

All the **ein**-type words, which indicate possession, can be used not only before nouns but on their own, to mean 'mine, ours, yours, his, hers, its, theirs'. The endings are exactly as above, except that the *m* singular SU adds **-er** and the *n* singular SU and DO add **-s**:

Leihen Sie mir bitte Ihren Bleistift. Meiner ist weg.
Lend me your pencil please. Mine has vanished (literally: *is away*).
Mein Fahrrad ist fünf Jahre alt. Wie alt ist Ihrs?
My bicycle is five years old. How old is yours?

Exercise 14

1 Geht er ohne seine Freundin ins Theater?
   Nein, er geht mit seiner Freundin ins Theater.

Continue the pattern, writing out your sentences in full.

2 Ist sie ohne ihre Schwester bei Müllers eingeladen?
   Nein, ...
3 Kommt der Vater mit unserem Geschenk für die Mutter?
   Nein, ...
4 Esse ich den Kuchen ohne eine Tasse Kaffee?
   Nein, ...
5 Geht er ohne seinen Stadtführer durch Frankfurt?
   Nein, ...
6 Mache ich das Abendbrot mit meiner Tochter?
   Nein, ...
7 Geht sie mit ihrem Bruder zur Tante?
   Nein, ...
8 Kaufen wir die Wurst mit einer Cola?
   Nein, ...

29 Adjectives preceding nouns

When adjectives are not used in isolation after the noun
(see the examples in Section 25), but become part of the
group of words directly preceding the noun, they require
special sets of endings similar to – but not identical
with – those of **d. .** and **ein**.

There are three sets to learn, according to whether (a) a
d. .-type word is also present, (b) an **ein**-type word is
also present, or (c) neither a **d. .** type nor an **ein**-type
word is present.

(a) *Adjectives after* **d.** *.-type words*

These have -**en** in all positions except for five with -**e**:

	singular			plural
	m	*f*	*n*	*m f n*
SU	der arm**e** Mann	die arm**e** Frau	das arm**e** Kind	die arm**en** Leute
DO	den arm**en** Mann	die arm**e** Frau	das arm**e** Kind	die arm**en** Leute
IO	dem arm**en** Mann	der arm**en** Frau	dem arm**en** Kind	den arm**en** Leuten†

†Plural nouns in the IO case always have -**n** added to the plural form unless the plural already ends in -**n** or is a foreign plural like **Autos**.

Summary of adjective endings after **d.** .-type words:

	singular			plural
	m	*f*	*n*	*m f n*
SU	-e	-e	-e	-en
DO	-en	-e	-e	-en
IO	-en	-en	-en	-en

(b) *Adjectives after* **ein**-*type words*

These have -**en** in all positions except five, but three of these undergo change compared with (a):

	singular			plural
	m	*f*	*n*	*m f n*
SU	ihr arm**er** Mann	seine arm**e** Frau	ihr arm**es** Kind	ihre arm**en** Kinder
DO	ihren arm**en** Mann	seine arm**e** Frau	ihr arm**es** Kind	ihre arm**en** Kinder
IO	ihrem arm**en** Mann	seiner arm**en** Frau	ihrem arm**en** Kind	ihren arm**en** Kindern

Summary of adjective endings after **ein.** .-type words:

	singular			plural
	m	*f*	*n*	*m f n*
SU	-er	-e	-es	-en
DO	-en	-e	-es	-en
IO	-en	-en	-en	-en

(c) *Adjectives not preceded by either* **d.** .- *or* **ein**–*type words*

All endings are now well differentiated, though easy to learn if you remember where they come from – see below:

	singular			plural
	m	*f*	*n*	*m f n*
SU	kalt<u>er</u>	kalt<u>e</u>	kalt<u>es</u>	kalt<u>e</u>
	Wein	Limonade	Bier	Getränke
DO	kalt<u>en</u>	kalt<u>e</u>	kalt<u>es</u>	kalt<u>e</u>
	Wein	Limonade	Bier	Getränke
IO	kalt<u>em</u>	kalt<u>er</u>	kalt<u>em</u>	kalt<u>en</u>
	Wein	Limonade	Bier	Getränken

Summary of adjective endings without **d.** .- or **ein**-type words:

	singular			plural
	m	*f*	*n*	*m f n*
SU	-er	-e	-es	-en
DO	-en	-e	-es	-en
IO	-em	-er	-em	-en

The principle behind the (b) and (c) sets of adjective endings is that any characteristic letters in the endings of **d.** . which may be lost in the combination **ein**-*type word* + *adjective* or when there is not even an **ein**-type word present MUST be preserved in the adjective ending. Thus, with **ein**, **-r** is lost with *m* singular SU case and **-s** is lost with *n* singular SU/DO cases. They are therefore transferred to the adjective. In the set (c) situation, all the **d.** . endings are lost, so they are all transferred to the adjective, with the sole modification that *n* singular SU/DO **d** + **as** becomes **-es** when transferred (as with the **d.** .-type words in Section 28).

30 Numerals: ordinal numbers and fractions

(a) The ordinal numbers ('first', 'second', 'third', etc.)
are as follows:

    (i) *first:* **erst** - so, as in English, unconnected with the
       cardinal ('one': **eins**).

    (ii) *second to nineteenth:* add -t to the cardinal number
       (Section 18), so 'second' is **zweit**; 'ninth', **neunt**; and
       'eighteenth', **achtzehnt**.

Exceptions:	*third*	**dritt**	(-ei- becomes -i-)
	seventh	**siebt**	(**sieben** loses the -en)
	eighth	**acht**	(**acht** does not get the additional -t)

    (iii) *twentieth* onwards: add -st to the cardinal number, so
       'thirty fifth' is **fünfunddreißigst**; 'hundredth',
       hundertst; and 'thousandth', **tausendst**.

The ordinals are mostly used as adjectives preceding nouns,
so they take the endings described in Section 29:

Die fünfte Person von rechts ist mein Vater.
The fifth person from the right is my father.
Ich nehme gern ein drittes Glas von dem herrlichen Wein.
I'd enjoy a third glass of that splendid wine.

The following usage is an extension of the Section 29(c)
endings:

Sie benutzen als erster (or **erste** if person spoken to is
female) **unsere neue Maschine.**
You're the first to use our new machine.
Ich bin als siebter mit der Prüfung fertig.
I'm the seventh to finish the test.

(b) Apart from 'half', **die Hälfte (-n)**, fractions are formed by adding **-el** to the ordinal number, which then becomes a *n* noun: for example, 'quarter', **das Viertel (-)**; 'tenth', **das Zehntel (-)**. So 'two-thirds' is **zwei Drittel**; 'three-eighths', **drei Achtel**.

'half (of) the ...' would often be **die Hälfte von ...** (or, instead of **von**, the possessor case, Section 50):

Die Hälfte von dem Geld gehört mir.
Half (of) the money belongs to me.

However, when 'half' is followed not by 'the' (or a similar indicator of particularity like 'this', 'my', 'each') but by 'a/an', you must use the adjective **halb**. Thus 'half anhour' is **eine halbe Stunde** and 'half a loaf' is **ein halbes Brot**.

Viertel, on the other hand, forms a lot of compounds, like 'a quarter of an hour', **eine Viertelstunde**; 'a quarter of a litre', **ein Viertelliter** (*m* or *n*, no change in the plural).

'one and a half' is **anderthalb** or **eineinhalb** or even **einundeinhalb,** and 'five and a half' is **fünfeinhalb** or **fünfundeinhalb**. These do not take any adjective endings even when they precede nouns.

31 Conversation between intimates

Conversation within the family, or between children, students and some groups of workers, etc. requires the use of *familiar* 2nd person pronouns ('you/your') and verb forms. These you have not yet met, and for the moment we shall deal only with the singular construction:

pronouns		ein-type word (possession)	verbs present tense	instructions/ requests
SU	du	dein (your)	of sein: bist	using sein: sei
DO	dich		of haben: hast	using other verbs:
IO	dir		of other verbs:	stem *only, no*
			stem + (e)st†	pronoun following
				(cf. Section 24)

†The (e) is added after stems ending in -t or -d.

32 Sequence of words (I)

The sequence of words in German was mentioned in Section 9 as an intriguing feature for the English learner. You have already begun to practise one aspect of this in Chapter 6, probably without being aware of it:

location	verb	SU
Auf dem Bild	sind	mehrere Sachen.
Auf einer Tischdecke	liegt	ein Brot.
Neben dem Brot	ist	ein Glas.
Hinter dem Brot	ist	eine Flasche mit einem Korken.
Auf der Flasche	ist	ein Etikett.

In simple *statements* of this sort (not questions or instructions) the 'natural' sequence of words in German can easily be exactly reflected in a 'natural' English translation, with first the locational (or temporal etc.) information, then the verb, and finally the SU.

In German, however, this mechanism of starting statements with something other than the standard SU can be taken much further, with for instance a DO or an IO at the beginning of the statement, to the extent that an English translation in the same sequence is impossible. The reason for this is that, whatever part of the statement comes first, *the verb must come second*. The only condition governing the part that comes first, if it is DO or IO, is that it must be or refer to something previously mentioned, or must at least be associated in the speaker's mind with something previously mentioned. Here are some good examples derived from sentences you have already met in their 'English' sequence:

DO	verb	SU	rest
zwei Cola	wollen	Sie	aber nur eine Wurst
den Theaterplatz	finden	Sie	dann sofort
so etwas	glaubt	kein Mensch	
viel Spaß	wünsche	ich	Ihnen heute abend
einen Stadtführer	suche	ich	
ihr	gefallen	rote Rosen	bestimmt
Ihnen	wünsche	ich	viel Spaß heute abend

Exercise 15

Insert the correct word from the column on the right in the following sentences. There may be more than one grammatical possibility, but you will see that not all are equally plausible.

1	... glaubt einem Verbrecher.	Solches
2	... Blumen sind für die Freundin?	Keiner
3	... Kuchen haben sie für das Kind.	Welches?/!
4	... Mann finde ich nett.	Jeder
5	... Wein schmeckt wunderbar.	Dieser
6	... Glück haben wir mit dem Wetter.	Welche?/!
7	... Buch aus der Hugo-Reihe kennen Sie?	Jede
8	... Hausbesitzer hat Schwierigkeiten.	Keinen
9	... Katze kommt ins Haus./?	Diesen

Exercise 16

Translate the following 'scene' into English. You will need these new words:

	einkaufen	to do the shopping
	jawohl!	(yes) certainly!
die	Einkaufsliste (-n)	shopping list
	alles	everything
	erst	first (of all)
	holen	to fetch, bring
der	Bäcker (-)	baker
das	Weißbrot (-e)	white loaf
	frisch	fresh
das	Brötchen (-)	roll
	billig	cheap
(der)	Marktkauf	(typical hypermarket name)
	fahren	to go (other than on foot)
	heute nachmittag	this afternoon
	dorthin	(to) there
	na gut!	all right (then)!
der	Metzger (-)	butcher
	halb	half
das	Pfund (-e)	pound
	((-) *after numbers*)	
das	Hackfleisch	mince
	gekocht	boiled
der	Schinken	ham
	bedienen	to serve
	man	one/they/people
	immer	always
das	Fleisch	meat
	lieber	rather
die	Altstadt	old town
	müssen	to have to
	dahin	(to) there
das	Gemüsegeschäft	greengrocer's
der	Kopfsalat (-e)	lettuce
	fest	firm
die	Gurke (-n)	cucumber
die	Bohne (-n)	bean
	grüne Bohnen	French beans
die	Sache (-n)	thing, item
der	Salat (-e)	salad
	ander..	other

das	**Gemüse**	vegetables
	eilen	to be urgent
	doch	after all
der	**Markt (:e)**	market
	unbedingt	definitely
das	**Ei (-er)**	egg
	Edeka	(chain of small super-markets)
	noch	still
	viele	many / a lot
	kriegen	to get

'She' tries to organise 'him' to do the shopping

Sie Gehst du bitte jetzt einkaufen?

Er Jawohl! Hast du eine Einkaufsliste für mich?

Sie Nein, ich sage dir alles … Erst hol bitte vom Bäcker ein kleines Weißbrot und zehn frische Brötchen.

Er Sie sind billiger bei Marktkauf, und wir fahren heute nachmittag dorthin.

Sie Na gut! Dann kauf beim Metzger ein halbes Pfund Hackfleisch und zweihundertfünfzig Gramm gekochten Schinken.

Er Beim Metzger bedient man mich immer schlecht. Ich kaufe Fleisch lieber in der Altstadt, und heute nachmittag müssen wir auch dahin.

Sie Na gut! Vom Gemüsegeschäft brauche ich dann einen Kopfsalat, anderthalb Pfund kleine feste Tomaten, eine schöne Gurke, zehn Pfund Kartoffeln und ein Pfund grüne Bohnen.

Er Die Sachen für den Salat und das andere Gemüse eilen nicht, und morgen ist doch Markt.

Sie Na gut, aber ich brauche unbedingt Eier von Edeka.

Er Nein, brauchst du nicht. Wir haben noch viele. Eier kriegen wir dann auch vom Markt.

Sie Na gut, dann brauchst du nicht einkaufen gehen.

Practise repeating the above conversation from memory, using the following key words as a guide.

Sie einkaufen?
Er Einkaufsliste?
Sie sage alles ... Bäcker ...Weißbrot ... Brötchen
Er Marktkauf fahren
Sie Metzger ... Hackfleisch ... Schinken
Er schlecht ... Altstadt ... nachmittag
Sie Gemüsegeschäft ... Kopfsalat ... Tomaten ... Gurke ... Kartoffeln ... Bohnen
Er eilen nicht ... Markt
Sie Eier
Er brauchst nicht ... noch viele ... Markt.
Sie nicht einkaufen

Exercise 17

*Construct a dialogue in which each pair of sentences is based on one of the pairs of items/locations listed. The first sentence should be an instruction to buy the item(s) somewhere; the second a response preferring (**lieber**) to buy the item(s) elsewhere. The first pair is done for you.*

1   anderthalb Pfund kleine feste Tomaten
    auf dem Markt
    Hol bitte anderthalb Pfund kleine feste Tomaten vom Gemüsegeschäft.
    Die Tomaten kaufe ich lieber auf dem Markt.

2   ein kleines Weißbrot
    bei Marktkauf
3   250 Gramm gekochter
    Schinken
    in der Altstadt
4   ein Kopfsalat
    auf dem Markt
5   zwanzig Eier
    auf dem Markt
6   eine schöne Gurke
    auf dem Markt
7   zehn frische Brötchen
    bei Marktkauf
8   ein halbes Pfund
    Hackfleisch
    in der Altstadt
9   zehn Pfund Kartoffeln
    auf dem Markt
10 ein Pfund grüne Bohnen
    auf dem Markt

Chapter 8

Chapter 8 looks at more complex German sentences.
It covers:

- *the order of words in a sentence with more than one verb*
- *the so-called auxiliary verbs – 'can', 'must', 'will', etc. – and how they are used with another, 'main' verb*
- *how to express quantities and measurements*
- *the various ways of saying where something 'is' and where something is 'put'*
- *the use of **da-** or **dar-** with prepositions to express 'on it', 'about them', etc.*

33 Sequence of words (II)

So far we have referred to 'the verb' as if – at least in a simple, straightforward sentence – there was no possibility of mistaking 'the verb'. Consider, however, the first sentence of the conversation in Chapter 7, Exercise 16:

Gehst du jetzt bitte einkaufen?

This group of words – which obviously all belong together, are spoken without a pause, and therefore constitute 'a simple sentence'– clearly contains two verbs: **gehst** is a verb matched up with **du** and so is a sort of personalised verb (often called a 'finite verb', because it is *restricted* to a particular person: 1st or 2nd or 3rd, singular or plural) and **einkaufen** is a verb which is not matched up with anything or anybody but completes the sense of **gehst. einkaufen** is, then, one of the (three) non-personalised forms of the verb and we shall call this form the '**-en** non-finite verb' and, when it has become familiar, simply the '**-en** form'. (Of course it is unhelpful that the form **einkaufen** can frequently be finite if it is matched up with **wir** or **Sie** or **sie**, which is not the case here!) The complete verb group means '(will you) go do the shopping' (i.e. 'go shopping').

The important point to note is that if a simple sentence contains a finite verb and a non-finite verb, the non-finite verb stands right at the end.

gehen can be combined with other verbs:

Ich gehe zweimal in der Woche schwimmen.
I go twice in the week swimming (i.e. *for a swim*).
Gehen wir morgen abend mit der Gruppe essen?
Shall we go tomorrow evening with the group eating (i.e. *out for a meal*)?

Meine Mutter geht immer früh schlafen.
My mother goes always early sleeping (i.e. *to bed*).
Manchmal gehen wir stundenlang im Wald spazieren.
Sometimes we go for hours in the forest walking (i.e. *for a walk*).

34 Finite (auxiliary) verb + -en non-finite verb

Finite **geh. .** + **-en** non-finite verb (Section 33) is the pattern also followed when the finite verb is one of the verbs similar to English 'will, can, must, may, shall', which have little specific meaning of their own, but which modify or colour the way in which the meaning of the main (following) verb is to be understood (and are therefore called 'auxiliary verbs'). These include a verb for expressing the future (**werden**) and another for expressing the idea of causing or permitting something to happen (**lassen**). Here is the complete set of eight, with all the forms of the present tense. (These verbs are all irregular in some way.)

	dürfen	können
	may, can (permission)	may, can (possibility)
ich/er/sie (she)/**es**	**darf**	**kann**
wir/Sie/sie (they)	**dürfen**	**können**
du	**darfst**	**kannst**

	mögen	müssen
	may, can (possibility), to like to	must, to have to
ich/er/sie (she)/**es**	**mag**	**muß**
wir/Sie/sie (they)	**mögen**	**müssen**
du	**magst**	**mußt**

	sollen	wollen
	must, to be to, to be said to	to want to, to intend to
ich/er/sie (she)/**es**	**soll**	**will**
wir/Sie/sie (they)	**sollen**	**wollen**
du	**sollst**	**willst**

	lassen	werden
	to get / allow (someone to), to have (something done)	will (future)
ich	**lasse**	**werde**
wir/Sie/sie (they)	**lassen**	**werden**
du	**läßt**	**wirst**
er/sie (she)/**es**	**läßt**	**wird**

35 Use of the auxiliary verbs (present tense)

(a) **dürfen:** *may/can (permission), (negative) mustn't*

Darf ich hier rauchen?
Can I smoke here?

Darf ich meinen Freund vorstellen?
May I introduce my friend?
In der Kirche darf man nicht laut reden.
One mustn't talk loudly in church.

(b) **können:** *may/can (possibility), be able to*

Für seine sechs Jahre kann er sehr gut schwimmen.
He can swim very well considering he's only six.
Seine Rede kann noch lange dauern.
His speech may go on for a long time yet.
Wir können seine Experimente nicht finanzieren.
We aren't able to finance his experiments.

(c) **mögen:** *may (possibility), to like to*

Er mag wohl reich sein, er kommt trotzdem nicht in den Klub.
He may have a lot of money, but he's still not going to get into the club.
Ich mag nicht über alles klagen, aber ...
I don't like complaining about everything, but ...

(d) **müssen:** *must, to have to, (negative) needn't, doesn't/don't have to*

Ich muß um zwölf zu Hause sein, sonst kommt das Mittagessen zu spät auf den Tisch.
I must be home at twelve, or else I shall be late with lunch.
Dieser Brief ist an dich. Du mußt nicht unbedingt antworten.
This letter is (addressed) to you. You aren't absolutely obliged to reply.

e) **sollen:** *must, to be supposed/expected to, to be to, to be said to*

Du sollst erst essen und dann ins Kino gehen.
You're to eat first and then go to the cinema.

Ich kann nicht länger auf ihn warten, er soll sofort kommen.
I can't wait for him any longer, he's to come at once.
Ich kann ihn empfehlen, er soll ein sehr guter Klavierlehrer sein.
I can recommend him. He's said to be a very good piano teacher.

(f)   **wollen:** *to want to, to be determined to, to intend to*

Er ist vollkommen satt, er will nichts mehr essen.
He's completely full. He doesn't want to eat another thing.
Er will gar nichts mehr von der Sache hören.
He doesn't want to hear anything more at all about the matter.
Er will seine Ferien in den Bergen verbringen.
He intends to spend his holidays in the mountains.

(g)   **lassen:** *to get (someone to), to make/have (someone do), to have (something done), to let/allow (someone (to) do)*

Der Chef läßt seine Sekretärin unwichtige Briefe unterschreiben.
The boss gets his secretary to sign unimportant letters.
Er läßt seinen Wagen alle zwei Tage waschen.
He has his car washed every other day.
Mein Vater läßt grüßen.
My father sends his regards.
Wir lassen unsere Tochter nicht alleine zur Schule gehen.
We don't let our daughter walk to school on her own.

(h)   **werden:** *shall/will (future), to be going to*

Ich mache es jetzt, ich werde in den nächsten Tagen keine Zeit haben.
I'll do it now. I shan't have any time in the next few days.
Es ist schrecklich dunkel, es wird bestimmt regnen.
It's terribly dark. It's going to rain for sure.

Vocabulary

Study the conversation that follows until you know all the sentences (and their meaning) by heart. You will need these new words:

	etwas	somewhat
das	Übergewicht	surplus weight
	abnehmen	to slim, lose weight
der	Urlaub (-e)	holiday(s)
	anziehen	to wear, put on
der	Sportler (-)	sportsman
	unbedingt	absolutely
	recht haben	to be right
	schwer	heavy
	hoffentlich	hopefully
	richtig	right, correct
	vorsichtig	careful, cautious
der	Arzt (¨e)	doctor
	mager	lean
der	Reis	rice
	passen	to fit
	vorig	last, previous
das	Jahr (-e)	year
	vernünftig	sensible
	weiß (from wissen)	to know
	schneiden	to cut
	lecker	delicious
die	Sahnesoße	cream sauce
	allein	on their own
	schmecken	to taste (good)
	achten (auf)	to pay attention (to), keep an eye (on)
der	Semmelknödel (-)	bread dumpling
das	Essen (-)	meal
das	Bierchen (-)	(nice) little beer
	Moment mal!	hold on!
	zunehmen	to put on weight

CONVERSATION

At Monday breakfast: discussing the menu for the day's main meal

Mutter Was *sollen* wir denn heute essen?

Tochter Nach dem Wochenende habe ich bestimmt etwas Übergewicht. Von heute an *muß* ich abnehmen.
In vier Wochen fahren wir in den Urlaub, da *will* ich meine Bikinis anziehen *können*. (*Zu ihrem Bruder*) Rudi, du bist Sportler, du *mußt* auch unbedingt abnehmen.

Sohn Ich *soll* bei meiner Figur Sportler sein!? Aber du hast recht, ich bin zu schwer. Ich *darf* in den nächsten Wochen keine Kartoffeln mehr essen. Und hoffentlich *lassen* wir kein Bier mehr ins Haus bringen!

Vater Ganz richtig. Mit fünfzig *muß* ich auch vorsichtiger sein. Der Arzt sagt, ich *soll* nur Fisch oder mageres Fleisch essen, dazu nur frisches Gemüse, keine Kartoffeln, keinen Reis.

M Was *soll* es denn geben? Ich passe nicht mehr in meine Sommerkleidung vom vorigen Jahr. Wir *müssen* vernünftig sein. Ich weiß was, ich *lasse* beim Metzger vier extra magere Steaks schneiden.

T Ja, und dann brauchen wir dazu nur eine leckere Sahnesoße.

S Fleisch und Sahnesoße allein schmecken nicht.

V Das *mag* sein, aber wir *müssen* auf die Kalorien achten.

S Vielleicht *können* wir dann ein paar Semmelknödel und Karotten in Buttersoße dazu essen.

V Zu so einem Essen *muß* man ein kaltes Bierchen trinken, nicht?

M Moment mal, *werden* wir nicht auch von diesem Essen zunehmen?

TRANSLATION

Mother	Well, what shall we eat today?
Daughter	I'm definitely somewhat overweight after the weekend. I must slim from today onwards. We're going on holiday in four weeks, and I want to be able to wear my bikinis. *(To her brother)* Rudi, you're a sportsman, you've absolutely got to lose weight too.
Son	What, I'm supposed to be a sportsman with a figure like mine!? But you're right, I'm too heavy. I mustn't eat any potatoes in the next few weeks. And hopefully we won't be having any more beer brought into the house!
Father	Quite right. At fifty I've got to be more careful too. The doctor says I must only eat fish or lean meat, and with it only fresh vegetables; no potatoes and no rice.
M	Well, what is it to be? I don't fit into my summer clothes from last year any more. We've got to be sensible. I know, I'll get four particularly lean steaks cut at the butcher's.
D	Yes, and then we only need a delicious cream sauce with them.
S	Meat and cream sauce don't taste good on their own.
F	That may be so, but we've got to keep an eye on the calories.
S	Perhaps we can also have a few dumplings and some carrots in butter sauce with them.
F	You have to drink a nice cold beer with a meal like that, don't you?
M	Hold on, aren't we going to put on weight from this meal too?

Exercise 18

Insert the correct form of **dürfen, können** *or* **müssen** *in the following sentences, choosing the auxiliary verb that best fits the sense:*

1 Sie _____ gut Englisch sprechen, ihre Lehrerin ist gut.
2 Wir _____ den Wein trinken, sonst wird er schlecht.
3 Er ist sechzehn Jahre alt, er _____ nicht Auto fahren.
4 Ich _____ ins Geschäft gehen und einkaufen, wir haben heute abend Freunde.
5 Er _____ kein Bier trinken, er will abnehmen.
6 Die kleine Tochter _____ den Film sehen, es ist Sonntag.
7 Das Mittagessen _____ warten, sie will erst den Sherry trinken.

36 Measurements, quantities, other units

Whereas English requires 'of' in expressions such as

two metres of string   (measurements)
a big pile of rubbish   (quantities)
some cans of beans   (other units)

the corresponding expressions in German place the two nouns together:

zwei Meter Bindfaden
ein großer Haufen Abfall
einige Dosen Bohnen

If the first noun is *m* or *n* it is always in the singular, even when the meaning is plural:

Ich brauche für dieses Rezept zwei Pfund Mehl.
I need two pounds of flour for this recipe.
Ich trinke jeden Abend drei Glas Rotwein.
I drink three glasses of red wine every evening.

37 'there is/are' + quantity/number/ location

In Section 27 we noted the use of **es gibt** for 'there is/are' when the idea of existence/availability predominates. When the existence/availability of something is taken for granted and the dominant idea is its quantity or number and its location, 'there is/are' is conveyed by **es ist/sind:**

Es ist ein Brief für dich da.
There's a letter for you (here).
Es sind zwei Zeitungen für meine Mutter da.
There are two newspapers (here) for my mother.

The **es** in these sentences is not like the **es** of **es gibt**. You will remember that **gibt** remains singular in all cases, with the noun to which it relates in the DO case. With **es ist/sind** the choice of **ist** or **sind** is made according to whether the real SU of the sentence (here **Brief** and **Zeitungen**) is singular or plural. This real subject is of course in the SU case.

38 Expressing specific location

In the examples in Section 37 the idea of location was rather weak (**da**) and could indeed be omitted in the translation. When the idea of location is more dominant and the information more precise, German has three verbs, in addition to **sein** ('be'), to express 'is/are'. These are in very common use; there is nothing lofty or poetic about them, as their literal English translations might suggest.

(a) *When something is upright:* **stehen**

   Auf dem Tisch steht eine alte Vase.
or   **Eine alte Vase steht auf dem Tisch.**
or   **Es steht eine alte Vase auf dem Tisch.**
   There's an old vase on the table.

Der Fernsehapparat steht in der Ecke.
The television set is in the corner.

(b) *When something is flat:* **liegen**

      Auf dem Boden liegt ein schmutziger Teppich.
or **Ein schmutziger Teppich liegt auf dem Boden.**
or **Es liegt ein schmutziger Teppich auf dem Boden.**
      There's a dirty carpet on the floor.
      Die Zeitung liegt auf dem Wohnzimmertisch.
      The newspaper is on the living-room table.

(c) *When something is inserted into/between or concealed:*
stecken

      Im Schloß steckt ein rostiger Schlüssel.
or **Ein rostiger Schlüssel steckt im Schloß.**
or **Es steckt ein rostiger Schlüssel im Schloß.**
      There's a rusty key in the lock.
      Was steckt hinter dem Vorhang?
      What's behind the curtain?

Sentences of this type beginning with **es** are only possible
when the real SU is a noun preceded either by **(k)ein** or by
some similar indefinite word (e.g. **einige**) or by nothing.

39 Expressing 'put'

Just as 'to be' in a location can be indicated in a general way
with **sein** or more precisely with **stehen**, **liegen** and **stecken**,
German can express 'put' in a generalised way with **tun** or
more precisely with **stellen**, **legen** and **stecken**:

	being in a location	putting in a location
generalised	**sein**	**tun**
upright	**stehen**	**stellen**
flat	**liegen**	**legen**
inserted	**stecken**	**stecken**

- Generalised 'put': **tun** (to do, put)

ich	**tue**
wir/Sie/sie (they)	**tun**
du	**tust**
er/sie (she)**/es**	**tut**

Er tut seine Bücher immer auf das falsche Regal.
He always puts his books on the wrong shelf.
Sie tut etwas Milch in die Milchkanne.
She's putting a little milk in the milk jug.

- 'put' so that something *stands*: **stellen**

Wir stellen den Nachttisch neben das Bett.
We'll put the bedside table next to the bed.
Er stellt die leeren Flaschen vor die Tür.
He puts the empty bottles outside the door.

- 'put' so that something lies *flat*: **legen**

Sie legt einen Fünfzigmarkschein auf die Theke.
She's putting a fifty-mark note on the counter.

- 'put' so that something is inserted *into/between* or
concealed: **stecken**

**Er steckt gerade einen Zehnmarkschein in deine
Manteltasche!**
He's just putting a ten-mark note in your coat pocket!

40 Preposition + 'it'/'them'/'this'/ 'these', etc.

When any of the prepositions you learnt in Section 26 (a)–(c),
except **ohne** and **seit**, is applied to a 3rd person pronoun
standing for anything *except* living beings, the pronoun itself
is not used but is represented by **da(r)-** followed by the

preposition, which thus becomes a *post*position. The two
bits form one word, with the stress on the preposition. The
-(r)- is used when the preposition begins with a vowel.

compare   **Ich lache über sie.**
I'm laughing at them (e.g. *my children,*
meine Kinder).

with   **Ich lache darüber.**
I'm laughing at them (e.g. *my mistakes,*
meine Fehler).

The particular case (DO or IO) normally required by the
preposition does not affect the **da(r)-** construction, which
may furthermore stand for a singular or a plural, or even for
no noun at all (but for a fact or an idea):

**A: Ich höre, er ist arbeitslos. B: Ja, aber er redet nie
darüber.**
A: I hear he's unemployed. B: Yes, but he never talks about it
(i.e. about being unemployed).

Some combinations of **da(r)-** + preposition have come to
acquire permanent meanings of their own, independent of
anything particularly evident in a context, though they can
naturally also be used in the way just described:

dafür	instead, on the other hand
dagegen	by contrast, on the other hand
daher	therefore
damit	so that (purpose), in order that
darum	therefore

ohne ('without') is simply followed by the standard pronouns
(Section 15), while to say 'since that', 'since it' (or 'since then')
using **seit** there is just one standard word: **seitdem**.

Exercise 19

*Insert the most appropriate word from the column on the right into the gap in each of the following sentences. You may need to juggle with the **da(r)-** words so as to use each one only once and to accommodate all of them.*

1 Er hat eine Feile in der Hand , _____ öffnet er die Tür.	dazwischen
2 Vor dem Einbrecher ist eine Treppe, _____ sitzt ein Skelett.	danach
3 Wir trinken ein Glas Wein, _____ gehen wir schlafen.	darauf
4 Ich esse eine Wurst, _____ trinke ich eine Cola.	daneben
5 Ich nehme fünf Rosen, _____ muß ich DM 12,50 bezahlen.	dahinter
6 Auf der Tischdecke liegt ein Brot, _____ steht ein Glas.	dazu
7 Der junge Mann ist zu schwer, _____ muß er etwas tun.	damit
8 Sie sehen die Kirche und das Gasthaus, Sie nehmen die Straße _____ .	dagegen
9 Das Haus steht direkt an der Straße, der Garten liegt _____ .	davor
10 Wir wollen einkaufen gehen, _____ müssen wir noch essen.	dafür

Exercise 20

*Complete the monologue below by filling the spaces with the appropriate words for 'be' and 'put'. Do this exercise twice, first using the generalised expressions **sein** and **tun**, and the second time choosing the more precise expressions as described in Sections 38 and 39. You will need to know these new words:*

paß auf!	now look!
der **Kühlschrank (⁼e)**	refrigerator
möglichst	as (far/much) as possible
freihalten	to keep clear

das	Hähnchen (-)	chicken
die	Himbeertorte (-n)	raspberry flan
das	Fertigessen (-)	oven-ready meal
das	Eisfach (⁻er)	freezer compartment
	morgen	tomorrow
	übermorgen	the day after tomorrow
der	Pflaumenkuchen (-)	plum tart
die	Schüssel (-n)	dish
die	Schlagsahne	(here) whipped cream, (but also) whipping cream
der	Becher (-)	(here) carton, (but also) beaker, mug
die	Packung (-en)	pack, packet
die	Leberwurst (⁻e)	liver sausage
	einzeln	singly, separately
das	Stück	piece (but with number can sometimes be omitted in translation)
	zum Weichwerden	to get soft
	flach	flat
der	Behälter (-)	container
der	Scheibenkäse	cheese in slices
der	Salat	(here) lettuce
die	Weintraube (-n)	grape
der	Beutel (-)	bag
die	Apfelsine (-n)	orange
der	Blumenkohl	cauliflower
der	Rosenkohl	brussels sprouts
das	Gemüsefach (⁻er)	vegetable compartment
das	Glas (⁻er)	jar
der	Honig	honey
die	Erdbeermarmelade	strawberry jam
	meine Güte!	my goodness!
das	Obst	fruit

A mother, about to leave her teenage son on his own for a few days, outlines to him the contents of the refrigerator, which she is stocking for him. (You will find the diagram on the next page helpful.)

Paß auf! Ich werde den Kühlschrank möglichst freihalten. Dann kannst du alles ganz leicht finden. Das Hähnchen für Sonntag, die gefrorene Himbeertorte und die beiden Fertigessen (1) _____ / _____ ich ins Eisfach. Die Fertigessen kannst du morgen und übermorgen essen. Der Pflaumenkuchen und die Schüssel mit Schlagsahne (2) _____ / _____ oben. Da (3) _____ / _____ ich auch die beiden Flaschen Wein hin … Ach, da ist gerade noch etwas Platz, den Becher Yoghurt kann ich dazwischen (4) _____ / _____ . Die vier Flaschen Bier (5) _____ / _____ ich unten in die Tür, und zwei Packungen Milch (6) _____ / _____ daneben. Ich (7) _____ / _____ die Packung gekochten Schinken, die Salami und die Leberwurst in die Mitte. Sie sind natürlich für abends … Eier? … Die Eier (8) _____ / _____ ich natürlich einzeln oben in die Tür, zwölf Stück. Zwei Stück Butter (9) _____ / _____ ich in das obere Fach in der Tür, das dritte lasse ich draußen zum Weichwerden. Der flache Behälter mit drei Sorten Käse (10) _____ / _____ in der Mitte, und dahinter liegen eine Tube Mayonnaise und der Scheibenkäse. Die Gurke, der Salat, die Weintrauben und die Tomaten (11) _____ / _____ unten, und den Beutel Apfelsinen, einen Kopf Blumenkohl und den Rosenkohl (12) _____ / _____ ich ins Gemüsefach ganz unten. Ein kleines Glas Honig und ein Glas Erdbeermarmelade (13) _____ / _____ ich weiter oben in die Tür … Meine Güte, ist der Kühlschrank wieder voll!

Eisfach

Oben

Mitte

unten

Obst-und Gemüsefach

Eier

oberes Fach.

für kleinere Gläser usw.

für Flaschen usw.

Exercise 21

Translate the monologue from Exercise 20.

Chapter 9

In this chapter you will learn:

- *some further meanings and uses of d. .*
- *more uses of the present tense and the exceptional present-tense forms of many common verbs*
- *the uses of a new tense, the 'pre-present', and how it is formed*
- *some words and expressions for giving time information, including frequency, months, days and dates, and times of day.*

41 Further uses of der, die, das, etc.

(a) **das** not only means 'the' before *n* nouns, but can stand alone without a noun to mean 'that':

(i) **A: Du sollst heute bezahlen.**   **B: Das weiß ich.**
   A: *You've got to pay today.*   B: *I know (that).*

(ii) **A: Zehn Brötchen kosten drei Mark.**
   B: Das ist zu teuer.
   A: *Ten rolls cost three marks.*   B: *That's too much.*

In the above, **das** – DO in (i) and SU in (ii) – stands for facts or ideas and not for identifiable nouns.

(b) **der** (*m*), **die** (*f*) and **die** (plural) can stand alone with out a noun to mean **er** (*m*), **sie** (*f*) and **sie** (plural):

(i) **A: Der Kellner hat unsere Bestellung seit einer Stunde.**
   A: *The waiter has had our order for an hour.*

B: Der ist aber langsam!
B: *My goodness, he's slow!*

(ii) **A: Ich warte auf die Schwester.**
A: *I'm waiting for the nurse.*
B: Die kommt heute nicht.
B: *She's not coming today.*

(iii) **A: Was kosten Bananen?**
A: *What's the price of bananas?*
B: Die sind diese Woche billig.
B: *They're cheap this week.*

This use of **der** and **die** so dominates the speech of some Germans as almost to replace **er** and **sie**. **der** and **die**, when used in this way as a substitute for **er** and **sie**, tend to be used to *start* sentences (and so are less common in questions, when this is not possible), and they always have some degree of *stress* (weight or emphasis) when spoken, as compared with their use to mean 'the'.

(c)   The uses described in (a) and (b) apply also to the DO and IO cases, producing the following scheme:

	singular			plural	
	m	*f*	*n*		
DO	den (ihn)	die (sie)	das	die (sie)	
IO	dem (ihm)	der (ihr)	dem	denen (ihnen)	

Examples:

A: Geben Sie mir den Schlüssel.
Give me the key.
B: Den finde ich im Augenblick nicht. (*m* DO)
I can't find it just at the moment.
A: Der Chef verspricht mir immer wieder mehr Geld.
The boss is always promising me more money.
B: Dem kann man gar nichts mehr glauben. (*m* IO)
You can't believe anything at all that he says.
A: Diese Milch ist sauer.
This milk is sour.

B: **Die müssen wir wegwerfen.** (*f* DO)
We'll have to throw it away.

A: **Frau Klimpel schwatzt sehr viel.**
Frau Klimpel gossips a lot.

B: **Ja, der erzähle ich nie (et)was.** (*f* IO)
Yes, I never tell her anything.

A: **Er verkauft sein Geschäft.**
He's selling his shop.

B: **Wie bitte? Das glaube ich nicht.** (*n* DO)
What! I don't believe it.

A: **Er hat zu viele Probleme mit seinem Geschäft.**
He has too many problems with his business.

B: **Dem ist er einfach nicht mehr gewachsen.** (*n* IO)
*He simply can't cope (i.e. with the general situation) any
more.*

A: **Drüben sitzen die neuen Nachbarn.**
The new neighbours are sitting over there.

B: **Die kennen wir leider noch nicht.** (plural DO)
Unfortunately we don't know them yet.

A: **Ich höre, die Kinder kriegen ein neues
Geschwisterchen.**
*I hear the children are going to get a new little brother or
sister.*

B: **Denen wollen wir aber eine Zeitlang noch nichts
davon sagen.** (plural IO)
We shan't tell them anything (about it) for a while, though.

(d) **der** and **die** are often used, particularly in spoken
German, before a forename or a family name, in referring
to individuals. With forenames this may – but need not –
imply intimacy, and with family names it may – but need
not – have pejorative overtones:

Der Rudi muß abnehmen.
Rudi's got to lose weight.
Ich sehe die Anna heute abend.
I'm seeing Anna this evening.
Dem Thomas schenke ich fünf Mark.
I'll give Thomas five marks.
Der Schmidt läßt seine Kunden immer warten.
Schmidt is always keeping his customers waiting.

While this usage has no parallel in English, perversely the English 'the' before a family name in the plural to mean the married couple or whole family with that name has no parallel in German:

Schmidts sind nicht zu Hause.
The Schmidts are not at home.

(e) In a list of nouns there is no question of a single **d. .** sufficing, and certainly not before nouns of mixed gender or mixed singular and plural. However, in both conversation and writing the common practice is to omit **d. .** altogether with groups of two or more nouns, even if separated by **und**:

Das Frühstück ist fertig. Brot, Butter, Eier, Marmelade, Honig, Kaffee, Milch, Zucker, Salz und Pfeffer stehen auf dem Tisch.
Breakfast is ready. The bread, butter, eggs, jam, honey, coffee, milk, sugar, salt and pepper are on the table.

Exercise 22

Insert the correct variant of **d. .** *in the following.*

1   *A* Wie geht es den Geschwistern?
    B Von _____ hören wir gar nichts.
2   *A* Wie lange müssen wir auf den Kaffee warten?
    B _____ ist schon lange fertig!
3   Der Junge bekommt immer soviel Geld von mir. _____ gebe ich jetzt nichts mehr.
4   *A* Bei diesem Wetter kann man gar nicht gut arbeiten.
    B _____ sage ich auch.
5   *A* Unsere Tochter heiratet nächste Woche.
    B _____ wünsche ich viel Spaß!
6   A Wie alt ist der Sohn von der Wirtin?
    B _____ weiß ich nicht.
7   *A* Wie alt ist der Sohn von der Wirtin?
    B _____ kenne ich nicht.

---

8   A Ich lese gern die BILD-Zeitung.
     B _____ lese ich auch gern.
9   A Meine Eltern sind krank, aber sie wollen nicht
       zum Arzt.
     B _____ kann man aber auch gar nicht helfen!
10   A Herr Schmidt verkauft mir saure Milch.
     B Bei _____ kaufe ich nichts mehr!

42 Uses of the present tense

(a) There are only two *real* tenses in German, the *present*
    and the *past*. The present tense is the only one you have
    learnt so far. (The future you learnt in Sections 34 and 35
    was a combination of the present tense of **werden** + the
    -en non-finite form.) The present tense covers both
    English ways of expressing 'present' ideas, as in:

    I *go* to my mother's twice a week.
    Don't delay me, *I'm going* home.

(b) It is also *very* much used, as are the two English con-
    structions in (a) above, to express 'future' ideas where
    the future is felt to be mapped out so clearly as to be
    virtually an extension of the present:

    I go to the States next month.
    Nächsten Monat fahre ich in die Vereinigten Staaten.
    I'm going on holiday with my brother.
    Ich fahre mit meinem Bruder in Urlaub.

    When the future is felt to be open-ended enough to justi-
    fy the sounding of a note of intention or conviction, the
    future with **werden** can be used:

    Ich werde nicht mehr so viel trinken.
    I'm going to start drinking less.
    Bei solcher Inflation wird alles bald viel mehr kosten.
    With inflation like this, everything's going to cost a lot more soon.

Sometimes the future with **werden** is necessary for clarity. The following request

Können Sie mir helfen, ich suche meine Koffer.
Can you help me? I'm looking for my suitcases.

could have the answer

Ich helfe Ihnen.
I'll help you.

Here the present tense has clear future meaning, the implication being **sofort** or **gleich**, 'at once', which might be added. But with a different answer to the same effect the present tense would be misleading and the future with **werden** is preferable:

Ich werde mein Bestes tun.
I'll do my best.

(c) Used together with a time reference – period of time or point in time – the present tense indicates a state of affairs continuing from the past into the present. This is quite logical, but English uses not the present tense but the pre-present, and this can lead to mistakes in German.

Ich kenne ihn seit sechs Jahren.
I have known him for six years.
Wie lange wohnen Sie schon hier?
How long have you been living here?
Wir wohnen hier seit 1982.
We've been living here since 1982.

43 Present tense: exceptional forms

Apart from the exceptional forms of the present tense described in Section 16 (**haben, sein**), Section 31 (familiar 2nd person singular of **haben, sein**), Section 34 (auxiliary verbs) and Section 39 (**tun**), there are some common verbs which are exceptional in the 2nd (familiar) and 3rd persons singular. These are easy to learn but *must* be learnt, and the most important are now listed, grouped according to the sound changes that take place. Only the 3rd person singular is given. The 2nd person is formed by inserting **-s-** before the final **-t** (unless the stem ends in **-s** or **-ß**):

-en form		3rd person singular
fahren	to go (other than on foot), travel	**fährt**
fallen	to fall	**fällt**
halten	to hold	**hält**
schlafen	to sleep	**schläft**
schlagen	to beat, strike	**schlägt**
tragen	to carry, wear	**trägt**
verlassen	to leave	**verläßt**
wachsen	to grow	**wächst**
laufen	to run	**läuft**
lesen	to read	**liest**
sehen	to see	**sieht**
stehlen	to steal	**stiehlt**
essen	to eat	**ißt**
geben	to give	**gibt**
helfen	to help	**hilft**
nehmen	to take	**nimmt**
sprechen	to speak	**spricht**
vergessen	to forget	**vergißt**
werfen	to throw	**wirft**

One common verb is exceptional throughout the singular:

wissen	to know (facts)	**ich/er/sie/es weiß**
		du weißt

44 The pre-present

You will remember that the auxiliary verbs (Sections 34 and 35) function as follows:

Start of sentence: End of sentence:
Finite auxiliary verb $\longrightarrow$ Non-finite main verb
(close to SU)   (**-en** form)

The pre-present follows a similar pattern. The finite verb is either **haben** or **sein**, which can be used as auxiliaries as well as independently. (For the choice of which to use, see Section 45.) In statements this finite verb is usually the second component of the sentence, and in questions either the first or the second, depending on the type of question.

The non-finite main verb is a type you have not met so far. In most cases it is made by taking the by now familiar **-en** form, replacing the **-en** by **-t**, and prefixing the stem with **ge-**: thus **machen** → **mach-en** → **ge-mach-t** → **gemacht**. (This type of non-finite verb stands in relation to the **-en** form as does English '(we have) *climbed*' to '(we can) *climb*'.) If the stem of the verb itself ends in **t** or **d**, it is necessary to insert an **-e-** before the added **-t**, simply so that it is pronounceable: thus **warten** ('to wait') → **wart-en** → **ge-wart-et** → **gewartet**. From now on we shall refer to this as the **ge_(e)t** form.

Wir haben ein Bild gemalt.

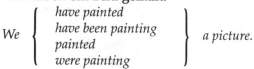

We $\left\{\begin{array}{l} \textit{have painted} \\ \textit{have been painting} \\ \textit{painted} \\ \textit{were painting} \end{array}\right\}$ *a picture.*

Wir sind in die Küche gerast.

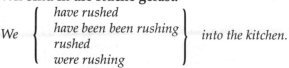

We $\left\{\begin{array}{l} \textit{have rushed} \\ \textit{have been been rushing} \\ \textit{rushed} \\ \textit{were rushing} \end{array}\right\}$ *into the kitchen.*

While the **-en** form is neutral in its perspective on the process represented by any particular verb, doing nothing more than *name* that process, the **ge_(e)t** form, in addition to naming the process, has the connotation of *completion,* and this is why and how it functions in the pre-present.

45 Pre-present auxiliary verb: sein or haben?

The rule is quite simple (though remembering to apply it is not!). Use **sein** as the auxiliary if the process denoted by the **ge_(e)t** main verb

(a) denotes a process involving motion or a change of state (e.g. **kommen,** 'to come'; **springen,** 'to jump'; **sterben,** 'to die'; **werden,** 'to become') without, however, taking or implying a DO (thus *excluding* such verbs as **bringen,** 'to take, bring'; **reichen,** 'to hand'; **schicken,** 'to send'; **ziehen,** 'to pull')
  or
(b) is one of the two verbs **sein,** 'to be', and **bleiben,** 'to stay, remain', which actually seem to imply the exact opposite of motion or a change of state.

Otherwise use **haben** as the auxiliary. Examples:

Ich bin hin und her gelaufen (motion).
I ran (or walked!) to and fro.
Ich bin zur Schule gegangen (motion), **aber mein Bruder ist zu Hause geblieben** (from **bleiben**).
I went to school but my brother stayed at home.
Meine Großmutter ist vier Wochen krank gewesen (from **sein**).
My grandmother was ill for four weeks.
Dann ist sie gestorben (change of state).
Then she died.

The rule does mean that a few verbs can require either **sein** or **haben,** according to the sense in which they are being used:

Wir sind immer mit dem Zug gefahren. (not implying a DO)
We always went by train.
Er hat einen eleganten Sportwagen gefahren. (taking a DO)
He was driving an elegant sports car.

46 Uses of the pre-present

Getting thoroughly familiar with the pre-present is invaluable, because it enables you to talk about almost any past event without ever having to use the second German tense, the *past tense* (Sections 59 and 66), which involves learning a fairly large number of new forms. For the pre-present you need only the present tense of **haben** or **sein,** which you are very familiar with already, and one **ge_(e)t** form for each verb you wish to use. The great advantage of the pre-present is that its coverage encompasses all the *four* English constructions in:

(x) (i)   *We have bought a house.*
     (ii)   *We have been buying a house.*
(y) (i)   *We bought a house.*
     (ii)   *We were buying a house.*

The German version for *all* the above is:

Wir haben ein Haus gekauft.

There is thus no provision in German for making the choice required in English between (x) and (y), nor is there (as we have already seen with the present tense, Section 42(a)) any means in the German verb or verb group for selecting between (i) and (ii) in either case. This does not mean that German cannot make such distinctions; they are simply accomplished by other means.

116

47 The ge_(e)t form

Most verbs follow the pattern **ge_(e)t**, which is to be regarded as the standard form. It is, for example, the pattern for most coinages from non-German sources (e.g. **gestartet, gestoppt, gelandet, geinterviewt, gecheckt**), and **ge_(e)t** will therefore always be used in this course as the symbol for this particular non-finite verb form, regardless of the fact that there are some divergences from it. Here are some examples of the standard pattern:

-en form		stem	ge_(e)t form
kaufen	to buy	**kauf**	**gekauft**
machen	to make, do	**mach**	**gemacht**
sagen	to say	**sag**	**gesagt**
zählen	to count	**zähl**	**gezählt**
baden	to bathe	**bad**	**gebadet**
blenden	to dazzle	**blend**	**geblendet**
bluten	to bleed	**blut**	**geblutet**
leisten	to achieve	**leist**	**geleistet**

(a) *Exceptional forms of* **ge_(e)t**

However, a number of verbs, including some of the commonest in the language, have exceptional forms. You can often be alerted to the presence of an exceptional form in German by an exceptional form in the English verb with which it has a common ancestry (e.g. 'to swim, swum': **schwimmen, geschwommen**). Here are some of the most important exceptional forms, grouped according to the changes that occur. Any particular oddities are underlined.

-en form		ge_(e)t form
brennen	to burn	**gebrannt**
bringen	to bring, take	**gebra<u>ch</u>t**
denken	to think	**geda<u>ch</u>t**

kennen	to know (people)	gekannt
wissen	to know (facts)	gewußt
essen	to eat	gegessen
fahren	to go (not on foot)	gefahren
fangen	to catch	gefangen
geben	to give	gegeben
halten	to hold	gehalten
kommen	to come	gekommen
laufen	to run	gelaufen
lesen	to read	gelesen
messen	to measure	gemessen
rufen	to call (out)	gerufen
schlafen	to sleep	geschlafen
schlagen	to hit, beat	geschlagen
sehen	to see	gesehen
stoßen	to bump	gestoßen
tragen	to carry, wear	getragen
treten	to step	getreten
wachsen	to grow	gewachsen
stehen	to stand	gestanden
gehen	to go	gegangen
brechen	to break	gebrochen
helfen	to help	geholfen
sprechen	to speak	gesprochen
sterben	to die	gestorben
treffen	to meet	getroffen
werden	to become	geworden
nehmen	to take	genommen
stehlen	to steal	gestohlen
leiden	to suffer	gelitten
pfeifen	to whistle	gepfiffen
schneiden	to cut	geschnitten
streiten	to quarrel	gestritten

bleiben	to stay, remain	**geblieben**
leihen	to lend	**geliehen**
scheinen	to seem, shine	**geschienen**
schreiben	to write	**geschrieben**
steigen	to climb	**gestiegen**
treiben	to drive, impel	**getrieben**
sitzen	**to sit**	**gese̲s̲sen**
schwimmen	to swim	**geschwommen**
finden	to find	**gefunden**
sinken	to sink	**gesunken**
springen	to jump	**gesprungen**
trinken	to drink	**getrunken**
bitten	to ask, request	**gebeten**
riechen	to smell	**gerochen**
schließen	to shut, close	**geschlossen**
liegen	to lie (recline)	**gelegen**
bieten	to offer	**geboten**
fliegen	to fly	**geflogen**
fliehen	to flee	**geflohen**
ziehen	to pull, draw	**gezogen**
lügen	to lie (fib)	**gelogen**
sein	to be	**gewe̲s̲en**

(b) *Effect of prefixes on the form of* **ge_(e)t**

Many German words are composite words consisting of a central core (or *root*) with a distinctive meaning, to the front or rear of which are attached (or *affixed*) further syllables of more generalised meaning. In the case of verbs the structure looks like this:

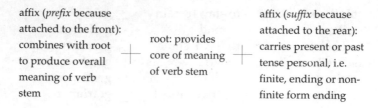

affix (*prefix* because attached to the front): combines with root to produce overall meaning of verb stem

root: provides core of meaning of verb stem

affix (*suffix* because attached to the rear): carries present or past tense personal, i.e. finite, ending or non-finite form ending

The nearest analogy in English would be a word like *returned*: *re-* (prefix), *-turn-* (root), *-ed* (suffix). The following now shows in a comprehensive way how the presence of a prefix affects the **ge_(e)t** non-finite form. The stressed (accented) syllables are marked with ', since observing the correct stress is the key to understanding the prefixes and their effects.

TYPE I:

-en form	**-en** form analysed			**ge_(e)t** form analysed		
	pre-fix	root	suf-fix	pre-fix	root	suf-fix
bekómmen to get	be	kómm	en	be	kómm	en
empfínden to feel	emp	fínd	en	emp	fúnd	en
entspréchen to correspond	ent	spréch	en	ent	spróch	en
erwárten to expect	er	wárt	en	er	wárt	et
gehören to belong	ge	hőr	en	ge	hőr	t
mißlingen to fail	miß	líng	en	miß	lúng	en
verstéhen to understand	ver	stéh	en	ver	stánd	en
widerspréchen to contradict	wider	spréch	en	wider	spróch	en
zerstören to destroy	zer	stör	en	zer	stör	t

TYPE II:

-en form	-en form analysed			ge_(e)t form analysed			
	prefix	root	suffix	prefixes		root	suffix
ánkommen to arrive	án	komm	en	án	ge	komm	en
aúfstehen to get up	aúf	steh	en	aúf	ge	stand	en
aúsmachen to switch off	aús	mach	en	aús	ge	mach	t
béitreten to join	béi	tret	en	béi	ge	tret	en
eínladen to invite	eín	lad	en	eín	ge	lad	en
gégenzeichnen to countersign	gégen	zeichn	en	gégen	ge	zeichn	et
míthelfen to assist	mít	helf	en	mít	ge	holf	en
náchholen to catch up	nách	hol	en	nách	ge	hol	t
vórbeugen to avert	vór	beug	en	vór	ge	beug	t
zúhören to listen	zú	hör	en	zú	ge	hör	t

If you study the two tables carefully, you will see that the TYPE I verb prefixes, which are unstressed, do not permit the **ge _ (e)t** form prefix **ge-** to be inserted between themselves and the root, i.e. they are inseparable from the root, and verbs with such inseparable prefixes do not take the **ge-** at all. The TYPE II verb prefixes, which are stressed, allow the additional prefix **ge-** to be inserted before the root, and so are said to be separable. The **ge_(e)t** forms of both types are written as single words, e.g. **verstanden, ausgemacht**. The suffix variations of both types of prefixed verbs **(-(e)t, -en)** result from what was explained in (a). That is, if the unprefixed verb is exceptional (e.g. **gestanden**), so are any prefixed forms derived from it (e.g. **aufgestanden,** 'got up', **verstanden,** 'understood').

The two tables contain the main prefixes used *exclusively* as inseparable or inseparable prefixes, but they are not exhaustive, and there are some prefixes (e.g. **über, um, unter**) which can appear in TYPE I or TYPE II verbs, producing in each case two verbs of completely different meaning (e.g. **umbáuen,** 'to build around, enclose'; **úmbauen,** 'to rebuild, convert').

To help you use prefixed verbs correctly, all prefixed verbs are labelled I or II in the Mini-dictionary and word lists.

(c) *Verbs ending in* **-ieren**

All verbs ending in (note the stress) **-íeren** (e.g. **telefoníeren, kontrollíeren, interessíeren, informíeren**) make the **ge_(e)t** form without the **ge-** but with the **-t** (e.g. **telefoníert,** etc.).

Exercise 23

For each sentence, insert the correct auxiliary verb for the pre-present (i.e. the correct form of **sein** *or* **haben***) in the first gap, and the* **ge_(e)t** *form of the given main verb in the second gap.*

1   Er _____ mir den Schlüssel _____. (bringen)
2   Mein Freund _____ heute in die Vereinigten Staaten
    _____. (fliegen)
3   Unsere Eltern _____ vor einigen Jahren _____.
    (sterben)
4   Meine Mutter _____ die Erdbeermarmelade in den
    Kühlschrank _____. (stellen)
5   Das Kind _____ vom Tisch _____. (springen)
6   Ich _____ heute den ganzen Tag zu Hause
    _____. (bleiben)
7   Dieses Jahr _____ die Miete für unsere Wohnung
    sehr _____ . (steigen)
8   Ich _____ meiner Wirtin einen Brief _____ .
    (schicken)
9   Wir _____ von meiner Schwester Geld _____ .
    (bekommen)
10 Du _____ wirklich sehr groß _____. (werden)

---

48 Time information

Learning a useful range of expressions for conveying time information is made easier by thinking of such expressions in groups:

(a) *Information about frequency*

nie	never
je (jemals)	ever
selten	rarely
einmal	once
zweimal (usw.)	twice (etc.)
ab und zu	occasionally
manchmal	sometimes
regelmäßig	regularly
immer wieder	again and again
immer	always

(b) *Indeterminate information related to 'now'*

jetzt	now (pure and simple: as in English can refer to what is happening or what is imminent)
nun	now (seen as the final step in a series: also has non-temporal sense of 'well now')
im Augenblick **augenblicklich** **im Moment** **momentan**	at the moment
eben **gerade**	just now (a moment ago); (exactly) now, just (at the moment); now (presently), just (in a moment) (as with English 'just', **eben** and **gerade** often have additional non-temporal connotations such as 'simply' or 'barely')
vorhin	a little time ago

neulich	recently (but only in the sense of a particular recent occasion in the speaker's mind)
letztens ⎫ in letzter Zeit ⎭	recently
vor einiger Zeit	some time ago
sofort ⎫ gleich ⎭	straight away, immediately, at once
bald	soon
nachher	afterwards

(c) *Indeterminate information related to 'then'*

dann	then
damals	at that time
davor ⎫ vorher ⎭	before that
kurz davor	shortly before that
danach	after that, afterwards
kurz danach	shortly afterwards
früher	formerly

(d) *Measured time information related to 'now'*

vor einem Monat	a month ago
vor einer Woche	a week ago
seit fünf Sekunden	for five seconds (i.e. starting five seconds ago, before 'now')
in drei Tagen	in three days (i.e. after three days)

(e) *Measured time information related to 'then'*

einen Monat davor ⎫ einen Monat zuvor ⎭	a month before, previously
seit vier Jahren	for four years (i.e. starting four years previously, before 'then')
nach zwei Wochen ⎫ zwei Wochen danach ⎬ two weeks later zwei Wochen später ⎭	

(f) *Information related to 'today'*

heute	today
gestern	yesterday
vorgestern	the day before yesterday
heute vor einer Woche ⎫ **heute vor acht Tagen** ⎭	a week ago today
gestern vor zwei Wochen ⎫ **gestern vor vierzehn Tagen** ⎭	a fortnight ago yesterday

morgen	tomorrow
übermorgen	the day after tomorrow

heute in drei Wochen	three weeks today
morgen in acht Tagen	tomorrow week

(g) *Named time information*

(i) Years: see also Section 18

> • NO preposition! (or preceded, more formally, by **im Jahre**)

1992 werde ich zwanzig.	*I'll be twenty in 1992.*
or	
Er hat im Jahre 1980 geheiratet.	*He got married in 1980.*
seit/vor/nach 1980	*since/before/after 1980*

(ii) Seasons:

> • preposition: **in** (all are *m* nouns, so usually **im**)

im ⎧	**Frühling**	*in* ⎧	*spring*
⎨	**Sommer**	⎨	*summer*
⎪	**Herbst**	⎪	*autumn*
⎩	**Winter**	⎩	*winter*

(iii) Months:

    • preposition: **in** (all are *m* nouns, so usually **im**)

im	{ **Januar** **Februar** **März** **April** **Mai** **Juni**	**im**	{ **Juli** **August** **September** **Oktober** **November** **Dezember**	*in* (month)

(iv) Days:

    • preposition: **an** (all are *m* nouns, so usually **am**)

am	{ **Sonntag** **Montag** **Dienstag** **Mittwoch** **Donnerstag** **Freitag** **Sonnabend** or **Samstag**	*on*	{ *Sunday* *Monday* *Tuesday* *Wednesday* *Thursday* *Friday* *Saturday*

(v) Dates:

    • without preposition:

Heute ist der 1. März. (erste)   *Today is the first of March.*
Donnerstag ist der 3. Mai. (dritte)
Morgen ist der 7. November. (siebte)
Freitag ist der 19. Juli. (neunzehnte)
Übermorgen ist der 20. Oktober. (zwanzigste)

    • dating a letter or document:

den 2. Januar 1985 (zweiten)   (DO case!)
den 30.8.1986 (dreißigsten achten)   (DO case!)

• preposition: an

Am 15. Juni fahren wir in Urlaub. (fünfzehnten)
We're going on holiday on 15th June.

(vi) Time of day:

  • preposition: **um**

8.00	**acht Uhr**
8.05	**fünf nach acht**
8.08	**acht Minuten nach acht**
8.10	**zehn nach acht**
8.15	**Viertel nach acht**
8.20	**zwanzig nach acht**
8.25	**fünf vor halb <u>neun</u>**
8.30	**halb <u>neun</u>**
8.32	**zwei Minuten nach halb <u>neun</u>**
8.35	**fünf nach halb <u>neun</u>**
8.40	**zwanzig vor neun**
8.45	**Viertel vor neun**

Um Viertel nach eins kommt der Arzt.
The doctor's coming at a quarter past one.

  • The 24-hour clock, which is in very widespread use for all sorts of formal purposes, is straightforward:

14.30   vierzehn Uhr dreißig
22.27   zweiundzwanzig Uhr siebenundzwanzig

Exercise 24

Establish in each case which of the sentences (a) (b) or (c) is most compatible with the initial statement.
1   Im Augenblick habe ich keine Zeit.
    (a) Ich spiele in zwei Stunden Tennis.
    (b) Ich habe jetzt viel Arbeit.
    (c) Ich schlafe im Augenblick.

2 In zwei Wochen fahre ich in die Vereinigten Staaten.
   (a) Ich bin für zwei Wochen in den Vereinigten Staaten.
   (b) Der Urlaub in den Vereinigten Staaten ist zwei Wochen.
   (c) Ich fahre heute in vierzehn Tagen in die Vereinigten Staaten.
3 Übermorgen muß ich beim Metzger einkaufen.
   (a) In zwei Tagen kaufe ich ein Pfund Hackfleisch.
   (b) Übermorgen verkauft der Metzger sein Geschäft.
   (c) Übermorgen verkaufe ich Gemüse.
4 Seit gestern vor vierzehn Tagen ist seine Mutter krank.
   (a) Seine Mutter ist in vierzehn Tagen krank.
   (b) Seine Mutter ist schon zwei Wochen krank.
   (c) Vor vierzehn Tagen ist seine Mutter im Bett geblieben.
5 Frau Schmidt ist eben in die Stadt gegangen.
   (a) Frau Schmidt ist momentan in der Stadt.
   (b) Gerade ist Frau Schmidt in die Stadt gefahren.
   (c) Frau Schmidt will gleich in der Stadt spazierengehen.
6 Früher hat Herr Kegel Bücher geschrieben.
   (a) Neulich hat Herr Kegel Bücher geschrieben.
   (b) Nachher schreibt Herr Kegel Bücher.
   (c) Herr Kegel hat damals gute Bücher geschrieben.

49 Reassurance tags

In English there is a range of reassurance tags, the choice being determined by the finite verb in each particular sentence ended by a tag:

He likes the painting, doesn't he?
So he likes the painting, does he?
He won't buy it, will he?
We shan't pay, shall we?
We're not going to pay, are we?

In German, on the other hand, the tag is extremely simple.

One tag does for all sentences, though it does vary from region to region and also according to the degree of casualness required.

In formal situations the tag would be **, nicht wahr?**, and this might well be found in writing. Most frequently used is the form **, nicht?** The initial comma is essential, otherwise the sentence itself becomes negative! Most casual of all is **, ne?** (pronounced as an English child might say the letter 'n' when spelling phonetically).

Regional variants are **, woll?** and **, gell?**

When the degree of reassurance being sought is stronger, the tag **, oder?** may be used, especially with negative sentences. However, this is much less common than the standard tag.

VOCABULARY

Study and learn the conversation below. You will need these new words:

die	**Ärztin (-nen)**	(female) doctor
	zum ersten Mal	for the first time
	jahrelang	for years
	plötzlich	suddenly
	unangenehm	unpleasant
der	**Schmerz (-en)**	pain
das	**Handgelenk (-e)**	wrist
	bemerken I	to notice
das	**Gelenk (-e)**	joint (here: wrist)
	steif	stiff
die	**Gelegenheit (-en)**	occasion
	passieren	to happen
der	**Schwager (-)**	brother-in-law
der	**Umzug (¨e)**	removal

	meinen	to say (give one's opinion)
der	Beruf (-e)	job
	benutzen I	to use
der	Maurer (-)	bricklayer
	etwa	(1) about; (2) perhaps (conjectural)
der	Fliesenleger (-)	tiler
	schon mal	ever
	von selbst	by itself
	röntgen	to X-ray
	wie gesagt	as (I) said
	erst mal	first of all
	untersuchen I	to examine
	allgemein	generally
das	Herz (-en)	heart
	abhören II	to check (heart, lungs)
der	Blutdruck	blood pressure
	messen	to measure
die	Blutprobe (-n)	blood test
	behandeln I	to treat
	überweisen I	to transfer, hand over
	schütteln	to shake

CONVERSATION

A doctor receives a new patient

Patient   Guten Tag, Frau Doktor!

Ärztin   Guten Tag, Sie sind zum ersten Mal bei mir, nicht?

P   Ja, ich bin jahrelang bei keinem Arzt gewesen.

Ä   Und was haben Sie denn jetzt so plötzlich?

P   Vor einigen Tagen habe ich sehr unangenehme Schmerzen im rechten Handgelenk bemerkt, und das Gelenk ist auch ganz steif geworden.

Ä   Bei welcher Gelegenheit ist das passiert?

P   Ich habe neulich meiner Schwester und meinem Schwager beim Umzug geholfen und sehr schwere Sachen getragen. Sofort danach habe ich es gemerkt. Die haben gemeint, ich soll zum Arzt gehen.

Ä   Haben Sie einen manuellen Beruf? … mit anderen Worten, benutzen Sie Ihre Hände viel?

P   Früher bin ich Maurer gewesen, aber seit etwa einem Jahr bin ich Fliesenleger.

Ä   Spielen Sie etwa Handball oder Tennis?

P   Ja, ab and zu beides.

Ä   Haben Sie schon mal Probleme mit dem Handgelenk gehabt?

P   Ja, vor etwa zwei Monaten, aber es ist von selbst besser geworden. Diesmal sind die Schmerzen viel stärker als vor zwei Monaten.

Ä   Hat man Ihnen das Handgelenk je geröntgt?

P   Nein, wie gesagt, ich bin lange nicht mehr zum Arzt gegangen.

Ä   Ich werde Sie erst mal allgemein untersuchen … Herz abhören … Blutdruck messen … Urin untersuchen … eine Blutprobe machen …

P   Warum denn das alles?

Ä   Sie waren doch so lange nicht beim Arzt… und dann das Handgelenk röntgen…

P   … und dann werden Sie das Handgelenk behandeln, nicht?

Ä   O nein! Dann überweise ich Sie an meinen Kollegen Henschel. Der ist Orthopäde!

P   (*Schüttelt den Kopf!*)

TRANSLATION

Patient   Hello, doctor.

Doctor   Hello. This is the first time you've come to see me, isn't it?

P   Yes, I haven't seen a doctor for years.

D   And what's the matter with you now all of a sudden?

P	A few days ago I noticed some very unpleasant pains in my right wrist, and my wrist also got quite stiff.
D	On what occasion did that happen?
P	I was helping my sister and brother-in-law with their house-moving recently and carrying very heavy things. I noticed it immediately afterwards. They said I must go to the doctor.
D	Do you have a manual job? ... in other words, do you use your hands a lot?
P	I used to be a bricklayer, but I've been a tiler for about a year.
D	Do you play, say, handball or tennis?
P	Yes, both now and again.
D	Have you ever had problems with your wrist before?
P	Yes, about two months ago, but it got better by itself. This time the pains are much worse than two months ago.
D	Has your wrist ever been X-rayed?
P	No. As I said, I haven't been to the doctor for a long time.
D	First I'll give you a general examination ... check your heart ... measure your blood pressure ... check your urine ... do a blood test ...
P	Why all those things?
D	Well, you said you hadn't seen a doctor for such a long time ... and then X-ray your wrist ...
P	... and then you'll give me some treatment for the wrist, won't you?
D	Oh no! Then I'll transfer you to my colleague Dr Henschel. He specialises in orthopaedics!
P	(*Shakes his head!*)

Chapter 10

Chapter 10 introduces the 'possessor' case and a group of
masculine nouns with unusual case endings. It also builds
on your knowledge of verbs, covering:

- more about the 'type II' verbs introduced in Chapter 9
- verb constructions with **zu** ('to'), **um ... zu, ohne ... zu** and
  statt ... zu
- how to express the 'obverse process' or passive
- auxiliary verbs in the pre-present tense
- the past tense of **haben**, **sein** and the auxiliary verbs.

50 Indicating possession: the possessor (PO) case

In English there are two ways of linking two nouns to
indicate that one is the possessor of the other:

(i) *Friday's paper*
     John's wife's aunt
     both companies' profits
     women's rights

(ii) *the tip of the iceberg*
     the opinion of the judge
     the end of the matter
     brother of the deceased

In (i) the possessor is marked by '(s) and precedes the
possessed item. In (ii) the nouns are linked by *of*, with the
possessed item preceding the possessor.

In German the usual sequence is that of (ii) (possessed item + possessor), but the method is like that of (i), i.e. marking the possessor noun and associated words in some way. Possessor status is expressed by case features similar to those for the SU, DO and IO cases, i.e. distinctive forms of **d. .**, of **ein**, of the adjective and – for *m* and *n* singular nouns only – of the noun itself:

die Schwägerin meines Freundes
my friend's sister-in-law
die Ansichten beider Rechtsanwälte
the views of both lawyers
der Ruf des ehemaligen Politikers
the former politician's reputation
der Wagen einer alten Dame
an old lady's car

All the required forms will be apparent from the following:

		singular			plural
		m	*f*	*n*	*m f n*
d. .		des	der	des	der
	(k)ein	**(k)eines**	**(k)einer**	**(k)eines**	**keiner**
d. .-type	**dies. .**	**dieses**	**dieser**	**dieses**	**dieser**
	jed. .	**jedes**	**jeder**	**jedes**	**–**
ein-type	**unser**	**unseres**	**unserer**	**unseres**	**unserer**
	Ihr	**Ihres**	**Ihrer**	**Ihres**	**Ihrer**
adjective after **d. .**		**-en** throughout			
adjective after **ein**		**-en** throughout			
adjective alone		<u>**-en**</u>	**-er**	<u>**-en**</u>	**-er**
noun ending		**-(e)s**	–	**-(e)s**	–

The (**e**) of the *m* and *n* singular noun endings is frequently inserted after monosyllabic noun stems.

51 Prepositions requiring the PO case

As mentioned in Section 26, each preposition in German requires the selection of a particular case for the noun or pronoun following. A few common prepositions require the PO case. To help you remember to associate them with the PO case, the English equivalents given here are all made to end with 'of':

außerhalb	outside *of*
innerhalb	inside *of*
jenseits	on the far side *of* (beyond)
statt	instead *of*
trotz	in spite *of*
während	in the course *of* (during)
wegen	because *of*, on account *of*

Though these prepositions are frequently used before nouns, there is no complete set of pronouns parallel to the SU, DO and IO pronouns for use after PO prepositions. Instead there are a number of idiosyncratic forms, of which these are the commonest:

stattdessen	instead (of it)
trotzdem	in spite of this, nevertheless
währenddessen	in the course of it / this
deswegen	because of this, consequently
meinetwegen	on my account, as far as I am concerned
unseretwegen	on our account
deinetwegen	on your account
usw.	etc.

Also very commonly heard is **wegen** followed by the IO pronouns:

wegen mir	because of me
wegen uns	because of us
wegen dir	because of you
wegen dem	because of him
usw.	etc.

52 Some exceptional masculine nouns

(a) We saw in Section 50 that *m* and *n* nouns add **-(e)s** for the singular PO case. However, a number of *m* nouns, including some very common ones, do not add **-(e)s** for the PO case, but do add **-(e)n** for all cases, singular and plural, except the SU singular, which is naturally the form in which they are now given:

der Automat	machine (e.g. vending)	(and other 'imported' nouns ending in **-at**)
der Bauer	farmer	
der Franzose	Frenchman	(and other *m* nationality designations ending in **-e** like **der Pole**, but NOT **der Deutsche**, which follows different rules; see Section 61)
der Held	hero	
der Herr	Mr, gentleman	(adds only **-n** in singular, **-en** in plural)
der Junge	boy	(the colloquial plural adds **-ns** throughout)
der Kollege	colleague	
der Kunde	customer	
der Mensch	person, human being, (plural) people	
der Nachbar	neighbour	
der Präsident	president	(and many other 'imported' nouns ending in **-ent**)
der Soldat	soldier	(see **Automat**)
der Student	student	(see **Präsident**)
der Tourist	tourist	(and other 'imported' nouns ending in **-ist**)

Many other nouns, particularly other categories of 'imported' nouns, behave in the same way as the above. All such nouns are followed in the Mini-dictionary not by the usual plural information but by '(PO **-n**)' or '(PO **-en**)': e.g. **der Tourist** (PO **-en**) tourist.

(b) A small but significant group of *m* nouns ending in **-e** add **-ns** for the singular PO case and **-n** in all other cases. Here is the singular SU case:

der	**Buchstabe**	letter (of the alphabet)
der	**Gedanke**	thought
der	**Glaube**	belief
der	**Name**	name
der	**Wille**	will (determination)

These are marked in the Mini-dictionary with '(PO **-ns**)'.

53 TYPE II verbs used as finite verbs

We have seen (Section 47(b)) that TYPE II verbs (those with separable prefixes) require the **ge-** of the **ge_(e)t** form to be inserted between the separable, stressed prefix and the root. The same principle applies if the **-en** form is preceded by **zu** ('to'), which is also inserted between the prefix and the root. (In both these cases the resultant sequence is spoken and written as one word: **áusgegangen, áuszugehen**.)

However, if a TYPE II verb is the finite verb of the sentence, the prefix is split off completely and appears *last of all* in the sentence:

Ich lade meine Freunde für Sonnabend ein. (éinladen)
I'm inviting my friends for Saturday.
Er schlägt ein kaltes Mittagessen mit Brot, Käse und Wein vor. (vórschlagen)
He suggests a cold lunch with bread, cheese and wine.
Ich helfe bei den Vorbereitungen für die Konferenz nicht mit. (míthelfen)
I'm not helping with the preparations for the conference.

Note that even **nicht**, which usually comes very late in a sentence, must precede the separated prefix.

TYPE I (inseparable prefix) verbs naturally remain intact under the circumstances just described:

Ich empfinde gar kein Mitleid mit dieser Frau. (empfinden)
I can feel no sympathy at all with this woman.

54 zu + -en form

You know already that if a simple sentence contains both a finite verb and an **-en** form, the **-en** form must stand right at the end of the sentence (Section 33):

Ich <u>gehe</u> zweimal in der Woche <u>schwimmen</u>.

Many constructions require the **-en** form to be accompanied by **zu**, like the 'to' which often accompanies the parallel English non-finite verb. Whereas in English the complete verb group (finite verb + 'to' + non-finite verb) tends to stick together, usually somewhere near the start of the sentence, **zu** clings to the **-en** form at the end of the sentence. Consequently there is no debate about the 'split infinitive' in German! It is simply not possible to insert anything between **zu** and the **-en** form, with even stressed prefixes being pushed out of the way:

Er hofft, morgen <u>zu</u> kommen.
He hopes to come tomorrow.
Wir versuchen, ein neues Haus <u>zu</u> finden.
We are trying to find a new house.
Ich habe vor, meine Freunde für Sonnabend ein<u>zu</u>laden.
I intend to invite my friends for Saturday.

Consider now some slightly more complex examples:

(a) (i)**Er wird immer zögern,**   **mir seine Sorgen zu erzählen.**
    He will always hesitate   *to tell me his worries.*

(ii) **Ich habe neulich versucht,**	**den Chef für Montag einzuladen.**
I recently tried	*to invite the boss for Monday.*
(b) (i) **Ich werde meine Mutter bitten,**	**uns ein Picknick vorzubereiten.**
I shall ask my mother	*to prepare a picnic for us.*
(ii) **Der Arzt hat mich überredet,**	**wegen des Handgelenks zum Orthopäden zu gehen.**
The doctor persuaded me	*to go to the orthopaedic specialist with my wrist.*

(Sentences (a) (ii) and (b) (i) show again how a TYPE II (separable prefix) verb opens up to allow the **zu** to slip between prefix and root.)

Each of the above sentences divides into two clear portions. No bits of either portion may stray across the division, so though the **ge_(e)t** or **-en** form of the first portion is required to stand last, this means *last in the relevant portion.*

As with the English versions, in the (a) sentences the SU of the first portion becomes the (implied) SU of the second portion (**er – zögern – erzählen; ich – versuchen – einladen**). This is NOT the case in the (b) sentences, however, where the implied SU of the second portion is the DO from the first portion (**ich – bitten – meine Mutter – vorbereiten; der Arzt – überreden – ich – gehen**).

Exercise 25

Complete the following by filling each double gap with the correct TYPE II verb from the column on the right. The short gap in each case is for the separable prefix, the long one for the rest of the verb.

Ich _____ _____, eine Party zu geben. Wir   anrufen
sind so viele, also _____ ich meine Wohnung   einladen
anders ____. Ich, _____ nur meine besten   einrichten
Freunde ____, aber wir sind fünfzig.   mithelfen
Diesmal _____meine Freunde mal nicht   vorhaben
____. Ich will alles alleine machen. Um 8 Uhr   vorschlagen
_____ ich sie ____. Dann können sie
kommen. Aber was sagen meine Freunde, sie
_____ stattdessen ____, gar nicht zu essen,
sondern den ganzen Abend lang zu trinken.

55 Expressing purpose: um ... zu

To express a purposive relationship between the two portions of a sentence – '(in order) to, (so as) to' – a modified
version of the bi-partite pattern from Section 54 is used: the
word **um** is placed at the *beginning* of the second portion of
the sentence. Here are the second portions of the sentences
from Section 54 modified in this way, with new first portions to make sense:

Er wird mich morgen besuchen,   **um mir seine Sorgen zu
erzählen.**
He's visiting me tomorrow   *(in order) to tell me his worries.*
**Ich bin zur Chefsekretärin
gegangen,**   **um den Chef für Montag
einzuladen.**
I've been to the boss's secretary   *(in order) to invite the boss for
Monday.*

**Ich werde etwas Aufschnitt
kaufen,**   **um uns ein Picknick
vorzubereiten.**
I'm going to buy some sliced meat   *(so as) to prepare a picnic for
us.*

**Ich muß besonders früh
aufstehen,**   **um wegen des
Handgelenks zum
Orthopäden zu gehen.**

I have to get up particularly early   *(so as) to go to the orthopaedic
specialist with my wrist.*

It would be idiomatic English to drop 'in order' or 'so as' and say only 'to', but if the second portion is the *purpose* of the first, the **um** is essential in German. Unlike the sentences without **um** and with only **zu**, the (implied) SU of the second (**um**) portion must always be the SU of the first portion. Also unlike the sentences without **um**, the order of the two portions can be reversed:

Um den Chef für Montag einzuladen,	**bin ich zur Chefsekretärin gegangen.**
Um mir seine Sorgen zu erzählen,	**wird er mich morgen besuchen.**

Note that in reverse order the former second portion, now coming first, has an effect on the sequence of words. As we noted in Section 32, whatever part of a statement comes first, *the verb must come second*, and the **um** portion counts as such a part, so that the verb, or more precisely the finite verb (here **bin** and **wird**) comes next, followed by the SU (here **ich** and **er**).

56 ohne ... zu (without ...-ing); statt ... zu (instead of ...-ing)

Like **um** in the construction described in Section 55, **ohne** and **statt** can be used to start the second portion of a sentence, with the meaning 'without (...-ing)' and 'instead of (...-ing)' respectively. Like the sentences containing **um**, **ohne** and **statt** sentences must have the same SU or implied SU in both portions, and the sequence of the portions can be reversed. Because these two constructions are more remote from the equivalent English than is **um ... zu**, a more deliberate effort has to be made to get them right.

Ich kann kein Picknick vorbereiten,	**ohne etwas Aufschnitt zu kaufen.**
I can't prepare a picnic	*without buying some sliced meat.*

Er wird mich morgen besuchen, statt mir seine Sorgen am Telefon zu erzählen.

He's going to visit me tomorrow *instead of telling me his worries on the telephone.*

Exercise 26

1 Die Dame geht in die Stadt. Die Dame geht in die
   Sie kauft ein. Stadt, um einzukaufen.

The following pairs of sentences make up a mini-story. Link the two sentences in each pair with **um ... zu, ohne ... zu** *or* **statt ... zu,** *as appropriate, on the lines of the above model.*

2 Fräulein Schmidt steht früh auf.
   Sie geht mit ihrem Hund spazieren.
3 Mittags kommt sie nach Hause und arbeitet im Garten.
   Sie ißt nicht.
4 Am Nachmittag geht sie ins Kino.
   Sie fragt ihre Mutter nicht.
5 Sie sieht gerne Filme.
   Sie kommt auf andere Gedanken.
6 Am Abend kommt ihr Freund.
   Er will sie ins Restaurant einladen.
7 Sie verläßt das Restaurant während des Essens.
   Sie bezahlt nicht.
8 Er bleibt im Restaurant sitzen und ißt beide Portionen.
   Er läuft nicht zu seiner Freundin.

---

57 Obverse process

You have seen in Section 44 how **haben** and **sein** are used as auxiliary finite verbs along with the **ge_(e)t** form to make the pre-present. You have also seen in Sections 34 and 35 (h) how **werden** is used as an auxiliary finite verb in combination with the **-en** form to make the future. There is also a further combination, of the auxiliary finite verb **werden** and the **ge_(e)t** form:

Das Haus wird in diesen Tagen eingerichtet.
The house is being furnished at present.
Ich werde oft mitten in der Nacht angerufen.
I'm often rung up in the middle of the night.

This is used to express the *obverse process,* where the process denoted by the verb, which logically proceeds from the 'doer' to things or persons affected (generally the DO), is turned upside down, so that the affected person or thing ('the house' and 'I' in the above sentences) becomes the SU of the obverse process ('is being furnished' and 'am rung up'). (The term *passive,* normally used for this construction, refers to the change whereby the affected item becomes the SU, but, apart from the difficulty of relating its everyday meaning to its grammatical meaning, it does not fit German since, as we shall show, there are obverse process constructions in German that have *no* SU, whether derived from a DO or anywhere else.)

The following shows the usual connection between the logical process and the obverse process:

$$\text{SU} \xrightarrow{\text{logical process}} \text{DO}$$ My father is showing the slides.

$$\text{SU} \xleftarrow{\text{obverse process}}$$ The slides are being shown (by my father).

As in English, the obverse process is useful *either* when it is desired to draw particular attention to the doer ('by my father' is more striking than 'my father' as SU) on the one hand, *or* when the doer is unworthy of attention (or even unidentifiable) on the other hand. These two situations appear in the following examples:

(i) *The slides are being shown by my father* (and not, say, by my brother).
     Die Dias werden von meinem Vater gezeigt.
(ii) *The slides are now being shown.*
     Jetzt werden die Dias gezeigt.

However, the use of the obverse process in German differs radically from English in two respects:

(a) In English not only a DO (pro)noun can be transformed into the SU of an obverse process:

The slides are being shown.

but also an IO (pro)noun can:

The guest is being shown the slides.

Although this same sequence of words is (almost) possible in German, any IO (pro)noun must stay in the IO case:

Dem Gast werden die Dias gezeigt.

and the SU remains what in the logical process would be the DO, i.e. **die Dias**, as can be seen from the plural finite verb **werden**.

(b) In English only verbs that can have DOs can be used in the obverse process, but in German the obverse process is possible with verbs that need only a 'doer'. If the 'doer' cannot be identified or consists of a collective, the obverse process can be used without a SU (or with only the impersonal **es** as SU):

	Heute abend wird gesungen.
or	**Es wird heute abend gesungen.**
	There's some singing this evening.
	Jetzt wird schnell gegessen!
or	**Es wird jetzt schnell gegessen!**
	Now you're going to eat fast!

A combination of the rules contained in (a) and (b) means that sentences like

The children are now being forgiven.
The students are being helped a lot.

which contain verbs which in German use the IO case
see Section 21) must be translated:

> **Den Kindern wird jetzt verziehen.**
> or **Es wird den Kindern jetzt verziehen.**
> **Den Studenten wird sehr geholfen.**
> or **Es wird den Studenten sehr geholfen.**

Because *both* the future *and* the obverse process are made
with **werden**, it is not usual to include **werden** twice in the
future obverse process:

**Wir werden nächste Woche in Französisch geprüft
(~~werden~~).**
We're going to be examined in French next week.

58 The pre-present of some auxiliary verbs

To form the pre-present of the sentence

Ich muß den Nachbarn helfen.
I have to help the neighbours.

it is of course the auxiliary finite verb **muß** that has to
become pre-present. However, the **ge_(e)t** form of **müssen** is
not used, but instead the **-en** form:

Ich habe den Nachbarn helfen <u>müssen</u>.
I had to help the neighbours.

Note that the **-en** form of the auxiliary stands right at the
end, even after the **-en** form of the main verb (here **helfen**).
The same applies to **dürfen, können, mögen, sollen, wollen**
and **lassen**. So, for instance, 'I got my car washed' would in
the pre-present be:

Ich habe meinen Wagen waschen lassen.

All of these verbs have an alternative **ge_(e)t** non-finite form which is used when they are not auxiliaries. Examples:

A: Kannst du geduldig warten?
A: Are you able to wait patiently?
B: Nein, das habe ich nie gekonnt.
B: No, I've never been able (to do) that.
Wir haben unser Gepäck am Bahnhof gelassen.
We left our luggage at the station.

All these 'independent' **ge_(e)t** forms begin with **ge-** and (except **lassen**) end with **-t**: **gedurft, gekonnt, gemocht, gemußt, gesollt, gewollt** and **gelassen**.

When **werden** is used as an auxiliary to form the obverse process, the **ge_(e)t** form is simply **worden,** but when **werden** is used independently ('to become') the **ge_(e)t** form is **geworden:**

Die Dias sind von meinem Vater gezeigt worden.
The slides were shown by my father.
Die Kunden sind heutzutage sehr frech geworden.
Customers have become very cheeky these days.

59 The past tense (I)

Apart from the advantages for the learner of using the pre-present as a means of referring to the past (Section 46), it is what Germans themselves are most likely to use in everyday conversation. However, its disadvantage is that it involves using at least two verbs, sometimes three (as in Section 58) and occasionally four.

The alternative is to use the second of the German true tenses, the *past tense*, which allows reference to the past to be made using one verb fewer than the equivalent pre-present.

The past tense is frequently used, even colloquially, when the main verb is **sein** or **haben**, thus avoiding two forms of the same verb in one sentence (e.g. **er ist ... gewesen; ich habe ... gehabt**). The past tense of the auxiliary verbs, too, is often preferred to the pre-present, so reducing the number of verbs in the sentence from a minimum of three to a minimum of two. Compare the following:

pre-present	past tense
Ich bin vier Wochen krank gewesen.	**Ich war vier Wochen krank.**

I was/have been ill for four weeks.

Wir haben viel Pech gehabt.	**Wir hatten viel Pech.**

We were/have been very unlucky.

Ich habe den Nachbarn helfen müssen.	**Ich mußte den Nachbarn helfen.**

Die Dias sind von meinem Vater gezeigt worden.	**Die Dias wurden von meinem Vater gezeigt.**

Here are the past tenses of **haben, sein** and the auxiliary verbs:

	haben	**sein**
ich/er/sie (she)/**es**	hatte	war
wir/Sie/sie (they)	hatten	waren
du	hattest	warst

	dürfen	**können**
ich/er/sie (she)/**es**	durfte	konnte
wir/Sie/sie (they)	durften	konnten
du	durftest	konntest

	mögen	**müssen**
ich/er/sie (she)/**es**	mochte	mußte
wir/Sie/sie (they)	mochten	mußten
du	mochtest	mußtest

	sollen	wollen
ich/er/sie (she)/es	sollte	wollte
wir/Sie/sie (they)	sollten	wollten
du	solltest	wolltest

	lassen	werden
ich/er/sie (she)/es	ließ	wurde
wir/Sie/sie (they)	ließen	wurden
du	ließest	wurdest

A look at the 1st and 3rd persons singular (which are *always* identical in the past tense) reveals four patterns in the above, of which two are significant for learning German past tenses in general (Section 66), while a third is typical of a further small group:

(a) **sein, lassen**   A new stem (**war, ließ**) appears and is used without any ending.

(b) **sollen, wollen**   The same stem as that of the **-en** form is used, followed by **-t-** and the ending **-e**.

(c) **haben, dürfen, können, mögen, müssen**   A new stem (**hat-, durf-, konn-, moch-, muß-**) appears and is followed by **-t-** and the ending **-e**.

(d) **werden**   This is an oddity. A new stem (**wurd-**) appears and is followed by the ending **-e**.

Pattern (a) is the one followed by the large number of verbs that take new stems for the past tense (like 'come/came', 'know/knew', 'see/saw'). We shall call these *new stem verbs*. Pattern (b) is the model for the bulk of verbs, which simply take the stem of the **-en** form and add **-t-**, always followed by an ending. These are *same stem verbs*, and are like 'rush/rushed', 'blame/blamed'. Pattern (c) is a mixture of (a) and (b), taking a new stem yet adding **-t-** always followed by an ending, somewhat akin to 'kneel/knelt', 'buy/bought'.

Vocabulary

Study and learn the conversation that follows. You will need these new words:

die	Freundin (-nen)	girlfriend
die	Silvesterfahrt (-en)	New Year's Eve trip
der	Winterprospekt (-e)	winter brochure
	anbieten II	to offer
	preiswert	reasonably priced
das	Allgäu	(mountainous area in Southern Bavaria)
der	Preis (-e)	price
	reichhaltig	varied
der	Ausflug (-̈e)	excursion
die	Abendveranstaltung (-en)	evening entertainment, event
das	Neujahrsfrühstück (-e)	New Year's Day breakfast
der	Sonderpreis (-e)	special price
die	Unterkunft (-̈e)	accommodation
das	Doppelzimmer (-)	double room
das	Einzelzimmer (-)	single room
das	Silvesterfestessen (-)	New Year's Eve banquet
die	Skimöglichkeit (-en)	opportunity for skiing
	hin und zurück	there and back, i.e. return (of a journey)
	sorgen für	to see to
die	Übernachtung (-en)	overnight stay
der	Hinweg (-e)	outward journey
das	Gleiche	the same
die	Rückfahrt (-en)	return journey
	unterwegs	on the way
	genügend	sufficiently
	anhalten II	to stop, pull up
	jeweils	each time
	einnehmen II	to eat, take, consume
die	Erfrischung (-en)	refreshment
der	Gasthof (-̈e)	inn
der	Löwe (PO -n)	lion

	unterbringen II	to accommodate
der	Grundpreis (-e)	basic price
	enthalten I	to contain, include
die	Dusche (-n)	shower
der	Zuschlag (-̈e)	additional charge
	nicht in Frage kommen	to be out of the question
die	Veranstaltung (-en)	item of entertainment, event
	einbegriffen	included
der	Geschmack (-̈e)	taste
	tagsüber	during the daytime
	tanzen	to dance
	gesellig	sociable
das	Beisammensein	being with other people
der	Gesellschaftsraum (-̈e)	lounge
	genießen I	to enjoy
die	Möglichkeit (-en)	opportunity
das	Skifahren	skiing
das	Festessen (-)	banquet
der	Tanz (-̈e)	dance
	veranstalten	to arrange, put on
	nach Wunsch	as required, to order
das	Feuerwerk	fireworks
	loslassen II	to set off
das	Sektfrühstück	champagne breakfast
	klingen	to sound
	beschränken I	to limit
	anstrengend	energetic, strenuous
der	Teilnehmer (-)	participant
die	Leute	people
das	Gegenteil	opposite
die	Gruppe (-n)	group
die	goldene Hochzeit (-en)	golden wedding
	feiern	to celebrate
	besprechen I	to discuss, talk over

CONVERSATION

Enquiring at a coach tour company about a short New Year holiday

Junger Mann	Meine Freundin und ich sind daran interessiert, eine Silvesterfahrt zu machen.
Fräulein	Gut, ich zeige Ihnen unseren Winterprospekt. Wir bieten dieses Jahr eine sehr preiswerte Fahrt mit Luxusbus nach Oberstdorf im Allgäu an, sieben Tage vom 28. Dezember bis zum 3. Januar inklusiv.
JM	(*Liest aus dem Winterprospekt.*)

> 7 Tage Silvesterfahrt mit Luxusbus ins Allgäu
>
> 5 Nächte in Oberstdorf
>
> reichhaltiges Programm mit Ausflügen, Abendveranstaltungen und Neujahrssektfrühstück
>
> Sonderpreis DM 950,-
>
> Unterkunft in Doppelzimmern Einzelzimmer DM 50,- extra Silvesterfestessen DM 25,- extra Skimöglichkeiten

JM	Was wird da alles für den Preis angeboten?
F	Ja, da ist erst mal die Fahrt hin und zurück im Luxusbus. Für alles wird gesorgt ... eine Übernachtung in einem netten Hotel auf dem Hinweg und das Gleiche auf der Rückfahrt ...
JM	Wie wird unterwegs gegessen?
F	Es wird natürlich genügend oft angehalten, und das Mittagessen wird jeweils während einer

längeren Pause in einem Gasthof eingenommen. Andere Erfrischungen werden im Bus serviert … Ja, und in Oberstdorf selbst wird man im Gasthof Zum Löwen untergebracht. Der Grundpreis enthält die Unterbringung in Doppelzimmern mit Dusche und Toilette, aber es werden auch Einzelzimmer angeboten für einen Zuschlag von DM 50,-. Aber das kommt für Sie wohl nicht in Frage ...?

JM   Was für Veranstaltungen sind im Preis einbegriffen?

F   Für jeden Geschmack wird gesorgt … Tagsüber werden drei kleinere Ausflüge gemacht, und jeden Abend wird getanzt, oder man kann das gesellige Beisammensein in der Bar oder im Gesellschaftsraum genießen. Es gibt auch Möglichkeiten zum Skifahren, aber das muß extra bezahlt werden.

JM   Und zu Silvester und am Neujahrstag selbst ...?

F   Silvester gibt es Tanz, und um elf Uhr wird eine besondere Show veranstaltet. Silvester wird auch um acht Uhr ein Festessen nach Wunsch serviert für einen Zuschlag von DM 25,-. Um Mitternacht wird dann das Feuerwerk losgelassen. Am 1. Januar wird ab neun Uhr ein Sektfrühstück eingenommen.

JM   Das klingt alles sehr schön. Und sind noch Plätze frei?

F   Ja, wir haben noch sechs Plätze frei. Wir mußten die Zahl der Teilnehmer wegen der Größe unseres Busses auf dreißig beschränken.

JM   Bei solch einem anstrengenden Programm sind die anderen Teilnehmer doch bestimmt alles junge Leute ...

F   O nein, ganz im Gegenteil! Sechzehn der Teilnehmer fahren als Gruppe, um Silvester eine goldene Hochzeit zu feiern.

JM   O! Das muß ich doch noch mal mit meiner Freundin besprechen ...

TRANSLATION

Young Man   My girlfriend and I are interested in doing a New Year's Eve trip.

Assistant   I'll show you our winter brochure. This year we're offering a very reasonable trip by luxury coach to Oberstdorf in the Allgäu, seven days from 28th December to 3rd January inclusive.

YM   (*Reads from the winter brochure.*)

---

7 day New Year's Eve trip
to the Allgäu by luxury coach

5 nights in Oberstdorf

Varied programme with excursions, evening entertainments and New Year's Day champagne breakfast

Special price DM 950.-

Accommodation in double rooms
Single room DM 50.- extra
New Year's Eve banquet DM 25.- extra
Opportunities for skiing

YM   What sort of things do you get for the price?

A   Well, first of all there's the outward and return journey in a luxury coach. Everything is taken care of … an overnight stop in a nice hotel on the way out and the same on the return journey ...

YM   How are the meals provided on the journey?

A   There are sufficient stops, of course, and lunch is always taken in an inn during a fairly long break. Other refreshments are served in the coach ... Well, and in Oberstdorf itself you're accommodated in the Lion Inn. The basic price includes accommodation in double rooms with shower and toilet, but single rooms are also available at an extra charge of DM 50.-. But you wouldn't be interested in that, I suppose ...?

YM What sort of entertainments are included in the price?

A Every taste is catered for ... In the daytime there are three shortish excursions, and there's dancing every evening, or you can enjoy the company in the bar or the lounge. There are also opportunities to ski, but you have to pay extra for that.

YM And on New Year's Eve and New Year's Day themselves ...?

A On New Year's Eve there's a dance, and at eleven o'clock a special show is put on. And on New Year's Eve there's also a banquet served to order at eight o'clock at an extra charge of DM 25.-. Then at midnight the fireworks are set off. On 1st January from nine o'clock onwards you can have a champagne breakfast.

YM That all sounds very nice. And are there still places available?

A Yes, we still have six places vacant. We have had to restrict the number of participants to thirty because of the size of our coach.

YM With such a strenuous programme I suppose the other participants are all young people ...

A Oh no, just the opposite! Sixteen of the participants are going as a group to celebrate a golden wedding on New Year's Eve.

YM Oh! I'll have to talk that over again with my girlfriend after all ...

Chapter 11

This chapter looks at three distinct areas:

- *the words used in front of nouns to express quantity (e.g. 'all the', 'a little', 'some') or to identify them (e.g. 'the same', 'another'), and how adjectives can be converted into nouns*
- *how sentences can be linked together in various ways, often by using joining words which affect the word order of the attached sentence*
- *the reflexive pronouns ('myself', 'yourself', etc.) and their use with verbs to form reflexive verbs, which are more numerous in German than in English.*

60 Quantifiers and identifiers

In addition to the **d. .-** and **ein**-type words of Section 28, there is a set of common expressions used before the (adjective +) noun which serve to quantify or identify the following noun. These are now arranged according to whether they are used (i) before any type of noun, (ii) before uncountable nouns (e.g. 'flour', 'anger'), (iii) before countable nouns in the singular (e.g. 'shop', 'mistake') or (iv) before countable nouns in the plural (e.g. 'shops', 'mistakes').

As these expressions vary in their requirements for endings, information is given for each, referring where necessary to the sets of endings (a), (b) and (c) from Section 29 (supplemented by Section 50 for the PO case). As with the units of measurement and quantity in Section 36, where there is an 'of' in English there is usually nothing in German.

(i) *Before any type of noun*

the same (identical)	**d. . selb. . ***	Written as one word, **d. .** with its usual endings, **selb. .** with set (a) endings.
the same (alike)	**d. . gleich***	Two separate words, **gleich** having set (a) endings.
all (of) the, the whole (of the)	**d. . ganz**	**ganz** means 'entire', so it can also follow **ein, mein**, etc. It takes set (a) or (b) endings as required.

* In practice there is a lot of overlap between **d. . selb. .** and **d. . gleich**

Ich bin in derselben Gruppe wie du.
I'm in the same group as you.
Ich habe das gleiche Kleid wie du gekauft.
I've bought the same dress as you.
Die ganze Arbeit hat er alleine geschafft.
He's managed all the work on his own.
Meine ganzen Bücher sind naß geworden.
All my books have got wet.
Ein ganzes Jahr hat er dafür gebraucht.
He took a whole year for it.

(ii) *Before uncountable nouns*

little	**wenig**	No ending required.
a little	**etwas**	No ending.
some	**einig. .**	Takes set (c) endings.
a bit of	**ein bißchen**	Really a *n* noun, so **ein** has its usual endings.
a drop of	**ein Tropfen**	A *m* noun, so **ein** has its usual endings.
enough	{ **genug** **genügend** }	No ending.
much, a lot of	**viel**	No ending required.

all (of) the, the whole (of the)	d. . ganz / all. .	See (i) above. Has the sense of 'all (*the*)'. Takes set (a) endings, but PO -en before *m* and *n* nouns with PO ending -(e)s.
all that/this, all my, etc.	all d. . /dies. / all mein, usw.	all has no ending.

für wenig Geld	*for little money*
mit etwas Salz	*with a little salt*
vor einiger Zeit	*some time ago*
mit einem bißchen Papier	*with a bit of paper*
mit einem Tropfen Öl	*with a drop of oil*
Wir haben genug Wein.	*We have enough wine.*
bei viel Arbeit	*with a lot of work*
bei allem guten Willen	*with the best will in the world*
trotz allen Komforts	*in spite of all the comfort*
wegen all der Unruhe	*because of all that noise*

(iii) *Before countable nouns in the singular*

the same	**d. . selb. .**	See (i) above.
any, some or other	**irgendein**	Endings of **ein.**
another (one more)	**noch ein**	**ein** has usual endings.
another (a different one)	**ein. . ander**	**ander** takes set (b) endings.
the whole (of the)	**d. . ganz**	See (i) above.

Heute kommt { **irgendein** / **noch ein** / **ein anderer** } **Vertreter von der Versicherung.**

Some representative or other } *from the insurance is*
Another representative } *coming today.*

(iv) *Before countable nouns in the plural*

a pair of	**ein Paar**	a *n* noun, so **ein** has its usual endings, and the following noun has the same case.
the two	**d.. beid..**	**beid..** takes set (a) endings.
both	**beid..**	Takes set (c) endings.
a few	**ein paar**	No endings, though a following IO noun may need **-(e)n.**
some	**einig..**	Takes set (c) endings.
	mehrer..	Takes set (c) endings.
many	**viel..**	Takes set (c) endings.
enough	{ **genug** **genügend** }	See (ii) above.
all (of) the	**all..**	Takes set (c) endings, but any following adjective adds **-en** in all cases.

von einem Paar alten Schuhen	*from an old pair of shoes*
wegen der beiden Damen	*because of the two ladies*
mit beiden Händen	*with both hands*
vor ein paar Wochen	*a few weeks ago*

für { **einige** **mehrere** **viele** } **gute Freunde**

for { *some* *several* *many* } *good friends*

für alle guten Freunde	*for all the good friends*

61 Converting adjectives into nouns

To a much greater extent than in English, adjectives in German are regularly converted into nouns. In English this is limited to denoting collective categories of people ('the disabled', 'the sick') and some abstracts, especially in set phrases ('the good, the bad and the indifferent'), but in German the usage is almost unrestricted – singular or plural; animate, inanimate, abstract. In the last Conversation there was the phrase

das Gleiche auf der Rückfahrt
the same on the return journey

Here the adjective **gleich,** given an initial capital letter, has become a *n* noun, the automatic gender for all *adjectival nouns* that do not refer specifically to male or female beings. Adjectival nouns take the appropriate *adjective* endings as described in Section 29. For instance, 'a German' is **ein Deutscher** if a man, but **eine Deutsche** if a woman, because the noun is derived from the adjective **deutsch.**

Adjectival nouns can be created as required. Many of them, whether well-established words that can be found in a dictionary as nouns or new creations required by a particular situation, are based on two non-finite forms of the verb: the **ge_(e)t** form, already familiar to you, and the **-end** form. Whereas the **ge_(e)t** form, as was noted in Section 44, has the connotation of completion, the **-end** form has the connotation of incompleteness, concurrence and simultaneity. So whereas **gefangen** means something like 'caught', 'captured', **überlebend** means something like 'surviving'. These two particular non-finite forms, used as adjectival nouns, become **der Gefangene** (or **die Gefangene**), 'prisoner', and **der Überlebende** (or **die Überlebende**), 'survivor'. Any such nouns listed in the Mini-dictionary are marked 'adj', to show that they must be given adjective endings.

Another common use of adjective as noun is in combination with **etwas,** 'something', and **nichts,** 'nothing'. In these cases the adjective has the endings given in Section 29 set (c).

Die Stunde soll mit etwas Einfachem anfangen.
The lesson must start with something simple.
Alles war ruhig, nichts Wesentliches ist geschehen.
Everything was quiet; nothing important happened.

On the other hand **alles,** 'everything', having the *n* **-es** already incorporated, is followed by an adjective-noun using the Section 29 set (a) endings:

Ich wünsche dir alles Gute zum Geburtstag.
I wish you all the best for your birthday.
In allem Praktischen war er der Klassenbeste.
In everything practical he was the best in the class.

62 Attached sentences

We have seen (Sections 54, 55, 56) how a sentence can contain a phrase which is attached to its core and yet has a separate and distinct identity. The first such phrases we looked at ended simply with **zu** + **-en** form. Other phrases enclosed their contents between link-words or *joiners* like **um, ohne** and **statt** and the **zu** + **-en** form. The meaning of these more elaborate phrases is given a particular slant by the joiner ('in order to', 'without ...-ing', 'instead of ...-ing'), and they can follow or precede the core of the sentence.

While we shall call the above 'attached phrases', we shall use the term 'attached sentences' for various types of word-sequences which differ from attached phrases in that, while they are also attached in some way to a central or core sentence, they contain a *finite verb* of their own.

(a) The simplest way of linking an attached sentence to a core sentence in such a way that the two are genuinely interdependent is to place the attached sentence directly next to the core sentence with nothing (except a comma) in between – and with no effect on the sequence of words (SU – verb – remainder) of either. Here are two examples from earlier chapters:

Der Arzt sagt, ich soll nur Fisch oder mageres Fleisch essen.
The doctor says I must only eat fish or lean meat.
Die haben gemeint, ich soll zum Arzt gehen.
They said I must go to the doctor.

Reverse the sequence of the sentences (the attached sentence remains the attached one even if it comes first) and the sequence of words in the core sentence changes:

Ich soll nur Fisch oder mageres Fleisch essen, sagt der Arzt.

The explanation is an extension of what was said in Section 32: the entire attached sentence constitutes the DO of the core sentence.

However, the scope offered by this method of linking is rather limited. It is widened immeasurably by the use of various categories of link-words or joiners to introduce the attached sentence.

(b) A small set of joiners:

und	and
aber	but
oder	or
sondern	but (on the contrary)
sondern … auch	but … also

which can be used to join any comparable bits of language to each other (pronoun or noun to pronoun or noun, adjective to adjective, finite verb to finite verb and so on) can also link sentence to sentence. Because they function very much like their English equivalents, most of them have already been used in this course without comment. They generally have no effect of their own on the expected sequence of words:

Es gibt auch Möglichkeiten zum Skifahren, <u>aber</u> das muß extra bezahlt werden.

It follows that if any of this small group of joiners are used to link sentences whose sequence of words has already been affected by some other factor (see Section 63 below) the altered sequence will be retained for the sentence attached by **und, aber**, etc.

Particular care is required when choosing between **aber** and **sondern,** both of which can translate English 'but'. If the sense is 'not only … but also', the German must be **nicht nur … sondern auch**. If the sense is 'not … but (on the contrary)', the German must be **nicht** (or another form of the negative, like **kein**) … **sondern:**

Er schickt keinen Brief, sondern er will mit mir persönlich sprechen.
He's not sending a letter but intends to speak to me personally.

(c) The joiner **denn** is in a class all by itself. Though like the joiners in (b) it does not affect the sequence of words, it cannot link anything except sentences. Though like the joiners described in Section 63 (c) it gives a quite special slant to the attached sentence it introduces, such an attached sentence is not free to stand *either* after *or* before the core sentence, but must stand after it.

Er kann mir nicht böse sein, denn er hat selbst Schuld daran.
He can't be cross with me, since it's his own fault.

Its meaning is, therefore, *explanatory*, and it may be translated by 'as', 'since' or 'for'.

63 Joiners affecting word sequence in the attached sentence

(a) **d. .** *joiners*

	singular			plural	translation
	m	*f*	*n*	*m f n*	
SU	**der**	**die**	**das**	**die**	who, which, that
DO	**den**	**die**	**das**	**die**	who(m), which, that (sometimes omitted in English but never in German)
IO	**dem**	**der**	**dem**	**denen**	to / for whom, to / for which
PO	**dessen**	**deren**	**dessen**	**deren**	of whom, of which, whose

These joiners are identical with the SU, DO and IO **d. .** words described in Section 41(a) – (c), plus **dessen** and **deren** for the PO case. They enable the attached sentence to relate to a particular noun in the core (or a preceding) sentence. The choice of **d. .** joiner is *either* singular, and if so *m*, *f* or *n*, *or* plural, exactly to match the intended noun in the core sentence, but the choice of *case* is determined by the role of the **d. .** joiner in the *attached sentence*, where it may stand by itself as SU, DO, IO or PO, or be in tandem with a preposition. The following examples, which include both arrangements, show the principles involved:

Case
SU **Ich bringe meinen Sohn, <u>der</u> nach Berlin fährt, zum Bahnhof.**
I'm taking my son, who's going to Berlin, to the station.
Das Fleisch, <u>das</u> auf dem Tisch liegt, kannst du für den Hund nehmen.
You can take the meat that's on the table for the dog.

DO **Mein Chef, <u>für den</u> ich seit zehn Jahren arbeite, ist sehr unsympathisch.**
My boss, for whom I've been working for ten years, is very unpleasant.
Wir haben den Urlaub, <u>den</u> wir auf Zypern verbracht haben, ganz toll gefunden.
We found the holiday (that) we spent in Cyprus quite fantastic.

IO **Meine Schwiegertochter, <u>der</u> ich gestern Blumen geschenkt habe, hat sie zum Blumengeschäft zurückgebracht.**
My daughter-in-law, to whom I gave some flowers yesterday, took them back to the florist's.
Der Verwandte, <u>bei dem</u> ich wohne, ist wie ein Vater zu mir.
The relative (who(m)) I live with is like a father to me.

PO **Hans, <u>dessen</u> Frau aus Ägypten kommt, lernt Chinesisch!**
Hans, whose wife comes from Egypt, is learning Chinese!
Die Frau, <u>deren</u> Auto falsch geparkt ist, versucht mit dem Polizisten zu flirten.
The woman whose car is illegally parked is trying to flirt with the policeman.

The crucial point to note is that as in all the above examples the *finite verb* of the attached sentence, i.e. the sentence introduced by the **d. .** joiner (sometimes accompanied by a preposition), must stand at *the end* of the attached sentence. This rule is valid for all the types of attached sentences described in this section.

Finally, when the attached sentence is related via a preposition to a noun in the core sentence, and that noun is not a living being, the **d. .** joiner has the alternative **wo(r)-**. (This is parallel to the **da(r)-** described in Section 40.)

| Die Fehler, | über die / worüber | ich gerade, lache, sind eigentlich überhaupt nicht witzig. |

The mistakes I'm just laughing about aren't really funny at all.

(b) **daß, ob** *and* w. . *joiners*

The w. . joiners are: **wann, warum, was, welch . ., wer, wen** ('whom'), **wessen** ('whose'), **wem** ('to whom'), **wie** and **wo.** The joiners in this group enable the entire contents of the attached sentence to be the SU or DO of the core sentence:

SU **Daß wir heute abend kein Essen im Haus haben, ist nicht meine Schuld.**

or **Es ist nicht meine Schuld, daß wir heute abend kein Essen im Haus haben.**
It's not my fault that we've no food in the house this evening.

DO **Kannst du mir sagen, ob er morgen kommt?**
Can you tell me whether he's coming tomorrow?

SU **Wann er morgen aufsteht, ist vollkommen egal.**

or **Es ist vollkommen egal, wann er morgen auf steht.**
It's completely immaterial when he gets up tomorrow.

DO **Weißt du zufällig, wessen Regenschirm hier liegt?**
Do you happen to know whose umbrella this is here?

This category of attached sentences includes cases where, because of ellipsis (the omission of an optional word), the attached sentence may not *appear* to be the object of the core sentence (although it really is):

Ich bin froh (darüber), daß er endlich zu Hause ist.
I'm glad (about the fact) that he's home at last.

In this example 'about the fact' sounds artificial, but the inclusion of the optional **darüber** would sound natural. This way of producing a 'complete' core sentence uses **da(r)-** to stand for the object, not directly of a verb, but of a preposition (here **über**). The full object is then stated in the attached sentence introduced by **daß**. When the preposition is essential to the sense of an idiom the construction with **da(r)-** in the core sentence is not optional but mandatory, as in the following:

Wir sind <u>dafür</u>, daß das Licht ausgemacht wird.
We are for the light being switched off.
Mein Vater ist <u>dagegen</u>, daß ich den Führerschein mache.
My father is against me (/my) taking my driving test.

Here the sense depends entirely on **für** and **gegen,** but there are also many combinations of verb + preposition and adjective + preposition where, though the sense is clear from the verb or adjective, usage requires the preposition to be stated (and therefore **da(r)-** in the core sentence), e.g. **bestehen auf**, 'to insist on'; **einverstanden mit**, 'agreeable to':

Ich bestehe <u>darauf</u>, daß er sofort bezahlt.
I insist on him (/his) paying immediately.
Er ist <u>damit</u> einverstanden, daß sie den Führerschein macht.
He's agreeable to her taking her driving test.

Nor is the **da(r)-** + preposition construction limited to cases where the attached sentence is introduced by the joiner **daß**. The expression **abhängen von**, 'to depend on', is often followed by attached sentences introduced by **ob, wo, wie,** etc:

Meine Entscheidung hängt davon ab, ob der Versuch gelingt.
My decision depends on whether the attempt succeeds.

Do not confuse **daß** with the **d. .** word **das; daß** is always a joiner!

Exercise 27

Revise the following mini-story by using the joiner **daß** *to introduce each attached sentence. The first one is done for you.*

1   Fritz schlägt vor, Ernst soll ihm helfen.
    Fritz schlägt vor, daß Ernst ihm helfen soll.
2   Ernst bittet darum, Fritz soll solche Vorschläge nicht machen.
3   Fritz besteht darauf, Ernst soll endlich mal etwas tun.
4   Ernst findet die Arbeit so anstrengend, er verletzt sein Handgelenk plötzlich.
5   Jetzt hat Fritz solches Mitleid, er schickt Ernst zum Arzt.
6   Der Arzt sieht sofort, Ernst ist einfach faul!

(c) *Prepositional joiners*

These function at the beginning of an attached sentence exactly as a preposition functions in front of a noun, and one or two are identical or nearly identical with the equivalent prepositions:

Bis fünf Uhr ...	(**bis** preposition)
Till five o'clock ...	
Bis er kommt, ...	(**bis** joiner)
Till he comes ...	
Während des Konzerts ...	(**während** preposition)
During the concert ...	
Während das Orchester spielt, ...	(**während** joiner)
While the orchestra is playing ...	
Nach dem Essen ...	(**nach** preposition)
After the meal ...	
Nachdem wir gegessen haben, ...	(**nachdem** joiner)
After we have dined ...	
Vor Weihnachten ...	(**vor** preposition)
Before Christmas...	
Bevor wir anfangen, ...	(**bevor** joiner)
Before we begin ...	

167

Others are more remote from the preposition with equivalent meaning:

Wegen des schlechten Wetters ... (**wegen** preposition)
Because of the bad weather ...
Weil das Wetter schlecht ist, ... (**weil** joiner)
Because the weather is bad ...
Trotz meiner Erkältung ... (**trotz** preposition)
In spite of my cold ...
Obwohl ich erkältet bin, ... (**obwohl** joiner)
Although I have a cold ...

Most prepositional joiners relate either to (i) time or to (ii) causality (or the absence of the latter). Here are the most important ones:

(i) *Time:*

als	when (single period or point of time in the past)
bevor	before
bis	till, until
nachdem	after
seitdem	since
sobald	as soon as
während	while
wenn	whenever (repeated periods or points of time in the past or present)

(ii) *Causal connection (or specific absence of causal connection):*

da	as, since
damit	so that, in order that (purpose)
obwohl	although
ohne daß	without
so daß	so that (effect), with the result that
statt daß	instead of
während	whereas
weil	because
wenn	if
wo	seeing that

168

It is important not to use **so daß** for every 'so that', but only where a consequence is being referred to:

Ich habe meinen Hausschlüssel verloren, so daß ich nicht ins Haus komme.
I've lost my front door key, so (that) I can't get into the house.

Where purpose or intention is meant, **damit** is the joiner to use:

Er hat das Schloß ausgetauscht, damit ich mit meinem Hausschlüssel nicht ins Haus komme.
He's changed the lock so that I can't get into the house with my front door key. (i.e. in order to prevent me)

ohne daß and **statt daß** are used when the SU of the attached sentence is different from the SU of the core sentence (cf. Section 56):

<u>Ich</u> kann kaum anfangen zu lesen, ohne daß mich eins der <u>Kinder</u> stört.
I can barely start reading without one of the children disturbing me.
<u>Meine Eltern</u> haben mir den Englischkurs bezahlt, statt daß <u>ich</u> mein eigenes Geld dafür nehmen mußte.
My parents paid for the English course for me instead of my having to use my own money for it.

Exercise 28

Rewrite the following so that each contains an attached sentence introduced by one of the joiners **bevor, bis, nachdem, obwohl, während, weil,** *as appropriate. The first one is done for you.*

1   Vor dem Essen muß man die Hände waschen.
    Bevor man ißt, muß man die Hände waschen.
2   Nach dem Essen soll man eigentlich nicht schlafen.
3   Während des Essens darf man nicht zu viel reden.
4   Trotz des vielen Redens hat er eigentlich nicht viel
    gesagt.

5   Wegen des schönen Wetters müssen wir endlich im Garten arbeiten.

6   Bis zum Anfang des Programms kannst du noch schön in der Küche helfen!

7   Wegen deines hohen Blutdrucks mußt du weniger arbeiten.

8   Trotz seines hohen Blutdrucks läuft er jeden Tag.

64 Reflexive pronouns

If the SU of a sentence needs to become also the DO (or IO) of the same sentence, i.e. to be turned back on itself (hence the term *reflexive*), English uses '(to / for) myself, yourself, themselves', etc.

For the 1st person, both singular and plural, and for the 2nd person singular, German quite logically – no confusion can arise from doing so – uses the DO and IO pronouns you learnt in Sections 15, 20 and 31:

		DO	IO
lst	singular	**mich**	**mir**
lst	plural	**uns**	**uns**
2nd	singular	**dich**	**dir**

Wir kaufen <u>uns</u> für nächsten Sommer einen Wohnwagen.
(IO)
We're buying (for) ourselves a caravan for next summer.

Du siehst furchtbar müde aus, du mußt <u>dich</u> mehr schonen. (DO)
You look terribly tired. You've got to spare yourself more.

A special form is necessary for the 3rd person, both singular and plural, and for the 2nd person 'plural' (which is of course a polite form based on the 3rd person plural), because it has to be clear that the pronoun relates back to the SU and not to some other 3rd person.

DO/IO

2nd	plural	\
3rd	singular	} **sich**
3rd	plural	/

Meine Eltern haben mir den Brief nicht gegeben, sondern ihn für <u>sich</u> behalten. (DO)
My parents didn't give me the letter but kept it for themselves.
Mein Bruder hat <u>sich</u> einen neuen Sportwagen angeschafft. (IO)
My brother has got himself (lit. *acquired for himself) a new sports car.*
Wenn Sie <u>sich</u> nicht etwas mehr schonen, machen Sie <u>sich</u> kaputt. (DO)
If you don't spare yourself a bit more you'll wear yourself out.

Notes:

(i) The plural reflexive pronouns, as well as meaning 'ourselves, yourselves, themselves', can also mean 'each other, one another':

   Weil wir im selben Alter sind, haben wir uns sofort geduzt.
   Because we're the same age we addressed each other with 'du' immediately.

(ii) The reflexive pronouns are used in all cases where the required pronoun relates to the SU of the sentence, even when English would not use a '-self' pronoun. This requires particular care to use the special reflexive pronoun **sich** and not the usual DO/IO pronouns for the 2nd plural and 3rd singular and plural:

   Er hat nicht genug Geld bei <u>sich</u> (NOT **ihm**).
   He hasn't got enough money on him.
   Jetzt haben Sie Ihren besten Freund gegen <u>sich</u> (NOT **Sie**).
   Now you've got your best friend against you.

(iii) The German equivalent of English 'myself' etc. used as a
reinforcer is **selbst:**

Probier diesen Kuchen, ich habe ihn selbst gemacht.
Try this cake — I made it myself.

65 Reflexive verbs

There are parallels between the use of reflexive pronouns in
combination with verbs in English and in German:

Er hat <u>sich verletzt</u> und muß zum Arzt (gehen).
He's <u>hurt himself</u> and has to go to the doctor.

However, there are also in German several categories of the
combination *verb + reflexive pronoun* (or *reflexive verb*) where
the English equivalent would not lead one to expect a reflexive verb.

(a) English 'get + -ed' non-finite verb, where the SU
    experiences a process which may be either deliberately
    brought about by the SU or be involuntary. Some
    common examples:

to get annoyed	**sich ärgern**
to get dressed (to dress)	**sich anziehen II**
to get drunk	**sich betrinken I**
to get excited	**sich aufregen II**
to get lost	**sich verirren I**
	sich verlaufen I
to get ready	**sich vorbereiten II**
to get shaved (to shave)	**sich rasieren**
to get undressed	**sich ausziehen II**
to get used / accustomed (to)	**sich gewöhnen (an) I**
to get washed (to have a wash)	**sich waschen**

Während mein Bruder sich wäscht, ⎤ **ziehe ich mich an.**
Während sich mein Bruder wäscht, ⎦
While my brother's having a wash, I'll get dressed.

Note that in attached sentences, where the finite verb stands last, the reflexive pronoun is quite likely to stand immediately after the joiner, thus coming before the SU it relates to.

(b) English 'be + -ed' non-finite verb (or an adjective with similar meaning), where the process indicated is often a state of mind. The commonest examples are:

to be ashamed	**sich schämen**
to be embarrassed	**sich genieren**
to be frightened (of)	**sich fürchten (vor)**
to be interested (in)	**sich interessieren (für)**
to be pleased (at)	**sich freuen (über)**
to be surprised	**sich wundern**

Er bittet seine Mutter nicht um Geld, weil er sich geniert.
He's not asking his mother for money because he's embarrassed.
Er findet die Ferien langweilig, denn er interessiert sich für nichts.
He finds the holidays boring, since he's not interested in anything.
Ich gratuliere, ich freue mich sehr über Ihren Erfolg.
I congratulate (you). I'm very pleased at your success.
Ich wundere mich, daß du bei so schönem Wetter im Haus bleibst.
I'm surprised that you're staying inside the house in such lovely weather.

(c) A range of miscellaneous English expressions, some referring to mental states or processes, of which the following are the commonest:

to apologise	**sich entschuldigen I**
to approach	**sich nähern**

to be, be situated	**sich befinden I**
to catch a cold	**sich erkälten I**
to complain	**sich beklagen I**
to feel (e.g. sad)	**sich fühlen**
to hurry	**sich beeilen I**
to imagine (delusion)	**sich (IO) einbilden II**
(mental image)	**sich (IO) vorstellen II**
to long (for)	**sich sehnen (nach)**
to look forward (to)	**sich freuen (auf)**
to remember	**sich erinnern (an) I**
to say thank you, express one's thanks	**sich bedanken I**

Der Junge ist noch so klein, ich habe ihn mir größer vorgestellt.
The boy is still so small. I imagined him taller.
Ich habe Hunger, ich freue mich sehr auf das Essen.
I'm hungry. I'm looking forward to the meal (lit. to the food).

(d) Some ideas which are conveyed in German by impersonal reflexive constructions with the SU **es.** These include

to be	
to be about	**sich handeln um**
to be a matter of	

which is very much used. Such constructions may, in spite of the presence of the reflexive pronoun, involve verbs that do not normally take a DO (or IO) and are therefore similar to the impersonal obverse process construction (Section 57(b)):

Ich muß Sie leider stören, es handelt sich um Ihren Sohn ...
I'm sorry to have to trouble you; it's about your son ...
Bei der Silvesterfahrt handelt es sich um eine Siebentagestour.
The New Year's Eve trip is (a matter of) a seven-day tour.

Im Allgäu lebt es sich sehr angenehm.
Life is very pleasant in the Allgäu.

Vocabulary

Study and learn the conversation that follows. You will need these new words:

der	**Fehler (-)**	fault
	sich beschweren I	to complain
	erscheinen I	to appear
der	**Kassenbon (-s)**	till receipt
der	**Kauf (-̈e)**	buying, purchase
die	**Reklamation (-en)**	complaint (here implying replacement or refund)
der	**Aufkleber (-)**	sticker
der	**Anfang (-̈e)**	beginning
	pfeifen	to whistle
der	**Pfeifton**	whistling
	auftauchen II	to turn up, appear
das	**Tonband (-̈er)**	(audio) tape
der	**Ton (-̈e)**	sound
	sich (DO) anhören II	to sound
das	**Gerät (-e)**	(piece of) equipment
	überhaupt	(here) actually
die	**Ordnung**	order
	einwandfrei	perfect
	genau	precisely, for certain
	versuchen I	to try
	allerdings	though, mind you
	ersetzen I	to refund
das	**Exemplar (-e)**	copy
	vorrätig	in stock
	bestellen I	to order
	sich (IO) anhören II	to listen to
	reichen	to hand
	sich vertun I	to make a mistake, slip up

175

CONVERSATION

A young (female) customer returns an apparently faulty audio cassette to the shop

Verkäufer	Ja, bitte schön?
Kundin	Guten Tag! Ich habe mir vorgestern bei Ihnen eine Kassette mit Popmusik gekauft, die leider einige Fehler hat. Da die Kassette ziemlich teuer war, wollte ich mich jetzt beschweren.
V	Um was für eine Kassette handelt es sich denn?
K	Es ist das neueste Konzert von den Twen-Tops, das gerade erst erschienen ist.
V	Darf ich mal den Kassenbon sehen, den Sie beim Kauf bekommen haben, denn ohne Bon gibt es keine Reklamation.
K	Das Dumme ist, daß ich den Bon einfach nicht finden kann, aber Sie sehen, der Aufkleber mit dem Preis befindet sich noch auf der Kassette.
V	Ja, aber trotzdem … Also, um welche Fehler handelt es sich denn?
K	Also, am Anfang gibt es einen hohen Pfeifton, der immer wieder auftaucht. Und dann hat das Tonband Stellen, wo man überhaupt nichts hört. Und wenn mal die Musik da ist, liegt das Ganze viel zu hoch im Ton.
V	Das hört sich nicht gut an, aber ist Ihr Gerät denn überhaupt in Ordnung?
K	O ja, das Gerät ist einwandfrei. Das weiß ich ganz genau, weil mein Bruder, der Musik studiert, seine Kassetten gespielt hat, nachdem ich es mit dieser versucht habe.
V	Na gut. Ich kann allerdings kein Geld ersetzen, sondern Ihnen nur ein neues Exemplar derselben Kassette geben, wenn wir sie noch vorrätig haben. Sonst muß ich sie bestellen … Aber erst muß ich mir selbst die

	Kassette anhören.
K	Bitte schön. (*Sie reicht ihm die Kassette, und er macht sie auf.*)
V	Aber das ist doch kein Twen-Tops-Konzert, sondern das Klarinettenquintett von Mozart!
K	O, da muß ich mich aber entschuldigen, ich habe mich vertan! Ich habe die Falsche mitgebracht!

TRANSLATION

Assistant	Yes please?
Customer	Hello! The day before yesterday I bought a cassette of pop music here, which unfortunately has some faults. As the cassette was rather expensive I wanted to complain now.
A	What sort of cassette is it?
C	It's the latest concert by the Twen-Tops, which has only just come out.
A	Can I see the till receipt that you got at the time of purchase, since we can't do anything about complaints without a receipt.
C	The stupid thing is that I just can't find the receipt, but you can see that the sticker with the price on it is still on the cassette.
A	Yes, but still … Well, what were the faults?
C	Well, at the beginning there's a high-pitched whistling sound that keeps coming back. And then there are places on the tape where you can't hear anything at all. And when the music actually is there, everything is pitched much too high.
A	That doesn't sound good, but is your equipment actually in order?
C	Oh yes, the equipment is perfect. I know that for certain, because my brother, who's a music student, played his cassettes after I

had been trying with this one.

A   Oh, all right. Mind you, I can't refund cash but only give you a fresh copy of the same cassette, if we still have it in stock. Otherwise I'll have to order it ... But first I've got to listen to the cassette.

C   Here you are. (*She hands him the cassette and he opens it.*)

A   But this isn't a Twen-Tops concert, it's Mozart's Clarinet Quintet!

C   Oh, I really must apologise. I've made a mistake! I've brought the wrong one!

Chapter 12

Chapter 12 concentrates on the past tense, telling you more about its uses and its formation. The chapter also introduces:

- the 'pre-past' tense (in English, 'had walked', etc.)
- the 'oblique past' tense of auxiliary verbs (in English, 'would', 'might', etc.)
- conditional statements, using the present (e.g. 'if he stays, we will ...'), the oblique past (e.g. 'if he stayed, we would ...') and the oblique pre-past (e.g. 'if he had stayed, we would have ...')
- the obverse or passive use of *zu* + *-en*
- the so-called affective words which indicate the speaker's attitude and are essential to idiomatic German.

66 The past tense (II)

This tense (already introduced for ten verbs in Section 59) is usually a genuine – and freely interchangeable – alternative to the pre-present for expressing past time. The choice of which to use depends on, for example, (i) the need to keep a sentence short by using one word fewer (the past tense instead of the pre-present), (ii) the usefulness or otherwise of having the main verb where otherwise only an auxiliary verb would stand, (iii) the advantage of variety in longer structures containing core sentences and attached sentences, (iv) the feel or speech rhythm of a sentence, and (v) regional speech habits. The choice is NOT (or very rarely) determined by whether the particular instance of past time concerned is viewed as isolated from the present (for which English must use the past tense) or as somehow involving the present (for which English must use the pre-present). German typically mixes the pre-present with the past tense.

Als ich ankam, **hat sie mich zu einer Tasse Kaffee eingeladen.**

  past tense   pre-present
When I arrived she invited me to (have) a cup of coffee.

As indicated in Section 59, two sets of endings are used,
(i) one for past tenses having the same stem as the **-en** form,
(ii) the other with past tenses having new stems:

	(i) same-stem verbs	(ii) new-stem verbs
singular		
1st } 3rd }	**-(e)te§**	no ending
2nd	**-(e)test§**	**-(e)st***
plural		
1st/2nd/3rd	**-(e)ten§**	**-en**

§ **e** is inserted when the stem ends in **-d** or **-t**

* **e** is inserted when the stem ends in **-s** or **-ß**

Was du lasest, kam von der Kirche.
What you were reading came from the church.
Die Kinder machten ziemlich viel Krach, während er redete.
The children were making rather a lot of noise while he was speaking.

While making the past tense of same-stem verbs is simple, the past tense stems of new-stem verbs have to be learnt (see Section 67 below).

There are a few new-stem verbs which take the same-stem verb endings (iii):

-en form		past tense stem
brennen	to burn	**brann-**
bringen	to bring, take	**brach-**
denken	to think	**dach-**
kennen	to know (people)	**kann-**
wissen	to know (facts)	**wuß-**

Daß du ihn kanntest, wußte ich nicht.
I didn't know that you used to know him.

67 Past tense new stems

Like the **ge_(e)t** form of exceptional verbs (Section 47(a)), these have to be learnt, and a good dictionary is useful. It can be a help to note that some past tense new stems are identical with the stem of the **ge_(e)t** form, while some change yet again. Here are most of the commonly used verbs listed in Section 47, now also grouped according to whether or not the stem is shared with the **ge_(e)t** form. The sub-grouping is as in Section 47.

(a) New stems shared with **ge_(e)t** form:

-en form		past tense stem
stehen	to stand	**stand**
leiden	to suffer	**litt**
pfeifen	to whistle	**pfiff**
schneiden	to cut	**schnitt**
streiten	to quarrel	**stritt**
bleiben	to stay, remain	**blieb**
leihen	to lend	**lieh**
scheinen	to seem, shine	**schien**
schreiben	to write	**schrieb**
steigen	to climb	**stieg**
treiben	to drive, impel	**trieb**
riechen	to smell	**roch**
schließen	to shut, close	**schloß**
bieten	to offer	**bot**
fliegen	to fly	**flog**
fliehen	to flee	**floh**

| ziehen | to pull, draw | zog |
| lügen | to lie (fib) | log |

(b) New stems NOT shared with the **ge_(e)t** form, which is therefore also given for comparison. It is very useful for learning new past tense stems to note that if the main vowel in the stem of the **-en** form is either **-e-** or **-i-** (but not the two together), the past tense stem is virtually certain to contain the vowel **-a-**. Though this is not true of **wissen** (**wuß-**) or **gehen** (**ging**), it works for all the other verbs in group (iii) of Section 66, for **stehen** in (a) of this section, and for the verbs in the following list.

-en form		past tense stem	ge_(e)t form
essen	to eat	aß	gegessen
fahren	to go (not on foot)	fuhr	gefahren
fangen	to catch	fing	gefangen
geben	to give	gab	gegeben
halten	to hold	hielt	gehalten
kommen	to come	kam	gekommen
laufen	to run, walk	lief	gelaufen
lesen	to read	las	gelsen
messen	to measure	maß	gemessen
rufen	to call (out)	rief	gerufen
schlafen	to sleep	schlief	geschlafen
schlagen	to hit, beat	schlug	geschlagen
sehen	to see	sah	gesehen
stoßen	to bump, push	stieß	gestoßen
tragen	to carry, wear	trug	getragen
treten	to step, kick	trat	getreten
wachsen	to grow	wuchs	gewachsen
gehen	to go	ging	gegangen
brechen	to break	brach	gebrochen
helfen	to help	half	geholfen
sprechen	to speak	sprach	gesprochen
sterben	to die	starb	gestorben
treffen	to meet	traf	getroffen

nehmen	to take	**nahm**	**genommen**
stehlen	to steal	**stahl**	**gestohlen**
sitzen	to sit	**saß**	**gesessen**
schwimmen	to swim	**schwamm**	**geschwommen**
finden	to find	**fand**	**gefunden**
singen	to sing	**sang**	**gesungen**
sinken	to sink	**sank**	**gesunken**
springen	to jump	**sprang**	**gesprungen**
trinken	to drink	**trank**	**getrunken**
bitten	to ask, request	**bat**	**gebeten**
liegen	to lie (recline)	**lag**	**gelegen**

Exercise 29

Rewrite the following pairs of sentences, turning the first one in each pair into an attached sentence introduced by the joiner **während**, *'while', and using the second as the core sentence. Use the past tense in the attached sentence and the pre-present in the core sentence. The first pair is rewritten for you.*

1 Ich laufe durch die Stadt.
   Meine Schwester schläft.
   Während ich durch die Stadt lief, hat meine Schwester geschlafen.
2 Fritz arbeitet im Garten.
   Sein Bruder hört sich Pop-Musik an.
3 Hanna schreibt einen Brief.
   Ihre Freundin geht schwimmen.
4 Otto trinkt Milch.
   Sein Bruder Bruno trinkt Schnaps.
5 Frau Krause spricht mit ihrem Nachbarn.
   Ein Einbrecher stiehlt ihr Geld vom Küchentisch.

6   Die Eltern streiten sich oben im Haus.
    Die Kinder halten unten im Haus eine Party.
7   Anton spricht mit den Eltern.
    Susanne stößt den Hund ins Wasser.

68 The pre-past

This runs parallel to the pre-present (Section 44) and is
formed with the *past tense* of **sein** or **haben** plus the **ge_(e)t**
form. (For the choice of **sein** or **haben** see Section 45.)

The pre-past is used as in English (e.g. 'had walked / had
been walking') to make clear the precise sequence of events:

When I arrived they had (already) eaten.
When I arrived they had (already) been eating.
Als ich ankam, hatten sie (schon) gegessen.

as against:

When (i.e. After) I arrived they ate.
Sobald ich ankam, aßen sie.

and:

When I arrived they were (already/just) eating.
Als ich ankam, aßen sie (schon/gerade).

It is also used to refer to situations or events *preceding* a particular point or period of time which is already in the past
and which is often stated explicitly but sometimes left
implicit:

**Bis vorgestern hatten wir keine Briefe von ihm
bekommen.**
*Up to the day before yesterday we hadn't received any letters
from him.*

184

69 The oblique past tense (I)

Most – but not all – English auxiliary verbs are available
in non-oblique / oblique pairs (e.g. 'will / would',
'may / might', 'can / could'), where the non-oblique member
of the pair comes over as direct, even blunt, by comparison
with the oblique member, which suggests deference,
hesitation, tentativeness, politeness.

Oblique verbs, which in English are distinguishable in only a
handful of auxiliary verbs ('could', 'might', 'ought', 'should',
'would', 'were' instead of 'was' in the singular, and old-fash-
ioned 'be' instead of 'am, is, are'), are abundant in German.
We begin here with the oblique past tense of eight of the ten
auxiliary verbs (already treated as special cases previously)
because these eight oblique past tenses are in constant
idiomatic use. Such use includes these verbs not just as auxiliaries (in tandem with a main verb in **-en** or **ge_(e)t** form)
but also as main verbs in their own right. Note that,
although the oblique past tense is obviously based on the
past tense, its *meaning* is NOT past but vaguely
present / future.

The 1st / 3rd singular is given; for the 2nd singular add **-st**,
for the plural add **-n**.

past tense	oblique past tense	nearest English equivalents
hatte	**hätte**	would have, might have
war	**wäre**	would be, were (as in 'if I were you ...')
wurde	**würde**	would
durfte	**dürfte**	might; (negative) shouldn't
konnte	**könnte**	could, might, would be able to
mochte	**möchte**	would like (to)
mußte	**müßte**	ought to, should, would have to
sollte	**sollte**	ought to

Hättest du etwas dagegen?
Would you have any objection?
An deiner Stelle wäre ich böse.
In your place I would be cross.
Würden Sie bitte warten?
Would you please wait?
Er dürfte eigentlich nicht Auto fahren.
He shouldn't really be driving.
Er könnte sich verletzen.
He might hurt himself.
Ich möchte bitte eine Tasse Kaffee.
1'd like a cup of coffee, please.
Dieser Brief müßte übermorgen schon ankommen.
This letter should arrive the day after tomorrow.
Du solltest nicht so schnell fahren.
You oughtn't to drive so fast.

70 The oblique past tense (II)

Apart from its idiomatic use with the auxiliary verbs, the
main use of the oblique past tense is in some types of conditional statements (see Section 71 below), and for this it is
necessary to know how to make the oblique past of *all* verbs,
not just auxiliaries.

Same-stem verbs (see Section 66) certainly have an oblique
past, but because it is identical with the past itself it tends to
be avoided and to be replaced by **würde (-st, -n)**, 'would',
plus the **-en** form of the verb required:

Wenn er ein neues Haus **baute ,...**
 bauen würde (preferred)
If he built a new house ...

New-stem verbs, among which are some of the most commonly used words in the language, are a different matter.
The 1st and 3rd singular oblique past is *always* distinguishable, and if the main vowel in the new stem is **a** or **o** or **u**, *all*

forms are distinguishable from those of the past tense, because these vowels become ä, ö and ü respectively. The new-stem verbs with same-stem endings behave similarly if the vowel is capable of change.

-en form		bleiben	kommen	ziehen	wissen
past tense new stem		blieb	kam	zog	wußte
singular					
1st/3rd	(¨)e	bliebe	käme	zöge	wüßte
2nd	(¨)est	bliebest	kämest	zögest	wüßtest
plural					
1st/2nd/3rd	(¨)en	blieben	kämen	zögen	wüßten

71 Conditional statements

A conditional statement consists of an attached sentence, usually – but not always – beginning with a joiner (**wenn**, 'if', or less commonly **falls**, 'in case'), to express the condition, and a core sentence to express the consequence if the condition is met. The sequence of attached sentence and core sentence is reversible.

Wenn sie zu Hause bleibt, bringen wir ihr etwas Schönes mit.
Wir bringen ihr etwas Schönes mit, wenn sie zu Hause bleibt.
If she stays at home we'll bring her something nice.
We'll bring her something nice if she stays at home.

If the attached (condition) sentence comes first:

(i) There is an alternative to using a joiner and placing the finite verb last (see Section 63). This is to start the attached sentence with the finite verb, followed immediately by the SU:

Bleibt sie zu Hause, bringen wir ihr etwas Schönes mit.

It is important not to mistake this structure for a question (see Section 22), but the presence of the core sentence precludes this.

(ii) The core sentence can start optionally with **so** or **dann**:

| **Wenn sie zu Hause bleibt,** | ⎫⎧ | **so** | ⎫ | **bringen wir ihr etwas** |
| **Bleibt sie zu Hause,** | ⎭⎩ | **dann** | ⎭ | **Schönes mit.** |

There are three types of conditional statement in German, corresponding roughly to three similar types in English.

(a) *Odds are even on the condition being met, so <u>neutral</u>*

Here the attached condition sentence has a finite verb in the present tense, and the core sentence a finite verb in the present tense or the future.

Wenn die Bäume schnell wachsen, bekommen wir in zwei Jahren die ersten Früchte.
If the trees grow fast we'll get the first fruit in two years.
Wenn man ihm die Wahl eines Instruments überläßt, wird er bestimmt Klavier lernen.
If the choice of an instrument is left to him he'll definitely learn the piano

(b) *Odds are against the condition being met, so <u>remote</u>*

Here the finite verbs of *both* the attached condition sentence *and* the core sentence can be

– *either* the oblique past tense of the main verb required (Section 70)

– *or* the oblique past tense of **werden** (**würde, -st, -n**) plus the **-en** form of the main verb required.

There is an absolutely free choice between those two options, in contrast with English, which requires the condition sentence always to have the past tense and the core sentence always to contain 'would' (the equivalent of **würde**). Since German is freer here than English, you need to concentrate only on incorporating one form or other of the oblique past tense in both sentences.

Wenn wir so einen Mann in den Klub aufnehmen würden, würden wir in Schwierigkeiten kommen. Wenn wir so einen Mann in den Klub aufnähmen, kämen wir in Schwierigkeiten.
If we accepted a man like that in the club we'd get into difficulties.

There is no need for consistency between the attached and core sentences, and indeed inconsistency is often preferred. **würde (-st, -n)** is, however, very common in everyday speech and also very handy for two reasons. First, many verbs have no distinguishable oblique past tense (Section 70) and sound faintly unsatisfactory in conditional statements. Second, if you are unsure of the (oblique) past tense of a new stem verb, you can get round it by using **würde (-st, -n)**.

(c) *The condition cannot be met, because it relates to an 'opportunity' now past, so hypothetical*

Here *both* the attached condition sentence and the core sentence contain the oblique *pre-past* (see Section 68 for the pre- past). This means using **hätte (-st, -n)** or **wäre (-st, -n)** as appropriate (Section 45) with the **ge_(e)t** form of the main verb required. Both **hätte** and **wäre** incorporate the idea of 'would' (Section 69), which is present only in the core sentence in English but not in the attached condition sentence, so care is needed.

Wenn wir das gewußt hätten, wären wir nicht gekommen.
If we had known that, we wouldn't have come.

Exercise 30

(a) *Write out the condition sentences from the left-hand column, adding to each the correct core sentence from the right-hand column.*

(b) *Write out the completed sentences a second time, deleting the joiner* **wenn** *and starting with the finite verb. The first is done for you in each case.*

1   Wenn Emil in den Film geht, ... dann wird es zu kalt für uns alle.

(a) Wenn Emil in den Film geht, dann sehe ich ihn mir auch an.

(b) Geht Emil in den Film, dann sehe ich ihn mir auch an.

2   Wenn du die Fahrkarte besorgen würdest, ... dann wäre sie schwierig.

3   Wenn Peter nicht das Fenster schließt, ... dann wird es Krach geben.

4   Wenn dieser Mann nicht den Klub verläßt, ... dann sehe ich ihn mir auch an.

5   Wenn die kleine Tochter nicht fernsehen dürfte, ... dann wirst du am Sonntag morgen schlafen können

6   Wenn der Vater in die Gaststube geht, ... dann hätten wir die Möglichkeit, am Wochenende in die Berge zu fahren.

7   Wenn du jetzt das Essen für Sonntag kochst, ... dann trinkt er immer zu viel.

72 zu + -en form expressing obverse process

You already know **zu** + **-en** form constructions in which the true or 'logical' SU of the **-en** form in the attached phrase is derived from the core of the sentence (Section 54):

Wir haben vor, morgen in die Berge zu fahren.
We intend to drive into the mountains tomorrow.
(we ... drive)
Ich mochte **dich** bitten, mir die Fahrkarte zu besorgen.
I'd like to ask you to obtain the ticket for me.
(you ... obtain)
Wir helfen **ihnen,** den Weg zu finden.
We'll help them to find the way.
(they ... find)

However, when this same **zu + -en** construction is in tandem
with **sein**, the force of the resulting expression is that of the
obverse process, with, in addition, an overlay of obligation
or permission or possibility:

Die Ergebnisse **sind** sofort nach der Wahl bekannt **zu**
machen.
The results are to be made known immediately after the election.
(the results must be made known)

Dieser Wein **ist** in jedem Supermarkt **zu bekommen.**
This wine is to be obtained at any supermarket.
(this wine can be obtained)

Dem Patienten **ist** nicht mehr **zu helfen.** (cf. Section 57(a))
*The patient is not to be helped any further. [Literal translation is
misleading.]*
(the patient cannot be helped)

Sogar über den Direktor **ist** Kritik **zu hören.**
Criticism is even to be heard of the director.
(criticism can be heard)

This structure needs special care, because the parallel
English one – 'to' + base form of verb – does not express the
obverse process, but only the future, or obligation, or both:

The meeting is to reconvene at 7.30.
(the meeting is going to/must reconvene)

73 Affective words

There are in German a number of short, generally (but not always) unstressed words, which are sometimes translatable into English, sometimes not, and which are not strictly necessary to the 'factual' meaning of a sentence. So far these have scarcely appeared in the dialogues, but it is essential to get to know them in order to be able not only to speak idiomatic German but also to understand the *full* meaning of what is being expressed.

The functioning of affective words in German can best be illustrated by some English expressions such as '(un)fortunately', 'sadly', 'clearly' and (nowadays) 'hopefully', which are included in a sentence not as part of its 'factual' meaning, but in order to show how the speaker *feels* about that 'factual' meaning (and, often, how he hopes to make the listener feel about it); hence the term *affective*.

Our friends clearly can't finance the undertaking.

means that the fact stated is 'clear' to the speaker, and 'clearly' here is different from the same word in

She stated her intentions clearly.

where it is part of the factual meaning. The same is true of the two different uses of 'hopefully' in the following pair.

Hopefully he'll pass his driving test this time.
He embarked hopefully on his third attempt at a balloon crossing of the Channel.

The range of such expressions extends to words like 'probably', 'possibly', 'certainly', etc., by which the speaker gives his assessment of the likelihood his proposition has of being realised. Such expressions, then, are the speaker's own comment on the content of what he is saying, and German has equivalent expressions like **wahrscheinlich**, 'probably', **offensichtlich**, 'clearly', and **hoffentlich**, 'hopefully', which do the same job and present no difficulty for the English-speaking learner.

However, German has in addition some much used short words of more *generalised* affective meaning than those with which we have illustrated the principle. They have scarcely any counterparts in English, except 'even', which conveys an attitude of generalised surprise.

Here are the commonest affective words in approximate descending order of frequency of use. We can give here only a rough description of the attitude each expresses, but you will find most of them used and underlined in the next Conversation.

doch	contradiction; objection; protest; persusion
ja	acknowledgement by the speaker that the 'fact' he is stating is well-known, accepted, obvious
wohl	belief that the 'fact' being stated,though not definite, is highly probable; assumption
mal	minimalisation of the 'fact' stated (cf. 'just')
denn	impatience/urgency for an answer/explanation
etwa	vagueness; uncertainty; disbelief
auch	mark or expectation of surprise at the inclusion of something in some notional category or other (cf. 'even')

schon	mark or expectation of surprise at the relative prematurity of something on some notional scale or other (cf. 'even')
noch	mark or expectation of surprise at the relative 'overdue-ness' of something on some notional scale or other (cf. 'even')
eben (N. German) ⎤ **halt** (S. German) ⎦	acceptance, acquiescence, resignation in face of the inevitability of the 'fact' being stated

The above 'definitions' are not to be understood in a literal sense and are only meant to assist you to home in on the force of affective words. Note, too, that all these affective words have other, non-affective, senses, some of which you will recognise, e.g. **(je)doch,** 'however'; **ja,** 'yes'; **wohl,** 'well'; **(ein)mal,** 'once'; **denn,** 'for'; **etwa,** 'about', **auch,** 'also'; **schon,** 'already'; **noch,** 'still'; **eben,** 'just (now)'.

Vocabulary

Study and learn the conversation that follows. You will need these new words:

der	**Film (-e)**	film
der	**Fotoapparat (-e)**	camera
	nämlich	you see
	voll	full
die	**Sommerferien** (plural)	summer holidays
das	**Bild (-er)**	photo, picture
	vorig	last
das	**Taschengeld**	pocket money
	sparen	to save
der	**Schulausflug (¨e)**	school outing
	na gut	(oh,) all right
	verschieden	various

das	Dia (-s)	slide
	richtig	proper
der	Augenblick (-e)	moment
	im Augenblick	at present
	überreden I	to persuade
	hinterher	afterwards
der	Abzug (-̈e)	print
der	Klassenkamerad (PO -en)	classmate
die	Aufnahme (-n)	exposure, photo
	vierundzwanziger	with twenty-four
	reintun II	to put in
	so was	that sort of thing
	überhaupt	at all, in general
der	Zähler (-)	counter
	sich bewegen I	to move
	weiterdrehen II	to wind on
der	Auslöser (-)	shutter release
	drücken	to press
	egal ob	regardless of whether
	abgesehen davon	quite apart from that
	mach dir nichts daraus	don't worry about it
	kriegen	to get

CONVERSATION

A teenager with a camera problem

Mädchen   Vati, sag mal, könntest du mir wohl bitte
einen Film für meinen Fotoapparat geben?
Meiner ist nämlich voll. Ich habe ihn schon
seit den Sommerferien darin und habe die
letzten Bilder vorige Woche auf der Hochzeit
von Marianne gemacht.

Vater   Ich verstehe, du möchtest wohl dein
Taschengeld sparen! Wenn ich dir einen Film
gebe, brauchst du natürlich keinen zu kaufen.

M Nein, so ist das nicht, aber wir haben heute einen Schulausflug, und ich möchte gern fotografieren können.

V Na gut. Ich habe verschiedene Filme. Was für einen wolltest du haben – für Dias oder richtige Bilder?

M Im Augenblick habe ich einen Diafilm drin. Du weißt, du hattest mich überredet, Dias zu machen. Aber ich habe richtige Bilder lieber, und die sind <u>auch</u> für einen Schulausflug besser. Ich könnte dann hinterher <u>auch</u> Abzüge für meine Klassenkameraden machen lassen.

V Gut. Wieviele Aufnahmen möchtest du <u>denn</u> haben? Möchtest du einen vierundzwanziger Film haben oder einen sechsunddreißiger?

M Gib mir <u>doch</u> einen vierundzwanziger, dann ist der Film schneller zu Ende, denn für einen Schulausflug brauche ich <u>doch</u> bloß zehn oder so.

V *(Er reicht ihr einen Film.)* So, da hast du deinen Film ...

M ... und Vati, könntest du <u>mal</u> bitte den alten Film herausnehmen und den neuen reintun? Du weißt <u>ja</u>, ich kann so was gar nicht gut ...

V Na gut ... *(Er öffnet den Fotoapparat.)* Aber hier ist <u>doch</u> überhaupt kein alter Film drin! Hast du <u>etwa</u> die ganze Zeit ohne Film fotografiert?!

M Was??!! O meine schönen Aufnahmen von der Hochzeit und überhaupt aus den ganzen Wochen seit den Sommerferien! Und ich dachte die ganze Zeit, es wäre ein Film drin! Der Zähler bewegte sich <u>doch</u> immer weiter.

V   Bei deinem Apparat geht der Zähler <u>eben</u>
    weiter, wenn man weiterdreht und den
    Auslöser drückt, egal ob ein Film drin ist
    oder nicht. Abgesehen davon wüßte ich nicht,
    wie ein Film überhaupt in deinem Apparat
    hätte sein konnen. Ich habe nämlich den
    alten Film am Ende der Ferien selbst
    herausgenommen.
    Aber mach dir nichts daraus! Du kriegst
    Abzüge von meinen Hochzeitsbildern!

TRANSLATION

Girl   Daddy, (tell me,) could you give me a film for
       my camera, please? (You see,) mine's full. I've
       had it in since the summer holidays, and I
       took the last photos last week at Marianne's
       wedding.
Father I see, you want to save your pocket money! If
       I give you a film you won't need to buy one,
       of course.
G   No, it's not (like) that, but we've got a school
       outing today, and I'd like to be able to take
       some photographs.
F   All right. I've got various films. What sort did
       you want (to have): for slides or proper
       photos?
G   At present I've got a slide film in. (You)
       remember, you'd persuaded me to take slides.
       But I prefer proper photos, and they're better
       for a school outing. Then I'd be able to get
       prints made for my classmates afterwards.
F   Fine. How many exposures would you like
       (to have)? Do you want a film with twenty-
       four or one with thirty-six?
G   Let me have one with twenty-four. (Then) the
       film will be finished more quickly, (since)
       I only need about ten for a school outing.

F   *(He hands her a film.)* Well, there's your film ...

G   ... and daddy, could you please just take the old film out and put the new one in? You know I'm no good at that sort of thing ...

F   Oh, all right ... *(He opens the camera.)* But there isn't any old film (at all) in here! Surely you haven't been taking photographs all this time without a film in?!

G   What??!! Oh, my lovely photos of the wedding, and from all these weeks since the summer holidays! And all the time I thought there was a film in it! But the counter kept moving on.

F   In your camera the counter does move on when you wind on and press the shutter release, regardless of whether there's a film in or not. Quite apart from that, I couldn't have imagined how a film could have been in your camera. (You see,) I took the old film out myself at the end of the holidays. But don't worry about it! You'll get prints of my photographs of the wedding!

Chapter 13

This final chapter introduces the oblique present tense and shows how this and other tenses are used when citing speech ('He said that ...'). It looks at the order of words in cited speech and in enclosed attached sentences. The chapter also covers:

- *ways of translating the English '-ing' form*
- *words such as 'therefore' and 'however', which link sentences into longer sequences of thought*
- *the familiar plural form*
- *word order in sentences with two -en verb forms*
- *the idiomatic use of impersonal expressions.*

74 by ...-ing; in spite of ...-ing

There are very few direct German equivalents for the various uses of the '-ing' non-finite form in English. The only major exception is the **-end** form, referred to in Section 61, used as an adjective in front of the noun:

der lachende Polizist   *the laughing policeman*

The extension of this usage is explained in Section 82(b) and (e).

Most other English '-ing' forms have to be rephrased before they correspond to what is possible in German, and usually there is a simple alternative:

After talking to him I changed my mind.
After I talked to him I changed my mind.
Nachdem ich mit ihm gesprochen hatte, habe ich meine Meinung geändert.

Before leaving I gave them my phone number.
Before I left I gave them my phone number.
Bevor ich wegging, habe ich ihnen meine Telefonnummer gegeben.

However, 'by … -ing' and 'in spite of …-ing' do not have obvious alternatives corresponding to the German, which requires constructions like those in Section 63(c)(ii).

(a) *by …-ing*

Use the joiner **indem** to introduce an attached sentence.

Ich konnte viel Geld sparen, indem ich Überstunden gemacht habe.
I was able to save a lot of money by doing overtime ('in that I did overtime').

(b) *in spite of …-ing*

Use the joiner **trotzdem** to introduce an attached sentence.

Ich konnte nicht viel Geld sparen, trotzdem ich Überstunden gemacht habe.
I wasn't able to save much money in spite of doing overtime ('in spite of that I did overtime').

These constructions make it easy for the core and attached sentences to have different subjects:

Wir konnten viel Geld sparen, indem du Überstunden gemacht hast.
We were able to save a lot of money by your doing overtime.

75 Line-of-thought pointers

The last Conversation contained two examples of **nämlich**, 'you see':

Meiner ist nämlich voll.
Ich habe nämlich den alten Film . . . selbst
herausgenommen.

nämlich is a line-of-thought pointer, indicating that the sentence containing it is an explanation of a previous sentence. Whereas the joiners you learnt in Section 63 enable attached sentences to be connected to core sentences (or other attached sentences), line-of-thought pointers enable sentences of all kinds to be bound into bigger chunks of German by pointing to the way a train or line of thought is developing.

Below are the most common line-of-thought pointers, grouped according to function and with the nearest English equivalents. They are given without examples, because they can only be properly illustrated in longer 'texts'. You will find many examples in the Conversation at the end of this chapter. Most of these expressions can stand at the start or in the middle of a sentence, but any restrictions are noted.

(a) *Consequential*

also	so
darum	thus
deshalb	therefore
daher	consequently
deswegen	
somit	
infolgedessen	

Note: German **also** NEVER means 'also', and German **so** on its own usually means 'in this way' (though in front of an adjective it means 'so').

(b) *Explanatory*

denn (start only)	⎫	⎰	for
nämlich (middle only)	⎭	⎱	you see

(c) *Additive*

außerdem	⎫	⎰ besides
überdies	⎪	⎱ furthermore
zudem	⎬	⎱ moreover
ebenfalls	⎪	
gleichfalls	⎭	likewise

(d) *Dismissive*

ohnehin	⎫	(middle only)	⎰ anyway
sowieso	⎭		⎱ in any case

(e) *Remonstrative*

immerhin	⎫	
schließlich	⎭	after all
wenigstens		at least
jedenfalls		at any rate

(f) *Reservational*

jedoch	
doch (start only)	however

(g) *Contrastive*

andererseits	⎫	⎰ on the other hand
dagegen	⎬	⎱ in contrast
hingegen	⎭	⎱ by comparison

(h) *Concessive*

		⎧ admittedly
allerdings	⎫	to be sure
freilich	⎭ .	though (final only)
		⎩ mind you

zwar ... aber	true ... but

Note: **zwar** in this sense is always followed by **aber, jedoch** or a similar reservational pointer in a subsequent sentence.

(i) *Provocative*

trotzdem ⎫	⎧ nevertheless
dennoch ⎭	⎩ nonetheless

(j) *Alternative*

sonst ⎫	otherwise
ansonsten ⎭	

es sei denn	⎧ unless
	⎩ except (that)

Note: **es sei denn** is very close in sense to the joiner **wenn** ('if') followed by a negative (**nicht** or **kein**).

Exercise 31

Add to the second sentence of each pair an appropriate line-of-thought pointer from the list below. Some sentences allow of more than one possibility, and in such cases the Key gives the mostapt one, with the others in brackets. Try putting the line-of-thought pointers at the start and in the middle, making any other necessary or desirable changes. The first is done for you.

allerdings	immerhin
andererseits	jedoch
außerdem	trotzdem
deshalb	

1   Emil weiß, daß Karl kommt.
    Er plant eine Busfahrt mit ihm.
    Deshalb plant er eine Busfahrt mit ihm.
    Er plant deshalb eine Busfahrt mit ihm.

2 Karl möchte zur Nordsee.
  Emil bucht eine Fahrt nach Berlin.
3 Berlin ist eine schöne Stadt.
  Es gibt sehr viele Touristen.
4 Die Nordsee ist ruhig.
  In Berlin gibt es viel zu sehen.
5 Das Brandenburger Tor ist sehr attraktiv.
  Es ist historisch und politisch wichtig.
6 Warum ist es historisch und politisch wichtig?
  Vor einiger Zeit war es das Tor zwischen Westen
  und Osten.
7 Karl wollte an die Nordsee.
  Er hat Berlin sehr interessant gefunden.

76 Conversation between intimates: the plural

In Section 31 the mode of addressing intimates was given only in the singular, i.e. for addressing just one person. If you are addressing more than one person you know intimately, or a group containing a significant proportion of people in that category, these forms are required:

pronouns		possessive (ein-type, cf. **unser**)
SU	**ihr**	**euer**
DO	**euch**	**euer**
IO	**euch**	**euer**

verbs -en form	present tense	past tense	oblique past tense	instructions/ requests
haben	**habt**	**hattet**	**hättet**	**habt**
sein	**seid**	**wart**	**wäret**	**seid**
dürfen	**dürft**	**durftet**	**dürftet**	–

sollen	sollt	solltet	solltet	–
lassen	laßt	ließt	ließet	laßt
sehen	seht	saht	sähet	seht
machen	macht	machtet	machtet	macht
reden	redet	redetet	redetet	redet

77 Attached sentences with two -en forms

Attached sentences where the finite verb must stand last
(Section 63) will contain two **-en** forms if the pre-present (or
pre-past) of certain auxiliary verbs is used (see Section 58). If
we take two examples from Section 58:

Ich habe den Nachbarn helfen müssen.
Ich habe meinen Wagen waschen lassen.

and turn them into attached sentences, where the finite verb
(here **habe**) would normally stand last, the finite verb stands
instead *immediately before* the two **-en** forms:

**Ich kam zu spät, weil ich den Nachbarn <u>habe</u> helfen
müssen.**
I came late because I had to help the neighbours.
**Obwohl ich meinen Wagen <u>habe</u> waschen lassen, sah er
hinterher immer noch schmutzig aus.**
Although I got my car washed, it still looked dirty afterwards.

78 Impersonal expressions

An impersonal expression comprises a process (i.e. a verb) in
combination with the SU **es** (not standing for an identifiable
n noun). German and English impersonal expressions often
coincide, but German has a range of impersonal idioms outside the scope of English usage, so if you cannot account for
an **es** expression you should bear in mind the 'impersonal'

possibility. You already know **es gibt** (Section 27) and **es handelt sich (um)** (Section 65(d)). Here are some further examples to illustrate the principle:

Bei Nacht <u>ging es</u> über die Grenze.
I [or whoever the context indicates] *crossed the frontier by night.*
Während der Revolution <u>kam es</u> zu gefährlichen Unruhen.
During the revolution some dangerous disturbances occurred.
Bei unseren Exportplänen <u>geht es</u> nur um den Kurs.
As regards our export plans, it's solely a matter of the rate of exchange.

In the above the **es** is obligatory, whereas with other idioms it is optional and more commonly omitted in everyday usage.

<u>**Es ist**</u> **mir zu warm,**⎫
Mir <u>**ist**</u> **zu warm,** ⎬ **mach bitte das Fenster auf!**
I'm too hot. Please open the window!

<u>**Es graut**</u> **mir** ⎫   **vor dem Schulanfang nach**
Mir <u>**graut**</u> ⎬   **den Ferien.**
I hate (the thought of) the start of school after the holidays.

79 The oblique present tense

This has a far more restricted use than the oblique past tense but is indispensable for producing and understanding the type of language described in Section 80. However, for all practical purposes (for reasons which will be apparent from that section) all you need to learn is the 3rd person singular. This is extraordinarily straightforward. Simply take the stem of the **-en** form and add **-e.** (The sole exception is **sein,** which has the oblique 3rd person singular **sei.**) This means that those verbs which are exceptional in the 3rd (and 2nd) person singular of the present tense are not so in the oblique present tense. The only plural form frequently used and therefore worth noting is **seien** (from **sein**). Some examples:

-en form	3rd person singular present tense	oblique present tense
haben	hat	habe
sein	ist	sei
dürfen	darf	dürfe
sollen	soll	solle
lassen	läßt	lasse
sehen	sieht	sehe
machen	macht	mache
reden	redet	rede
tun	tut	tue

80 Indirect citation of speech

Directly quoted speech in German is no different from that in English, with the speaker's actual words placed within quotation marks. However, particularly in newspapers, direct quotation is used less than indirect citation along the lines of 'He said (that) ...', which is also, of course, much used in everyday conversation.

In indirect citation the original words actually spoken undergo certain changes in both English and German. Some of these are self-evident. For instance, if the speaker says "I ... ", this becomes 'he' or 'she' in the citation, while "here" will either remain 'here' or become 'there', depending on the location of the citer.

However, some changes are more problematical. If, for example, the speaker says "The repairs are going to be expensive", do we cite this as 'He said the repairs were going to be expensive' or as 'He said the repairs are going to be expensive'? The answer is that it may depend partly on the citer's time-location in relation to the timing of the repairs, and partly on the extent to which the citer identifies with the speaker's opinion. The same sorts of dilemma arise in German, but in the context of the way German handles citation, which is to use the oblique tenses throughout for recounting what someone else has said.

The big difference, therefore, between indirect citation in English and German lies in what happens to the verbs, and the best plan is to forget altogether what you would do with the verbs in English and to observe the following guidelines:

(a) Every *present tense verb* in the speaker's actual words (thus including the present tenses of **haben** and **sein** used as part of the pre-present, and of **werden** as part of the future or obverse process) is replaced by EITHER the *oblique present tense* OR the *oblique past tense*. It does not in principle matter which, though it may do so in practice.

The prime aim is that the replacement verb should if at all possible demonstrably be an oblique tense. Consequently, many oblique present tense forms are no use, because they are identical with the non-oblique present tense itself. In these cases the oblique past tense (even if it is the same as the non-oblique past tense) is preferable.

However, the oblique present tense does have one form that is much used for indirect citation, the 3rd person singular (Section 79), which is always distinct from the 3rd person non-oblique present because it ends in **-e** instead of **-t**. This form constantly occurs in newspapers and on radio and TV, much less so in everyday conversation.

Examples:

Actual words	**Der Minister: „Ich nehme die ganze Verantwortung auf mich, denn der Fehler wird schwere Folgen haben. "**
Citation	**Der Minister sagte, er nehme die ganze Verantwortung auf sich, denn der Fehler werde schwere Folgen haben.**

The Minister said he was taking the whole responsibility
upon himself, for the error would have grave conse-
quences.

Actual   **Monika: „Ich nehme keinen Regenschirm mit,**
words   **sonst lasse ich ihn bestimmt irgendwo liegen."**

Citation **Monika sagte, sie** $\begin{Bmatrix} \text{nehme} \\ \text{nähme} \end{Bmatrix}$ **keinen Regenschirm**

mit, sonst $\begin{Bmatrix} \text{lasse} \\ \text{ließe} \end{Bmatrix}$ **sie ihn bestimmt**

irgendwo liegen.
Monika said she wasn't taking an umbrella. Otherwise
she would be certain to leave it somewhere.

Actual   **Die Freunde: „Wir sind heute zu euch gekommen,**
words   **weil wir euch seit langem nicht gesehen haben."**

Citation **Unsere Freunde sagten, sie** $\begin{Bmatrix} \text{(seien)} \\ \text{wären} \end{Bmatrix}$ **heute**

(/gestern?/am ...tag?) zu uns gekommen, weil sie
uns seit langem nicht gesehen hätten.
Our friends said they had come to (see) us today (/yester-
day?/ on ...day?) because they hadn't seen us for a long
time.

Notes:

(i) Other things being equal, the oblique *past* tense is preferred in everyday conversation.
(ii) Just as the oblique past tense of **werden** – **würde (-st, -n,**
-t) – plus the **-en** form of the main verb was shown to be a
useful alternative to the oblique past tense of the main verb
in remote conditional statements (Section 71(b)), so it is a
very handy substitute in indirect citations in colloquial
German. It is particularly valuable when no demonstrably
oblique form is available:

Actual words	**Die Nachbarn: „Wir erwarten unsere Tochter mit Mann und Kindern aus Würzburg für die Weihnachtsferien."**
Citation	**Unsere Nachbarn sagten, sie würden ihre Tochter mit Mann und Kindern aus Würzburg für die Weihnachtsferien erwarten.** *Our neighbours said they were expecting their daughter with her husband and children from Würzburg for the Christmas holidays.*

(b) Every *past tense verb* in the speaker's actual words is replaced by the **ge_(e)t** form of that verb together with EITHER the *oblique present tense* OR the *oblique past tense* of **haben** or **sein,** whichever is appropriate. The rule for the choice of auxiliary is the same as for the pre-present (Section 45):

Actual words	**Peter: „Ich fand nur drei Kunden vor, als ich das Geschäft aufmachte."**

Citation **Peter sagt, er** $\left\{\begin{array}{l}\text{habe}\\\text{hätte}\end{array}\right\}$ **nur drei Kunden**

vorgefunden, als er das Geschäft aufgemacht $\left\{\begin{array}{l}\text{habe.}\\\text{hätte.}\end{array}\right.$

Peter said he found only three customers (waiting) when he opened the shop.

Actual words	**Die Zwillinge: „Wir gingen zusammen bis zum Markt, wo wir uns dann trennten."**

Citation **Die Zwillinge sagten, sie** $\left\{\begin{array}{l}\text{seien}\\\text{wären}\end{array}\right\}$ **zusammen bis zum Markt gegangen, wo sie sich dann getrennt hätten.**
The twins said they went together as far as the market, where they then separated.

If the speaker's actual words already contain the past tense of **haben** or **sein** as part of the pre-past (see Section 68), these are simply replaced by their oblique past tenses:

Actual words	Die Gäste: „Wir waren zum Strand gegangen, und als wir uns zum Sonnen hingelegt hatten, fing es plötzlich an zu regnen."
Citation	Die Gäste sagten, sie wären zum Strand gegangen, und als sie sich zum Sonnen hingelegt

hätten, $\begin{Bmatrix} \text{habe} \\ \text{hätte} \end{Bmatrix}$ es plötzlich angefangen zu regnen.

The guests said they had gone to the beach and when they had lain down to sunbathe it suddenly started raining.

(c) When a speaker's actual words contain one of the instruction/request forms of the verb, there is no hard and fast rule about how to cite this indirectly. The natural and instinctive way is to use either the oblique past tense **möchte** or some form of **sollen,** oblique or non-oblique, as seems to fit the case.

Actual words	Arzt: „Essen Sie nur Fisch oder mageres Fleisch!"
Citation	Der Arzt sagt, ich soll nur Fisch oder mageres Fleisch essen.
	The doctor says I must only eat fish or lean meat.

Actual words	Schwester und Schwager: „Geh zum Arzt!"
Citation	Die haben gemeint, ich soll zum Arzt gehen.
	They said I must go to the doctor.

Actual words	Sprechstundenhilfe: „Herr Doktor, schauen Sie bitte doch noch einmal bei Herrn Sinke vorbei."
Citation	Meine Sprechstundenhilfe hat gesagt, ich sollte bei Ihnen noch einmal vorbeischauen.
	My receptionist told me to visit you again.
Actual words	Hempels: „Bitte besuchen Sie uns doch, sobald wir das Haus eingerichtet haben!"
Citation	Hempels haben gesagt, wir möchten sie besuchen, sobald sie das Haus eingerichtet hätten.
	The Hempels said we must visit them as soon as they had furnished the house.

81 Sequence of words in indirect citation

Most of the examples in Section 80 required no change in the
sequence of words when actual speech was cited indirectly.
This is because no joiners were used to introduce the
attached citation sentences. This is only possible with *statements* and *instructions*. Even these are often introduced by
the joiner **daß**, and all cited questions *must* start with one of
the joiners from Section 63(b). In all such cases the finite verb
of the attached citation sentence must stand at the end:

Actual words   **Mann: „Ich halte gar nichts von den Freunden unserer Kinder."**
Citation   **Mein Mann sagt, daß er gar nichts von den**

Freunden unserer Kinder │ **halte.**
                              │ **hielte.**
*My husband says that he doesn't think much of our
children's friends.*

Actual words   **Er: „Wie lange wirst du noch einkaufen?"**
Citation   **Er fragte sie, wie lange sie noch**

einkaufen │ **werde.**
              │ **würde.**
He asked her how long she would go on shopping.

Actual words   **Ich: „Geben Sie meinem Sohn noch eine Chance?"**
Citation   **Ich fragte ihn, ob er meinem Sohn noch eine**

Chance │ **gebe.**
        │ **gäbe.**
*I asked him whether he would give my son
another chance.*

Exercise 32

*For each example of indirect citation, say which of the statements
(a) (b) or (c) comes closest to the situation described.*

1 Der Minister sagt, er habe den Brief vor drei Wochen
zwar gesehen, aber er sei nicht überzeugt gewesen.
(a) Es gibt einen Brief.
(b) Es gibt keinen Brief.
(c) Ein Brief ist angekommen.

2 Monika sagt, sie habe ihren Regenschirm zuerst an der
Schule liegengelassen, ihn dann aber später abgeholt.
(a) Sie hat ihren Regenschirm verloren.
(b) Sie bringt ihren Regenschirm zur Schule.
(c) Sie hat ihren Regenschirm noch.

3 Die Freunde sagen, sie hätten uns lange nicht gesehen
und würden uns gern besuchen.
(a) Die Freunde besuchen uns.
(b) Die Freunde möchten uns besuchen.
(c) Die Freunde möchten uns nicht sehen.

4 Die Nachbarn sagen, ihre Tochter spiele im Orchester
die Klarinette und ginge bald auf eine Reise nach
England.
(a) Die Tochter geht auf Ferien nach England.
(b) Die Tochter spielt Klarinette in England.
(c) Die Nachbarn fahren nach England.

5 Peter sagt, er habe nur zwei Kunden am Morgen
gehabt; am Nachmittag seien noch vier schwierige
Kunden gekommen, und er sei deshalb am Abend
sehr müde gewesen.
(a) Peter hat sechs nette Kunden gehabt.
(b) Peter ist froh, daß es Abend ist.
(c) Peter bedient seine Kunden freundlich.

6 Die Zwillinge sagen, sie seien auf den Markt gegangen
und hätten sich Pullover gekauft; einer von ihnen habe
noch ein T-Shirt gekauft.
(a) Die Zwillinge haben zwei Pullover und zwei
T-Shirts gekauft.
(b) Die Zwillinge haben sich auf dem Markt getrennt.

(c) Einer der Zwillinge hat einen Pullover und ein
     T-Shirt.
7   Die Gäste sagen, sie hätten sich erst am Strand sonnen
     wollen; sie hätten dann einen Ausflug machen wollen,
     aber die Sonne sei für alles zu heiß gewesen.
     (a) Die Gäste haben einen Ausflug gemacht.
     (b) Die Gäste haben sich gesonnt.
     (c) Die Gäste konnten das alles nicht machen.

82 Enclosed attached sentences

Section 63(a) on **d. .** joiners showed how such joiners relate
the attached sentence which they introduce to a particular
noun in a preceding sentence. Certain attached sentences
can, in modified form, be placed directly *in front of* the noun
to which they relate instead of after it.

The first condition is that attached sentences placed in front
of the noun must have that noun as their SU. That is, in their
more familiar place after the noun they would start with a
d. . joiner in the SU case. The principles underlying
enclosed attached sentences will be clear if we take one of
the examples from Section 63(a) where the **d. .** joiner is in
the SU case:

**Das Fleisch, das auf dem Tisch liegt, kannst du für den
Hund nehmen.**
You can take the meat that's on the table for the dog.

The attached sentence here can appear alternatively as follows:

**Das [auf dem Tisch liegende] Fleisch kannst du für den
Hund nehmen.**

Three things have happened to the attached sentence:
(i)   the joiner **das** has gone,
(ii) the finite verb **liegt** has changed into the **-end**

non-finite form **liegend** (see Sections 61 and 74 for this form), and

(iii) **liegend** has acquired the ending needed by adjectives after **d.** . words (Section 29(a)), since although **liegend** is not an adjective it has to be treated like one on the analogy **das frische Fleisch** → **das ... liegende Fleisch**.

Otherwise the sequence of words is exactly as in the original attached sentence, with **liegend** occupying the position of the finite verb **liegt**. The change from finite verb to non-finite verb means that the feature *tense* has disappeared, so that any 'time' associated with **liegend** is simply concurrent with the 'time' suggested by the core sentence (since this is the connotation of the **-end** form (Section 61)). The enclosed attached sentence would be the same if the 'time' of the whole changed:

Das Fleisch, das auf dem Tisch lag, konntest du für den Hund nehmen.
Das [auf dem Tisch liegende] Fleisch konntest du für den Hund nehmen.
You were able to take the meat that was on the table for the dog.

There are restrictions on the types of word which may appear as the last word in enclosed attached sentences (which we call 'enclosed' because they fit between any **d.** .- or **ein**-type word and the noun they relate to). Each type of final word corresponds to a different type of original sentence with its own particular characteristics.

Here are the five permissible categories with examples (always showing first the original attached sentence from which the enclosed attached sentence is derived) and notes:

(a) *Adjective*

Der Verlust der Reisepässe war eine Angelegenheit, die dem Reiseleiter äußerst unangenehm war.
The loss of the passports was a matter that was extremely embarrassing to the courier.

Der Verlust der Reisepässe war eine [dem Reiseleiter äußerst unangenehme] Angelegenheit.

Here the verb **war** from the original attached sentence has disappeared in the enclosed attached sentence, which is not surprising since **sein** as a finite verb shows tense and person (1st singular, etc.) but has no 'meaning'.

(b)   **-end** *form of almost any verb except* **sein** *and the auxiliary verbs (in their auxiliary function)*

Teilnehmer, die bis morgen auf ihre Ergebnisse hier warten, werden eingeladen, im Hotel zu übernachten.
Participants who are waiting here until tomorrow for their results are invited to spend the night in the hotel.
[Bis morgen auf ihre Ergebnisse hier wartende] Teilnehmer werden eingeladen, im Hotel zu übernachten.

This particular example shows that an enclosed attached sentence may not *appear* to be enclosed at the front end if the noun it relates to has no **d. .**- or **ein**-type word. Here, only the **d. .** joiner and the finite features of **warten** (i.e. tense and person) disappear.

(c)   **ge _(e)t** *form of any verb capable of having a DO*

Das östliche Mittelmeer, das oft von meinen Bekannten als Lieblingsreiseziel ausgesucht wird, werde auch ich mir dieses Jahr vornehmen.
This year I'm also going to visit the eastern Mediterranean, which is often chosen by my friends as a favourite destination.
Das [oft von meinen Bekannten als Lieblingsreiseziel ausgesuchte] östliche Mittelmeer werde auch ich mir dieses Jahr vornehmen.

Zündkerzen, die zu selten ausgewechselt wurden, können einen dann im Stich lassen.
Spark plugs that have been changed too infrequently can (then) leave you in the lurch.

[Zu selten ausgewechselte] Zündkerzen können einen dann im Stich lassen.

Here, the attached sentence loses not only the **d. .** joiner, but also the finite auxiliary verb **werden**, one of the two components of the obverse process, when it becomes an enclosed attached sentence.

(d) **ge_(e)t** *form of any verb making the pre-present with* **sein**

Die Stadt wird von einer Krankheit bedroht, die in der Gegend noch nie vorgekommen ist.
The town is threatened by a disease that has never before appeared in the area.
Die Stadt wird von einer [in der Gegend noch nie vorgekommenen] Krankheit bedroht.

This type of enclosed sentence loses the **d. .** joiner and the finite auxiliary verb **sein** from the original attached sentence. The process represented by the **ge_(e)t** form has here NO connection with the obverse process of (c). It has the connotation of *completion* (Sections 44, 61).

(e) **zu + -end** *form of any verb capable of having a DO*

To understand this properly you should first look again at Section 72, from which the following examples are derived:

Die Ergebnisse, die sofort nach der Wahl bekannt zu machen sind, werden im Rathaus ausgehängt.
The results, which are to be made known immediately after the election, will be posted in the town hall.

Die [sofort nach der Wahl bekannt zu machenden] Ergebnisse werden im Rathaus ausgehängt.

Die Kritik, die über den Direktor zu hören war, war unberechtigt.
The criticism that was to be heard about the director was unfounded.

Die [über den Direktor zu hörende] Kritik war unberechtigt.

Here, the **d. .** joiner and the finite verb **sein** disappear when the attached sentence becomes an enclosed one.

With all the above types (a) to (e) it is essential first to isolate the enclosed attached sentence (which is why it is shown in [ ] in all our examples), then to establish which type of standard attached sentence it is akin to, finally to understand it along the same lines as our translations of the 'source' attached sentences. Any attempt to understand or translate without following this method will end in confusion, and since enclosed attached sentences are found in profusion in all types of writing (and not rarely in speaking), there is a great incentive to face the challenge they pose.

Vocabulary

Study the conversation that follows, trying to relate each step in the discussion to what you have learnt. You will need these words:

vorhaben II	to have planned, have (got) on
genau	precisely
hier ist nichts los	nothing's going on here
um … herum	about
erzählen	to tell
zustehen II	to be due
vorschießen II	to advance (money)
meines Erachtens	in my opinion
wahnsinnig	crazy
umgehen (mit) II	to deal (with)
das **Verhältnis (-se)**	(plural) means
ausgeben II	to spend
grillen	to grill
geeignet	suitable
je	each

	besorgen I	to obtain
	so (et)was	things like that
die	Tiefkühltruhe (-n)	(chest) freezer
	toll	great
	sich verschulden I	to get into debt, go into the red
	überübermorgen	the day after the day after tomorrow
	übernachten I	to stay the night
	aufkommen II	to (be liable to) pay
	was = etwas	something
	übrigens	by the way
der	Eintritt	admission
	dabei wegkommen (mit) II	to get away (with)
	nicht in Frage kommen	to be out of the question
der	Vorschuß (¨(ss)e)	advance
	gewiß	certainly
	anspruchslos	undemanding
die	Unterhaltung (-en)	entertainment
	in die Tasche greifen	to dip into one's pocket
	losfahren II	to set out, come out
	abholen II	to collect, pick up
die	Erziehung	education, bringing up
die	Sparsamkeit	thrift

CONVERSATION

A family controversy over the expenditure requirements of the younger generation

Vater Was habt ihr denn heute abend vor?

Sohn Das wissen wir noch nicht ganz genau. Hier in Voßdorf ist heute nichts los, aber in Wunsdorf soll es eine große Disko geben. Die wäre allerdings ziemlich teuer, so um die zwanzig Mark herum pro Person, hat uns die Brigitte erzählt ...

Mutter	... und deswegen wollt ihr also nicht hin ...
Tochter	... O doch, wenn ihr uns das uns für die nächsten vier Wochen zustehende Taschengeld vorschießen würdet.
V	Ihr habt eine meines Erachtens wahnsinnige Art, mit Geld umzugehen. Ihr lebt total über euere Verhältnisse. So viel braucht ihr doch wohl nicht für einen einzigen Abend auszugeben!
M	Ja, Vater hat ganz recht!
S	Es geht leider nicht nur um heute abend! Morgen gibt's nämlich ein Barbecue bei Eckels, und der Franz hat gesagt, wir möchten doch etwas zum Grillen geeignetes Fleisch und je zwei Liter Bier besorgen.
M	So was braucht ihr doch nicht zu kaufen! Ich werde für euch ein paar Sachen aus der Tiefkühltruhe holen, und Bier könnt ihr auch von hier mitnehmen.
T	O, das wäre toll! Ich glaube, wir müssen uns trotzdem verschulden, denn überübermorgen gibt die Brigitte eine tolle Party bei sich, und da wir auch dort übernachten dürfen, müssen wir ihrer Mutter natürlich ein Geschenk mitbringen.
M	Wenn es sich um ein Geschenk für die Mutter handelt, braucht ihr doch nicht dafür aufzukommen! Ich besorge morgen was Schönes in der Stadt.
V	Was möchtest du denn sonst noch finanzieren, Ilse?
S	Übrigens brauchen wir für heute abend nicht nur den Eintritt sondern auch das Geld für ein Taxi hinterher von Wunsdorf bis nach Hause. Das sind immerhin fünfzehn Kilometer, und mit weniger als vierzig Mark kommen wir nicht dabei weg.
V	Das kommt zusammen auf etwa achtzig Mark. Das kommt überhaupt nicht in Frage, mit oder ohne Vorschuß!
M	Was Vater sagt, ist ganz gewiß richtig, ihr müßtet viel anspruchsloser sein. Andererseits, für eine

harmlose Unterhaltung mit Freunden einmal in
der Woche braucht ihr nicht in euere eigene
Tasche zu greifen. Den Eintritt können wir
bezahlen. Außerdem sagt Vater immer, er führe
nachts ganz gern los, um euch von irgendwo
abzuholen. Also könnt ihr auch das Taxigeld
sparen!

V   Und das soll nun Erziehung zu Sparsamkeit sein!

TRANSLATION

Father   So what have you got on this evening?
Son   We don't quite know yet. There's nothing
going on here in Voßdorf, but there's supposed
to be a big disco in Wunsdorf. It's pretty
expensive though, about twenty marks per
person, so Brigitte told us …

Mother   … and so therefore you're not intending to go …
Daughter   Oh we are, if you'd advance us the pocket
money that's due to us for the next four weeks.

F   You've got a way of dealing with money that's
crazy in my opinion. You're living completely
beyond your means. You're not telling me that
you need to spend that much on a single
evening!

M   Yes, father's absolutely right!

S   Unfortunately it's not just a matter of this
evening. You see, tomorrow there's a barbecue
at the Eckels, and Franz said could we get some
meat that's suitable for grilling and two litres
of beer each.

M   But you don't need to buy things like that! I'll
take a few things out of the freezer for you,
and you can take some beer from here, too.

D   Oh, that would be great! I think we'll have to
go into the red even so. You see, the day after
the day after tomorrow Brigitte's putting on a
fantastic party at her house, and as we're

allowed to stay the night there we've obviously got to take her mother a present.

M If it's a present for the mother, you don't have to spend your money on it! I'll get something nice in the town tomorrow.

F And what else were you thinking of under-writing, Ilse?

S By the way, for this evening we don't only need the admission but also the money for a taxi home from Wunsdorf afterwards. After all, that's fifteen kilometres, and we shan't get away with less than forty marks.

F That comes to about eighty marks. That's quite out of the question, with or without an advance!

M What father says is certainly right. You ought to be a lot less demanding. On the other hand you don't need to dip into your own pockets for a bit of harmless entertainment with friends once a week. We can pay the admission charge. Moreover, father's always saying how he's happy to come out at night to pick you up from somewhere or other. So you'll even be able to save the taxi fare!

F And that's what you call bringing them up to be thrifty!

Reading Practice

Chapters 5/6

Hier geht es um die Wurst

Was ist älter: das Frankfurter Würstchen oder das Wiener Würstchen?

Richtige Antwort: das Frankfurter Würstchen.

Metzger Johann Georg Lahner kommt aus Frankfurt und ist Erfinder vom Frankfurter Würstchen. 1904 geht er nach Wien. Sein 'Frankfurter' Würstchen ist sehr bald in Wien bekannt als *Wiener Würstl*.

Vocabulary

die	Antwort (-en)	answer
der	Erfinder	inventor
	Wien/Wiener	Vienna/Viennese
das	Würstchen (-)	diminutives of **die Wurst:**
das	Würstl (-) (Austrian)	sausage

London auf die Schnelle

Piccadilly Circus, Hyde Park, Big Ben, Madame Tussaud und die Tate Gallery. Das sind die bekanntesten Stellen in London für den Ausländer. Der neue London-Katalog von ATLASTRIPS bietet in Ko-operation mit British Air Holidays Kurztrips in die britische Metropole. Individuell und flexibel kann der Gast seinen Urlaub planen.

Theater und Musicals am Abend, Sightseeing-Touren, Lunch im "Planet Hollywood" oder Shopping auf der Portobello Road. London bietet Unterhaltung pur. Ein gemütliches Hotel ist da sehr wichtig. Es gibt über 30 Hotels: vom simplen bis zur Luxusklasse. Eine Übernachtung mit englischem Frühstück im 2-Sterne-Hotel Tunnicliffe kostet etwa 53 Mark; das 3-Sterne-Hotel Regal nimmt für Übernachtung und Frühstück etwa 75 Mark. Das 5-Sterne-Hotel Gresham House direkt am Hyde Park ist luxuriös und kostet etwa 290 Mark.

Man kann von London auch relativ schnell in die Universitätsstädte Oxford und Cambridge kommen. Sie sind wunderschön und so typisch englisch. London, Oxford und Cambridge sind eine Reise wert.

Vocabulary

	bieten	to offer
	gemütlich	cosy, comfortable
die	Reise (-n)	trip, journey
	auf die Schnelle	at speed
	über	more than
	wert	worth

Wein ist im Kommen

Die Deutschen trinken wieder öfter ein Glas Wein statt ein Glas Bier oder ein Glas Sekt. Der Weinkonsum steigt wieder nach der Stagnation in den letzten Jahren. Solche Präferenzen gehen oft Hand in Hand mit Gesundheitstrends. Milch und Fruchtsäfte profitieren in diesem Jahr auch.

Der nasse Sommer ist schlecht für die Brauereien und für die alkoholfreien Getränkehersteller. Man hat einfach nicht solchen Durst. Jeder Deutsche trinkt etwa 3,2 Liter weniger Bier und etwa 1,6 Liter weniger Mineralwasser als im letzten Jahr.

Aller Alkoholkonsum außer Wein ist jetzt niedriger, er steht bei 163,6 Liter pro Person, das sind etwa 2,8 Liter weniger als im letzten Jahr. Dasselbe ist der Fall bei alkoholfreien Getränken, die Deutschen trinken 1,9 Liter weniger und sind jetzt bei 225,5 Liter pro Kopf.

Absolutes Lieblingsgetränk der Bundesbürger aber ist Bohnenkaffee mit 164,5 (Vorjahr 164,6) Litern pro Kopf. Der Teekonsum steigt um 0,5 auf 25,5 Liter.

Vocabulary

	außer	except
die	**Brauerei (-en)**	brewery
	dasselbe	the same
der	**Durst**	thirst
die	**Gesundheit**	health
	letzt	last
der	**Saft (–̈e)**	juice
	steigen (um ... auf)	to increase (by ... to)
das	**Vorjahr**	previous year

Versteigerung bei der Lufthansa

Der Auktionator von der Lufthansa: "Hundert Mark zum ersten, hundert Mark zum zweiten und niemand mehr?" Der Versteigerer schwingt den Hammer. "... hundert Mark zum dritten." Es ist kurz nach zwölf Uhr mittags. Die Auktion in Mannheim beginnt gerade. Etwa 150 Koffer und Taschen, mehrere Kinderwagen, Dutzende von Sonnenschirmen und Tennisschlägern liegen vor ihm. Das dauert fünf bis sechs Stunden ohne Pause, und er arbeitet so schnell wie möglich.

Einmal im Monat, immer am Samstag ab zwölf Uhr, versteigert der Auktionator für die Deutsche Lufthansa AG herrenloses Fundgut. Die Lufthansa wartet drei Monate auf die Besitzer dieser Sachen. In der Zeit sucht die Lufthansa die Besitzer, aber eben meistens vergeblich. Scheinbar gehören diese Sachen niemandem.

Die Koffer z.B. kauft man immer geschlossen, also mit allem Inhalt. Das ist am interessantesten. Keiner kennt den Inhalt. Ist der Koffer "schwer" oder "sehr schwer" oder "nicht so schwer"? Der Preis für einen geschlossenen Koffer ist etwa 100 Mark. Die Preise sind selten höher als 150 Mark. Es sind ja genug Koffer da.

Vierzig Millionen Gepäckstücke transportiert die Lufthansa im Jahr. Nur jedes Zehntausendste ist herrenlos trotz intensiver Suche nach dem Besitzer. Von einer Million Koffern und Taschen gehen also etwa einhundert verloren.

Die Adressen von den Besitzern in den Koffern sind willkommener als nasse Handtücher oder stinkende Nahrungsmittel... Und der Zoll sucht im Fundgut Waffen und Rauschgift. Wirklich wertvolle Sachen und Geld sind fast nie in den Koffern. Trotzdem kann der neue Käufer für seine 100 Mark eben Glück oder Pech haben.

Vocabulary

	AG (Aktiengesellschaft)	plc
	arbeiten	to work
der	Auktionator (-en)	auctioneer
	beginnen	to begin
	(zum) Beispiel, z.B.	for example, e.g.
das	Fundgut	lost property
das	Gepäckstück (-e)	piece of luggage
der	Hammer (-)	hammer
das	Handtuch (¨er)	towel
	herrenlos	ownerless
der	Kinderwagen (-)	pram
	meistens	generally
	mittags	noon
	möglich	possible
das	Nahrungsmittel (-)	food
das	Rauschgift (-e)	drug
	scheinbar	apparently
	schwingen	to swing
der	Sonnenschirm (-e)	parasol
	stinken	to stink
die	Suche	search
die	Tasche (-n)	bag
der	Tennisschläger (-)	tennis racquet
	vergeblich	in vain
	verloren gehen	to get lost
der	Versteigerer (-)	auctioneer
	versteigern I	to auction
die	Versteigerung	auction
die	Waffe (-n)	weapon
	wertvoll	valuable
	willkommen	welcome
	wirklich	really
der	Zoll (¨e)	customs

LEISTUNGSTEST FÜR DEUTSCHE SCHULEN

Die Kultusminister wollen ihre Schulen regelmäßig testen lassen. Im internationalen Vergleich sind deutsche Schulen jetzt schlechter als die im Ausland. Am schlechtesten sind die Leistungen in Mathematik, dann folgen die Naturwissenschaften und dann Lesen. Später folgen Fremdsprachen, Geschichte, Geographie und Schreiben. Bei einer internationalen Vergleichsstudie in der achten Klasse in Mathematik erreichen deutsche Schüler nur den 16. Platz unter 26 Ländern – deutlich hinter Rußland und Tschechien.

Außerdem sind sie im Schnitt älter als Schüler in anderen Ländern. Ein deutscher Schüler beginnt sein Schulleben erst mit sechs Jahren. Normalerweise soll er mit 18 Jahren fertig sein, aber ein deutscher Schüler kann 'sitzenbleiben' und muß dann das Schuljahr wiederholen. Das ist viel üblicher als in anderen Ländern. Dadurch wird ein deutscher Schüler vielleicht erst mit 20 Jahren fertig.

In Nordrhein-Westfalen beginnt die Schulministerin mit einem eigenen Programm. Noten und Zeugnisse sollen vergleichbar sein. Fachlehrer sollen die Arbeiten in Parallelklassen korrigieren. Keine Schule soll 'leichter' als eine andere sein.

Vocabulary

die	**Arbeit (-en)**	piece of work, (examination) paper
das	**Ausland**	abroad
	deutlich	clearly, significantly
	erreichen	to attain, reach
der	**Fachlehrer (-)**	specialist teacher
die	**Fremdsprache (-n)**	foreign language
die	**Geschichte**	history
die	**Klasse (-n)**	class
	korrigieren	to correct, mark
der	**Kultusminister (-)**	education minister
die	**Leistung (-en)**	performance
das	**Lesen**	reading
die	**Naturwissenschaft (-en)**	natural sciences, biology
	normalerweise	normally
die	**Note (-n)**	mark
	Rußland	Russia
im	**Schnitt**	on average
das	**Schreiben**	writing
das	**Schuljahr (-e)**	school year
	sitzenbleiben II	to repeat a year
	Tschechien	the Czech Republic
	üblich	usual
der	**Vergleich (-e)**	comparison
	vergleichbar	comparable
	wiederholen I	to repeat
das	**Zeugnis (-se)**	report, certificate

Jeder vierte Deutsche ist Allergiker

Jeder vierte Deutsche über 14 Jahren leidet bereits unter Allergien. Dies findet man in einer Krankenkassenstudie. Am meisten ist es der Heuschnupfen. Etwa sechs Millionen Bundesbürger leiden daran. Etwa 2,3 Millionen leiden an einer Sonnenallergie; 2,2 Millionen reagieren allergisch auf Tierhaare. 1,9 Millionen haben eine Allergie gegen bestimmtes Essen, 2,1 Millionen gegen Staub im Haus.

Die Hälfte der Allergiker hat jetzt einen anderen Lebensstil. Neun Prozent fahren nur noch zu bestimmten Zeiten in den Urlaub, sieben Prozent essen nur noch ganz normal, fünf Prozent haben keine Haustiere mehr. Allergien sind außerdem teuer: Ein Drittel der Allergiker bezahlt 50 Mark im Monat mehr für die Bekämpfung der Symptome.

Vocabulary

die	Bekämpfung	alleviation
	bereits	already
die	Krankenkasse (-n)	health insurance (organisation)
	reagieren	to react
der	Staub	dust

230

Die Sucht nach dem Handy

Macht das Handy den Körper kaputt? "Elektroskeptiker" vermuten Gefahren für die Gesundheit durch den Mobilfunk. Gibt es wirklich ein Risiko? Ein Forscherteam aus Kamp-Lintfort will darüber informieren. Die ersten Resultate sollen im nächsten Jahr bekannt werden.

Das Handy erwärmt Körperzellen beim Gebrauch. Zu viel Wärme bringt Gefahren. Der Biologe Wojtysik erklärt: "Da gehen die Zellen kaputt, das Eiweiß verklumpt. Wie ein gebratenes Schnitzel, das ist ver gleichbar." Doch keine Angst, das Handy röstet seinen Besitzer nicht.

Seit einem dreiviertel Jahr wollen nun die Forscher genauer sein. Freiwillige Studenten oder Wissenschaftler lassen mit sich experimentieren. Es gibt Zellversuche, aber keine Tierversuche.

Australische Forscher haben Experimente mit Tieren gemacht. In einer Studie im Auftrag der australischen Telekom haben Mäuse 'Strahlen' von Mobilfunkgeräten bekommen, und die Wissenschaftler haben vermehrten Krebs festgestellt.

Vocabulary

im	Auftrag	on behalf (of)
	Australien	Australia
der	Biologe (-n)	biologist
	braten	to fry
das	Eiweiß	protein
	erwärmen I	to heat
	experimentieren	to experiment
das	Handy (-s)	mobile phone
	feststellen II	to discover
der	Forscher (-)	researcher
	freiwillig	voluntary
der	Gebrauch	use
die	Gefahr (-en)	danger
der	Körper (-)	body
der	Krebs (-e)	cancer

die	Maus (¨e)	mouse
das	Mobilfunkgerät (-e)	mobile phone
das	Resultat (-e)	result
	rösten	to roast
das	Schnitzel (-)	cutlet, schnitzel
der	Skeptiker (-)	sceptic
der	Strahl (-en)	ray, emission
die	Sucht (¨e)	addiction
das	Tier (-e)	animal
	verklumpen I	to get lumpy
	vermehrt	increased
	vermuten I	to suspect
der	Versuch (-e)	experiment
die	Wärme	heat
der	Wissenschaftler (-)	scientist
die	Zelle (-n)	cell

Erdbeeren: Hoher Gesundheitswert

Der hohe Gesundheitswert von Erdbeeren basiert nicht nur auf dem großen Vitamingehalt, vor allem an Vitamin C, sondern auch auf dem Reichtum an den verschiedenen lebenswichtigen Mineralstoffen wie z.B. Kalium, Calcium, Magnesium, Phosphat und Silizium.Erdbeeren sind auch sehr gut für die Verdauung (harntreibend und entschlackend) und für die Darmtätigkeit aufgrund des Pektingehaltes.

Vocabulary

	aufgrund	by virtue (of)
	basieren auf	to be based on
die	Darmtätikgeit	bowel activity
	entschlackend	purgative
die	Erdbeere (-n)	strawberry
der	Gehalt	content
	harntreibend	diuretic
	lebenswichtig	important (to life)
der	Mineralstoff (-e)	mineral
der	Reichtum	richness
die	Verdauung	digestion

Größeres Drogen-Risiko: 1712 Opfer in einem Jahr

Die Drogensituation in Deutschland hat sich sehr verschlechtert: Zum ersten Mal ist die Zahl der Rauschgifttoten im lez-
ten Jahr wieder angestiegen – auf 1712 Todesopfer. Gleichzeitig hat der Konsum synthetischer Modedrogen wie Ecstasy durch immer jüngere Konsumenten in alarmierender Weise zugenommen.

Damit wurden 147 Menschen mehr als im Vorjahr Opfer ihrer Sucht – ein Anstieg um fast zehn Prozent. Zwanzig junge Menschen sind durch Ecstasy gestorben. Von den fast 17 200 registrierten Erstkonsumenten nahmen 44 Prozent synthetische Drogen. Die höchste Konsumrate war LSD (plus 54,3 Prozent), danach Amphetamin-Derivate mit 52,2 Prozent. Ecstasy gehört dazu.

Die Ecstasy-Menge, die die Polizei gefunden hat, ist explosionsartig um 80 Prozent gewachsen. Bei allen anderen Rauschgiften sind die Fundmengen gesunken – bei Heroin von 933 auf 898 Kilo.

Die politischen Parteien auf der Linken kritisieren. Die jungen Drogensüchtigen haben mehr Angst vor polizeilicher Verfolgung als den Wunsch nach Hilfe. Dies treibt sie in die Kriminalität. Die Parteien auf der Rechten lehnen jede Entkriminalisierung des Drogenkonsums ab. Stattdessen

Vocabulary

	ablehnen II	to reject
	ansteigen II	to increase
der	Anstieg (-e)	increase
die	Droge (-n)	drug
die	Entkriminalisierung	decriminalisation
	explosionsartig	explosively
	fast	almost
die	Fundmenge (-n)	quantity found
	gleichzeitig	simultaneously
die	Hilfe	help
der	Konsument (PO -en)	consumer
die	Kriminalität	crime
	kritisieren	to criticise
die	Linke (see Section 61)	the Left
das	Opfer (-)	victim
die	Partei (-en)	(political) party
	polizeilich	by the police
das	Präventionsangebot (-e)	preventive measure
das	Rauschgift (-e)	drug
die	Rechte (see Section 61)	the Right
das	Risiko (-s/Risiken)	risk
das	Therapieangebot (-e)	therapeutic measure
das	Todesopfer (-)	fatality, death
der	Tote (see Section 61)	dead person
die	Verfolgung	pursuit
sich	verschlechtern I	to deteriorate
die	Weise (-n)	way, manner
der	Wunsch (¨e)	wish
	zunehmen II	to increase

Reizende Leute

Weder Hopfers noch Bremsers haben erwartet, daß sie nach nur drei Tagen ihres Ferienaufenthaltes so gute Freunde finden. Als sich Hopfers in ihrem Zimmer über die erste Begegnung mit Bremsers unterhalten haben, hat er gesagt: "Da haben wir wirklich die richtigen Leute kennengelernt. Der Mann ist wirklich interessant im Gespräch, und die Frau finde ich einfach reizend. Und die Großzügigkeit, mit der sie uns an der Bar bewirtet haben!" Und die so hochgelobten Bremsers haben zur gleichen Zeit etwas ähnliches über die Hopfers gesagt.

Nicht daß sich Hopfers und Bremsers nur während der ersten Ferienwoche sehr oft getroffen haben. Auch in der zweiten Woche haben sie jeden Abend zusammen gesessen, geredet, gelacht und getrunken. Herr Hopfer hat gemeint: "Am nettesten sind Bremsers, wenn sie beschwipst sind, dann macht sie die überraschendsten Kommentare, und er wirkt so komisch mit schwerer Zunge. Aber durch diese Trinkabende wird unser Geld bald nicht mehr reichen, und ich glaube, daß die Bremsers auch langsam zu wenig Geld für diese teuren Abende haben." Ähnliche Gedanken bei Bremsers, die dann angefangen haben, sich Abende mit Hopfers ohne Wein recht langweilig vorzustellen.

In der dritten Woche haben sich beide Paare gegenseitig einfach langweilig, dumm und geizig gefunden. Am Ende der Woche haben sie sehr herzlich Abschied genommen und sich versprochen, in Verbindung zu bleiben ...

Vocabulary

	Abschied nehmen	to say farewell / goodbye
der	**Aufenthalt (-e)**	stay
die	**Begegnung (-en)**	meeting, encounter
	beschwipst	tipsy
	bewirten I	to invite, entertain

	gegenseitig	one another
	geizig	mean, miserly
die	Großzügigkeit	generosity
	hochgelobt	highly praised
	kennenlernen	to get to know
	komisch	funny
	reichen	to last
	reizend	delightful, charming
	überraschend	surprising
sich	unterhalten	to converse
die	Verbindung (-en)	contact
	weder ... noch	neither ... nor
	wirken	to have an effect
die	Zunge (-n)	tongue

Was Männer abtörnt
Aussehen ist wichtiger als Charakter

Nun wissen wir, was Männer an Frauen absolut nicht mögen: Frauen, die alles besser wissen (und damit vielleicht die eigene Meinung vehement vertreten können?) sind für Männer doch tatsächlich "Abtörner Nummer eins". Dicht darauf folgen Körpergeruch (68 Prozent) und schlechte Zähne (62 Prozent). Auch vulgäre Sprachgewohnheiten gefallen den Männern nicht. So lautet jedenfalls das Resultat einer Umfrage, die das Münchner Magazin "freundin" veröffentlicht hat.

Die angeblich weibliche Vorliebe, langfristige Zukunftspläne zu machen, hält fast jeder zweite Mann für "absolut unsexy". Nach der Umfrage ist der Kaufrausch vieler Frauen immerhin noch für 42 Prozent der Männer ein Ärgernis.

Nicht weiter überraschend: Die Herren legen viel Wert auf das Aussehen. Optische Gesichtspunkte wie eine gute Figur (61 Prozent) oder Miniröcke (59 Prozent) – natürlich mit langen Beinen (58 Prozent) – stehen ganz oben auf ihrer Wunschliste.

237

Vocabulary

	angeblich	allegedly
das	Ärgernis (-se)	(source of) irritation
das	Aussehen (-)	appearance
das	Bein (-e)	leg
	dicht	close
	folgen	to follow
der	Gesichtspunkt (-e)	point of view
die	Gewohnheit (-en)	habit
der	Kaufrausch	spending mania
der	Körpergeruch	body odour
	langfristig	long-term
	lauten	to say
die	Liste (-n)	list
	(eine) Meinung	to express (an) opinion
	vertreten I	
	Münchner	(of / from) Munich
der	Rock (⁻e)	skirt
die	Umfrage	opinion poll
	veröffentlichen I	to publish
die	Vorliebe	preference
	weiblich	female, feminine
	Wert legen auf	to set store by
der	Zahn (⁻e)	tooth
die	Zukunft	future

Autoklau nahm deutlich ab

Die Zahl der Kfz-Diebstähle hat wegen elektronischen Wegfahrsperren im letzten Jahr weiter deutlich abgenommen. Offiziellen Informationen zufolge lag der Rückgang bei 14,6 Prozent. Danach wurden im letzten Jahr 110 764 Fahrzeuge gestohlen, im Jahr davor waren es 129 652. Während im letzten Jahr davon 40 090 auf Dauer verschwunden blieben, waren es im vorletzten 46 301. Dies ist eine Abnahme von 9,1 Prozent.

Bei Langfingern waren die Marken VW (12 237), Mercedes (6 227), BMW (4 220) und Audi (3 955) am gefragtesten. In der Luxusklasse gingen die Diebstähle in den vergangenen Jahren bereits drastisch zurück. Im letzten Jahr lag die Zahl der entwendeten und weiter gesuchten Porsche bei 302. Jedes dritte gestohlene Fahrzeug wurde im Ausland entwendet.

Die Entwicklung zeigt, daß sich der serienmäßige Einbau der Wegfahrsicherung, der seit über einem Jahr für alle Neufahrzeuge vorgeschrieben ist, sehr gelohnt hat. Seitdem ist der Polizei kein Fall bekannt, in dem ein Dieb diese Sicherung überwunden hat und mit dem Auto wegfahren konnte.

Nachforschungen ergaben, daß in solchen Fällen entweder ein Diebstahl vorgetäuscht, das Fahrzeug abgeschleppt oder der Schlüssel entwendet worden war.

Vocabulary

	abnehmen II	to decrease
	abschleppen	to tow away
der	Autoklau	car theft
der	Dieb (-e)	thief
der	Diebstahl (¨e)	theft
der	Einbau	installation, fitting
	entwenden I	to steal
die	Entwicklung (-en)	development, situation
das	Fahrzeug (-e)	vehicle
der	Fall (¨e)	case

	gefragt	in demand
das	Kfz (Kraftfahrzeug)	vehicle
der	Langfinger (-)	thief
	lohnen sich	to be worth while
die	Marke (-n)	type, make
der	Rückgang (⁀e)	decrease
	serienmäßig	standard
	überwinden I	to defeat
	vergangen	past
	verschwunden bleiben	to disappear permanently
	vorletzt	last but one
	vorschreiben II	to prescribe
	vortäuschen II	to fake
	wegfahren II	to drive away
die	Wegfahrsicherung	immobiliser
die	Wegfahrsperre	immobiliser
	zufolge	according (to)

Unruhestand: Jeder elfte Rentner geht noch zur Arbeit

Jeder elfte Rentner geht noch zur Arbeit. Dies ist das Zwischenergebnis einer Langzeitstudie von drei Professoren. Sie hatten 2 000 Männer und Frauen aus Wuppertal, Solingen und Remscheid im Alter von 60 bis 80 Jahren befragt.

Grund für die Studie sei die ständig wachsende Zahl älterer Menschen in der Gesellschaft, erklärte Professor Wächter, der die Untersuchung leitet. Man habe das Freizeitverhalten der Rentner näher beobachten wollen. Doch was Wächter und seine Kollegen fanden, hatte mit "Ruhestand" oft nichts zu tun. Dabei sei das Geldverdienen für arbeitende Rentner nicht das Hauptmotiv. Älteren Leuten gehe es oft um "soziale Anerkennung".

"Auf der anderen Seite rechnen viele Betriebe fest mit der günstigen Rentnerarbeit", sagte die wissenschaftliche Mitarbeiterin Eva Walter. Bei 610-Mark-Jobs bekämen die Sozialversicherungskassen keinen Pfennig. Stundenlöhne seien sehr niedrig: Urlaubs-, Weihnachts- oder Krankengeld würden normalerweise nicht bezahlt. Dabei sei die Rentnerarbeit oft erstklassig. Walter: "Die Leute haben Berufserfahrung, sind pünktlich und zuverlässig. Das wünscht sich jeder Personalchef."

"Die von uns befragten Rentner kamen oft durch Zeitungsannoncen an ihren Job." Vielfach sei die Nachfrage der Betriebe so groß gewesen, daß die Rentner zwischen mehreren Angeboten auswählen konnten.

Vocabulary

die	Anerkennung	recognition
das	Angebot (-e)	offer
	auswählen II	to choose
	befragen I	to question
	beobachten I	to observe
die	Berufserfahrung (-en)	(job) experience
der	Betrieb (-e)	firm
	erklären I	to explain
	erstklassig	first class
das	Freizeitverhalten	leisure behaviour
die	Gesellschaft (-en)	society
	günstig	good value
das	Hauptmotiv (-e)	main motive
das	Krankengeld (-er)	sick pay
die	Langzeitstudie (-n)	long-term study
	leiten	to lead
die	Mitarbeiterin (-nen)	(female) colleague
die	Nachfrage (-n)	demand
	pünktlich	punctual
der	Rentner (-)	pensioner
der	Ruhestand	retirement
die	Sozialversicherungs-kasse (-n)	social insurance fund
	ständig	constantly
der	Stundenlohn (-̈e)	hourly pay
der	Unruhestand	(pun) non-retirement state, state of restlessness
die	Untersuchung (-en)	investigation
	wissenschaftlich	academic
die	Zeitungsannonce (-n)	newspaper advert
	zuverlässig	reliable
das	Zwischenergebnis (-se)	provisional result

Türkei diskriminiert Deutsche

Nach der Kritik des türkischen Ministerpräsiadenten an der "Diskriminierung" von Türken in Deutschland hat der Bundestagsabgeordnete Hirsch am Montag die "Diskriminierung" von Deutschen in der Türkei beklagt.

Die Lage von deutschen Frauen, die mit Türken verheiratet seien, stehe trotz jahrelanger Kritik immer noch in "krassem Gegensatz" zu den Lebensumständen von Türken in der Bundesrepublik, erklärte Hirsch, der mehrere Benachteiligungen auflistete.

So müßten deutsche Frauen alle zwei Jahre ihre Aufenthalts- und Arbeitserlaubnis gegen hohe Kosten erneuern lassen. Beim Tod des Ehemannes oder einer Scheidung gebe es keine gesicherte Aufenthaltsrechte. Auch ein Wahlrecht werde nicht gewährt.

"Diese Diskriminierung kann nicht länger toleriert werden und wird die Beziehungen zwischen beiden Staaten belasten."

Vocabulary

die	Arbeitserlaubnis (-se)	work permit
die	Aufenthaltsgenehmigung (-en)	residence permit
	belasten I	to burden
die	Benachteiligung (-en)	disadvantage
die	Beziehungen (pl)	relations
der	Bundestagsabgeordnete (adj)	(German) MP
	diskriminieren	to discriminate against
der	Ehemann (-̈er)	husband
	erneuern I	to renew
	gewähren I	to grant
die	Lage (-n)	situation
die	Lebensumstände (pl)	living conditions
der	Ministerpräsident (PO -en)	prime minister
die	Scheidung (-en)	divorce
der	Tod	death
	tolerieren	to tolerate
die	Türkei	Turkey
	türkisch	Turkish
das	Wahlrecht	right to vote, franchise

Key to Exercises

LESSON 3

Exercise 4: 1 Der Vater liebt die Wirtin. 2 Es ist harmlos! 3 Er kauft die Zeitung. 4 Sie macht die Betten. 5 Die Tochter holt das Auto. 6 Sie ruft die Katze und den Hund. 7 Die Katze und der Hund kommen. 8 Die Wirtin bringt Wasser. 9 Vater, Wirtin, Tochter, Hund und Katze trinken das Wasser.

LESSON 4

Exercise 5: 1 Sie kaufen ein Haus und machen Wohnungen. 2 Eine Wohnung hat keine Küche. 3 Das ist ein Problem, und sie bauen eine Küche. 4 Eine Wohnung hat kein Wasser. 5 Das ist auch ein Problem, aber der Vater installiert ein Wassersystem. 6 Eine Wohnung hat keine Elektrizität. 7 Das ist kein Problem. Der Sohn ist Elektriker. 8 Eine Wohnung hat eine Küche, Wasser, Elektrizität und (einige) Schränke, aber keine Fenster. 9 Das ist kein Problem, es ist eine Katastrophe.

Exercise 6: 2 Zwei Brote kosten DM 9,60 (neun Mark sechzig). 3 Zwei Würste kosten DM 6,50 (sechs Mark fünfzig). 4 Zwei Uhren kosten DM 170,00 (hundertsiebzig Mark). 5 Zwei Zeitungen kosten DM 5,00 (fünf Mark). 6 Zwei Betten kosten DM 976,00 (neunhundertsechsundsiebzig Mark). 7 Zwei Schränke kosten DM 1 010 ((ein)tausendzehn Mark). 8 Zwei Messer kosten DM 15,00 (fünfzehn Mark). 9 Zwei Rosen kosten DM 7,50 (sieben Mark fünfzig). 10 Zwei Autos kosten DM 36 000,00 (sechsunddreißigtausend Mark).

Exercise 7: Ich bringe meinem Vater ein Buch. Ich gebe es ihm im Flur. Ich schenke meinem Bruder einen Hund und wünsche ihm einen guten Tag.

LESSON 5

Exercise 8: 1 Was 2 Wann 3 Wen 4 Wo 5 Wer 6 Wie 7 Warum

Exercise 9:
Verkäufer Bitte schön ...?
Fremde Guten Tag. Haben Sie einen Führer?
V Was für einen Führer?
F Einen Stadtführer.
V Ich weiß es nicht. Fragen Sie bitte den Chef.
F Guten Tag. Ich suche einen Stadtführer. Haben
Sie so etwas?
Chef Ja sicher. Die Stadtführer sind drüben. Gucken
Sie dort ...
F Es ist verrückt. Ich finde Stadtführer von
Frankfurt, Gießen, Marburg und Kassel, aber ich
finde keinen Stadtführer von Bunsenheim.
C Natürlich nicht. Warum brauchen wir Stadtführer
von Bunsenheim? Wir wohnen hier und kennen
die Stadt!

Exercise 10: 2 größer 3 jünger 4 klüger 5 wärmer 6 länger
7 netter

LESSON 6

Exercise 11: Der Verbrecher steht mit einem Pinsel und einer
Palette in der Hand vor einem Bild. Auf dem Bild sind
mehrere Sachen. Auf einer Tischdecke liegt ein Brot, neben
dem Brot ist ein Glas, und hinter dem Brot ist eine Flasche
mit einem Korken. Auf der Flasche ist ein Etikett. Was ist
aber für den Verbrecher am wichtigsten? Die Feile in
dem/im Brot, natürlich!

Exercise 12: Der Einbrecher geht bis an die Haustür. Er
klopft an die Tür. Niemand kommt zur Tür. Er geht um das
Haus und guckt durch die Fenster. Er findet ein Auto ohne
Nummernschild zwischen dem Haus und der Garage. Er
geht zurück an die Haustür. Er steckt eine Feile zwischen die
Tür und den Rahmen. Er öffnet die Tür mit der Feile und
geht in den Flur. Ihm gegenüber auf der Treppe sitzt ein
Skelett mit einer Axt in der Hand.

Exercise 13:

Hotelgast	Was gibt es im Fernsehen heute abend?
Kellner	Ich weiß es nicht.
H	Gucken sie bitte in die Fernsehzeitung.
K	Es gibt keine Fernsehzeitung diese Woche.
H	Gibt es eine Tageszeitung?
K	ja, hier ist eine Tageszeitung … aber sie ist leider von gestern.

LESSON 7

Exercise 14: 2 Nein, sie ist mit ihrer Schwester bei Müllers eingeladen. 3 Nein, der Vater kommt ohne unser Geschenk für die Mutter. 4 Nein, ich esse den Kuchen mit einer Tasse Kaffee. 5 Nein, er geht mit seinem Stadtführer durch Frankfurt. 6 Nein, ich mache das Abendbrot ohne meine Tochter. 7 Nein, sie geht ohne ihren Bruder zur Tante. 8 Nein, wir kaufen die Wurst ohne eine Cola.

Exercise 15: 1 Keiner, (Jeder) 2 Welche 3 Keinen, Diesen 4 Keinen, Diesen 5 (Jeder), Dieser 6 Solches, Welches 7 Welches 8 Jeder, Dieser 9 Welche, Jede

Exercise 16:

She	Will you please go and do the shopping?
He	Certainly! Have you got a shopping list for me?
She	No, I'll tell you everything … First please bring a small white loaf and ten fresh rolls from the baker.
He	They're cheaper at Marktkauf, and we're going there this afternoon.
She	All right. Then buy half a pound of mince and 250 grams of boiled ham at the butcher's.
He	They always serve me badly at the butcher's. I would rather buy meat in the old town, and we also have to go there this afternoon.
She	All right. Then I need lettuce, one and a half pounds of small, firm tomatoes, a nice cucumber, ten pounds of potatoes and a pound of French beans from the greengrocer's.

He	The things for the salad and the other vegetables aren't urgent, and after all there's (a) market tomorrow.
She	All right, but I definitely need eggs from Edeka.
He	No, you don't need (them). We still have a lot. We'll (then) get eggs from the market, too.
She	All right, then you don't need to go shopping.

Exercise 17: 2 Hol bitte ein kleines Weißbrot vom Bäcker. Das Weißbrot kaufe ich lieber bei Marktkauf. 3 Hol bitte 250 Gramm gekochten Schinken vom Metzger. Den gekochten Schinken kaufe ich lieber in der Altstadt. 4 Hol bitte einen Kopfsalat vom Gemüsegeschäft. Den Kopfsalat kaufe ich lieber auf dem Markt. 5 Hol bitte zwanzig Eier von Edeka. Die Eier kaufe ich lieber auf dem Markt. 6 Hol bitte eine schöne Gurke vom Gemüsegeschäft. Die Gurke kaufe ich lieber auf dem Markt. 7 Hol bitte zehn frische Brötchen vom Bäcker. Die Brötchen kaufe ich lieber bei Marktkauf. 8 Hol bitte ein halbes Pfund Hackfleisch vom Metzger. Das Hackfleisch kaufe ich lieber in der Altstadt. 9 Hol bitte zehn Pfund Kartoffeln vom Gemüsegeschäft. Die Kartoffeln kaufe ich lieber auf dem Markt. 10 Hol bitte ein Pfund grüne Bohnen vom Gemüsegeschäft. Die grünen Bohnen kaufe ich lieber auf dem Markt.

LESSON 8

Exercise 18: 1 kann 2 müssen 3 darf 4 muß 5 darf 6 darf 7 kann

Exercise 19: 1 damit 2 darauf 3 danach 4 dazu 5 dafür 6 daneben 7 dagegen 8 dazwischen 9 dahinter 10 davor

Exercise 20: 1 tue/stelle 2 sind/liegen 3 tue/lege 4 tun/stellen 5 tue/stelle 6 sind/stehen 7 tue/lege 8 tue/stecke 9 tue/lege 10 ist/liegt 11 sind/liegen 12 tue/lege 13 tue/stelle

Exercise 21: Now look! I'll keep the refrigerator clear as far as possible. Then you'll be able to find everything quite easily. I'm putting the chicken for Sunday, the frozen raspberry flan and the two oven-ready meals into the freezer compartment. You can eat the oven-ready meals tomorrow and the day after. The plum tart and the dish with cream are at the top. I'm also putting the two bottles of wine there ... Oh, there's just a little space there still, I can put the carton of yoghurt in between. I'm putting the four bottles of beer in the bottom of the door, and two cartons of milk are next to them. I'm putting the packet of boiled ham, the salami and the liver sausage in the middle. They're for evenings, of course ... Eggs? ... I'm putting the eggs singly in the top of the door, of course, twelve of them. I'm putting two pieces of butter in the top compartment in the door. I'll leave the third one out to get soft. The flat container with three sorts of cheese is in the middle, and a tube of mayonnaise and the sliced cheese are behind it. The cucumber, the lettuce, the grapes and the tomatoes are at the bottom, and I'm putting the bag of oranges, one cauliflower and the sprouts in the vegetable compartment right at the bottom. I'll put a little jar of honey and a jar of strawberry jam a little higher in the door ... My goodness, how full the refrigerator is again!

Exercise 22: 1 denen 2 der 3 dem 4 das 5 der 6 das 7 den 8 die 9 denen 10 dem

Exercise 23: 1 hat/gebracht 2 ist/geflogen 3 sind/gestorben 4 hat/gestellt 5 ist/gesprungen 6 bin/geblieben 7 ist/gestiegen 8 habe/geschickt 9 haben/bekommen 10 bist/geworden

Exercise 24: 1 (b) 2 (c) 3 (a) 4 (b) 5 (a) 6 (c)

LESSON 10

Exercise 25: Ich habe vor, eine Party zu geben. Wir sind so viele, also richte ich meine Wohnung anders ein. Ich lade nur meine besten Freunde ein, aber wir sind fünfzig. Diesmal helfen meine Freunde mal nicht mit. Ich will alles alleine machen. Um 8 Uhr rufe ich sie an. Dann können sie kommen. Aber was sagen meine Freunde, sie schlagen stattdessen vor, gar nicht zu essen, sondern den ganzen Abend lang zu trinken.

Exercise 26: 2 Fräulein Schmidt steht früh auf, um mit ihrem Hund spazierenzugehen. 3 Mittags kommt sie nach Hause und arbeitet im Garten, statt zu essen. 4 Am Nachmittag geht sie ins Kino, ohne ihre Mutter zu fragen. 5 Sie sieht gerne Filme, um auf andere Gedanken zu kommen. 6 Am Abend kommt ihr Freund, um sie ins Restaurant einzuladen. 7 Sie verläßt das Restaurant während des Essens, ohne zu bezahlen. 8 Er bleibt im Restaurant sitzen und ißt beide Portionen, statt zu seiner Freundin zu laufen.

LESSON 11

Exercise 27: 2 ..., daß Fritz solche Vorschläge nicht machen soll. 3 ..., daß Ernst endlich mal etwas tun soll. 4 ..., daß er sein Handgelenk plötzlich verletzt. 5 ..., daß er Ernst zum Arzt schickt. 6 ..., daß Ernst einfach faul ist!

Exercise 28: 2 Nachdem man gegessen hat, soll man eigentlich nicht schlafen. 3 Während man ißt, darf man nicht zu viel reden. 4 Obwohl er viel geredet hat, hat er eigentlich nicht viel gesagt. 5 Weil das Wetter schön ist, müssen wir endlich im Garten arbeiten. 6 Bis das Programm anfängt, kannst du noch schön in der Küche helfen! 7 Weil du hohen Blutdruck hast, mußt du weniger arbeiten. 8 Obwohl er hohen Blutdruck hat, läuft er jeden Tag.

LESSON 12

Exercise 29: 2 Während Fritz im Garten arbeitete, hat sich sein Bruder Pop-Musik angehört. 3 Während Hanna einen Brief schrieb, ist ihre Freundin schwimmen gegangen. 4 Während Otto Milch trank, hat sein Bruder Bruno Schnaps getrunken. 5 Während Frau Krause mit ihrem Nachbarn sprach, hat ein Einbrecher ihr Geld vom Küchentisch gestohlen. 6 Während sich die Eltern oben im Haus stritten, haben die Kinder unten im Haus eine Party gehalten. 7 Während Anton mit den Eltern sprach, hat Susanne den Hund ins Wasser gestoßen.

Exercise 30: 2 (a) Wenn du die Fahrkarte besorgen würdest, dann hätten wir die Möglichkeit, am Wochenende in die

Berge zu fahren. (b) Würdest du die Fahrkarte besorgen, dann hätten wir die Möglichkeit, am Wochenende in die Berge zu fahren. 3 (a) Wenn Peter nicht das Fenster schließt, dann wird es zu kalt für uns alle. (b) Schließt Peter nicht das Fenster, dann wird es zu kalt für uns alle. 4 (a) Wenn dieser Mann nicht den Klub verläßt, dann wird es Krach geben. (b) Verläßt dieser Mann nicht den Klub, dann wird es Krach geben. 5 (a) Wenn die kleine Tochter nicht fernsehen dürfte, dann wäre sie schwierig. (b) Dürfte die kleine Tochter nicht fernsehen, dann wäre sie schwierig. 6 (a) Wenn der Vater in die Gaststube geht, dann trinkt er immer zu viel. (b) Geht der Vater in die Gaststube, dann trinkt er immer zu viel. 7 (a) Wenn du jetzt das Essen für Sonntag kochst, dann wirst du am Sonntag morgen schlafen können. (b) Kochst du jetzt das Essen für Sonntag, dann wirst du am Sonntag morgen schlafen können.

LESSON 13

Exercise 31: 2 Jedoch bucht Emil eine Fahrt nach Berlin. Emil bucht jedoch eine Fahrt nach Berlin. (trotzdem, allerdings) 3 Allerdings gibt es sehr viele Touristen. Es gibt allerdings sehr viele Touristen. (deshalb, jedoch, außerdem) 4 Andererseits gibt es in Berlin viel zu sehen. In Berlin gibt es andererseits viel zu sehen. (jedoch) 5 Außerdem ist es historisch und politisch wichtig. Es ist außerdem historisch und politisch wichtig. (andererseits) 6 Immerhin war es vor einiger Zeit das Tor zwischen Westen und Osten. Es war immerhin vor einiger Zeit das Tor zwischen Westen und Osten. 7 Trotzdem hat er Berlin sehr interessant gefunden. Er hat trotzdem Berlin sehr interessant gefunden. (jedoch, allerdings, andererseits)

Exercise 32: 1 (a) 2 (c) 3 (b) 4 (b) 5 (b) 6 (c) 7 (c)

Mini-dictionary

Numbers are not included in the Mini-dictionary. The cardinal numbers are to be found in Section 18 and the ordinal numbers in Section 30. I indicates TYPE I (inseparable prefix) verbs; II indicates TYPE II (separable prefix) verbs.

ab und zu occasionally, now and again

der **Abend (-e)** evening

das **Abendbrot (-e)** supper

abends in the evenings

die **Abendveranstaltung (-en)** evening entertainment/event

aber but

der **Abfall (-̈e)** rubbish, waste, garbage

abgesehen (davon) apart (from that)

abhängen II **(von)** to depend (on)

abholen II to collect, pick up

abhören II to listen to, check (e.g. heart)

abnehmen II to lose weight

der **Abzug (-̈e)** print, copy

ach! oh!

achten (auf) to pay attention (to), keep an eye (on)

(das) Ägypten Egypt

die **Ahnung (-en)** idea, clue, notion

all all

alle zwei Tage every other day

allein(e) alone

allerdings admittedly, mind you, ...though

alles everything

das **Allgäu** (mountainous area in Southern Bavaria)

allgemein general, in general

als than, as, when

also so, therefore, well

alt old

das **Alter (-)** age

die **Altstadt** old (part of) town

am = an dem

an at, on, to, by, on to, up to

anbieten II to offer

ander.. other, different

andererseits on the other hand

ändern to change, alter

anderthalb one and a half

der **Anfang (-̈e)** beginning, start

anfangen II to begin, start

der **Anfänger (-)** beginner

die **Angelegenheit (-en)** matter, affair, business

angenehm pleasant

die **Angst (-̈e)** fear, anxiety, worry

anhalten II to stop, pull up

anhören II **sich** to listen to, sound

ankommen II to arrive

anrufen II to ring up, call, telephone

anschaffen II to get, acquire, obtain, buy

die **Ansicht (-en)** view, opinion
ansonsten otherwise, apart from that
anstatt instead (of)
anstrengend strenuous, energetic
antworten to answer
anziehen II to put on (clothes)
anziehen II **sich** to get dressed
die **Apfelsine (-n)** orange
der **April** April
arbeitslos unemployed
ärgern sich to get annoyed
arm poor
der **Arzt (ˉe)** doctor (male)
die **Ärztin (-nen)** doctor (female)
auch also, too, even
auf on, on top of, on to
der **Aufkleber (-)** sticker
aufkommen II to (be liable to) pay
aufmachen II to open
die **Aufnahme (-n)** exposure, photo, shot
aufnehmen II to accept, admit
aufpassen II to pay attention, take note, watch
aufregen II **sich** to get excited/worked up
der **Aufschnitt** sliced (cold) meat
aufstehen II to get up
auftauchen II to turn up, appear
der **Augenblick (-e)** moment, instant
im Augenblick at the moment
augenblicklich at the moment

der **August** August
aus out of, from
der **Ausflug (ˉe)** excursion, outing
ausgeben II to spend
ausgehen II to go out
aushängen II to post, put up, display
der **Ausländer (-)** foreigner
der **Auslöser (-)** shutter release
ausmachen II to put out, switch off
aussehen II to look, appear
außerdem besides, moreover, furthermore
außerhalb outside (of)
äußerst extremely
die **Aussicht (-en)** view, prospect
aussuchen II to choose, select
austauschen II to exchange
auswechseln II to replace
ausziehen II **sich** to get undressed
das **Auto (-s)** car
der **Automat (PO -en)** machine (e.g. vending)
die **Axt (ˉe)** axe

der **Bäcker (-)** baker
baden to bathe, swim
der **Bahnhof (ˉe)** station
bald soon
die **Banane (-n)** banana
die **Bar (-s)** bar
bauen to build
der **Bauer (PO -n)** farmer
der **Baum (ˉe)** tree
der **Becher (-)** cup, mug, carton
bedanken I **sich** to say 'thank you', express one's thanks

bedeuten I to mean
bedienen I to serve
bedrohen I to threaten
beeilen I sich to hurry (up)
befinden I sich to be, be situated
begegnen I to meet
behalten I to keep
der Behälter (-) container
behandeln I to treat
bei with, at, in
beid.. both, two
das Beisammensein being with people, get-together
beitreten II to join
bekannt known, well-known, acquainted
der Bekannte (adj) acquaintance, friend
beklagen I sich to complain
bekommen I to get, obtain
bemerken I to notice
benutzen I to use
der Berg (-e) mountain, hill
der Beruf (-e) job, trade, profession, occupation
beschränken I to limit, restrict
beschweren I sich to complain
der Besitzer (-) proprietor, owner
besonder.. special
besonders especially
besorgen I to get, obtain
besprechen I to discuss, talk over
besser better
bestehen I (auf) to insist (on)
bestellen I to order
die Bestellung (-en) order
am besten best of all

bestimmt definite
besuchen I to visit, attend
betrinken I sich to get drunk
das Bett (-en) bed
der Beutel (-) bag
bevor before
bewegen I sich to move
bezahlen I to pay for
das Bier beer
das Bierchen (-) (nice) little beer
bieten to offer
das Bild (-er) picture, photograph
billig cheap, inexpensive
der Bindfaden string
bis until, up to
ein bißchen a bit
bist (you) are
bitte please
bitten (um) to ask (for), request
bitte schön? yes please?
bitte schön! here you are!
der Bleistift (-e) pencil
blenden to dazzle
die Blume (-n) flower
das Blumengeschäft (-e) florist's
der Blumenkohl cauliflower
der Blutdruck blood pressure
bluten to bleed
die Blutprobe (-n) blood test
der Boden (¨) floor, ground
die Bohne (-n) bean
grüne Bohnen French beans
böse angry, naughty, wicked
brauchen to need
brechen to break
breit wide
brennen to burn
der Brief (-e) letter
bringen to bring, take
das Brot (-e) bread, loaf

253

das **Brötchen (-)** roll
der **Bruder (¨)** brother
das **Buch (¨er)** book
der **Buchstabe (PO -ns)** letter (of
the alphabet)
der **Bus (-se)** bus, coach
die **Butter** butter
die **Buttersoße** butter sauce
die **Chance (-n)** chance
checken to check
der **Chef (-s)** boss
die **Chefsekretärin (-nen)** boss's
secretary, personal assistant
chinesisch Chinese
die **Coca-Cola (-)** Coca-Cola

d. . the
d. . selb. . the same
da there, then, as
das **Dach (¨er)** roof
dafür for it, instead
dagegen against it, on the
other hand
daher from there, therefore
dahin (to) there
dahinter behind it
damals then, at that time
die **Dame (-n)** lady
damit with it, in order that,
so that
danach after that, afterwards
daneben next to it
danke (schon)! thank you!
dann then
darüber over it, above it,
about it
darum round it, therefore, so
das that
dauern to last
davor before it
dazu to it, with it

dazwischen between them
die **Decke (-n)** ceiling
denken to think
denn for, as, since, then
dennoch nevertheless, yet
deren whose, of whom
deshalb therefore
dessen whose, of whom
deswegen on account of it,
therefore
der **Deutsche** (adj) German
der **Dezember** December
das **Dia (-s)** slide
dich you
der **Dienstag** Tuesday
dies. . this
dir to / for you
der **Direktor (-en)** director
doch but, however, after all
der **Donnerstag** Thursday
das **Doppelzimmer (-)** double
room
dort there
dorthin (to) there
die **Dose (-n)** can, tin, jar
draußen outside
das **Drittel (-)** third
drüben over there
der **Druck (¨e)** pressure
drücken to press
du you
dumm silly, stupid
dunkel dark
durch through, by
dürfen may, to be
allowed / able
die **Dusche (-n)** shower
duzen to say 'du'

eben just, just now, simply
ebenfalls likewise

ebenso just as
die **Ecke (-n)** corner
Edeka (chain of small supermarkets)
egal all the same, immaterial, regardless
ehemalig former
das **Ei (-er)** egg
eigen own
eigentlich really, actually
eilen to be urgent
ein a, one
einbegriffen included
einbilden II **sich** to imagine
der **Einbrecher (-)** burglar
einfach simple
eingeladen invited
einig. . some, a few
einkaufen II to do the shopping
die **Einkaufsliste (-n)** shopping list
einladen II to invite
einmal once
einnehmen II to eat, take, consume
einrichten II to furnish, arrange
der **Eintritt (-e)** admission
einverstanden agreed
einwandfrei perfect, faultless, flawless
einzeln separate, one by one, single
das **Einzelzimmer (-)** single room
das **Eisfach (-̈er)** freezer compartment
elegant elegant
der **Elektriker (-)** electrician
die **Elektrizität** electricity
empfehlen I to recommend

empfinden I to feel
endlich finally, at last
der **Englischkurs (-e)** English course
enthalten I to contain, include
die **Entscheidung (-en)** decision
entschuldigen I **sich** to apologise
Entschuldigung! excuse me!
die **Entschuldigung (-en)** excuse, apology
entsprechen I to correspond
er he
meines Erachtens in my opinion
die **Erdbeermarmelade** strawberry jam
der **Erfolg (-e)** success
die **Erfrischung (-en)** refreshment
das **Ergebnis (-se)** result
erinnern I **sich (an)** to remember
erkälten I **sich** to catch a cold
erkältet sein to have a cold
die **Erkältung (-en)** cold
erscheinen I to appear
ersetzen I to replace
erst first, only
erwarten I to expect, await
erzählen I to tell, relate
die **Erziehung** education, bringing up, upbringing
es it
essen to eat
das **Essen (-)** food, meal
das **Etikett (-en)** label
etwa about, perhaps, say
etwas something
so etwas something / anything like that

euch you
euer your
das **Exemplar (-e)** copy
das **Experiment (-e)** experiment
der **Export (-e)** export
extra extra, on purpose, deliberately

das **Fach ("-er)** compartment, subject
fahren to go (not on foot), travel
die **Fahrkarte (-n)** ticket
das **Fahrrad ("-er)** bicycle
die **Fahrt (-en)** journey, trip
fallen to fall
falls in case
falsch wrong
fangen to catch
die **Farbe (-n)** colour, paint
der **Februar** February
feiern to celebrate
die **Feile (-n)** file
der **Fehler (-)** mistake, error
das **Fenster (-)** window
die **Ferien** (plural) holiday(s)
der **Fernsehapparat (-e)** television set
das **Fernsehen** television
die **Fernsehzeitung (-en)** TV magazine
fertig ready, finished
das **Fertigessen (-)** oven-ready meal
fest firm
das **Festessen (-)** banquet
das **Feuer (-)** fire
das **Feuerwerk** fireworks
die **Figur (-en)** figure
der **Film (-e)** film
finanzieren to finance

finden to find
der **Fisch (-e)** fish
flach flat, shallow
die **Flasche (-n)** bottle
das **Fleisch** meat
fliegen to fly
fliehen to flee
der **Fliesenleger (-)** tiler
flirten to flirt
der **Flur (-e)** hall
die **Folge (-n)** consequence
der **Fotoapparat (-e)** camera
die **Frage (-n)** question
in Frage kommen to be possible
nicht in Frage kommen to be out of the question
fragen to ask
der **Franzose (PO -n)** Frenchman
französisch French
die **Frau (-en)** woman, wife, Mrs
frech cheeky
frei free, vacant
freihalten II to keep clear
freilich admittedly, to be sure
der **Freitag** Friday
freuen sich auf to look forward to
freuen sich (über) to be pleased (at)/glad (about)
der **Freund (-e)** friend
die **Freundin (-nen)** girlfriend
freundlich kind, friendly
frisch fresh
froh glad
die **Frucht ("-e)** fruit
früh early
früher earlier, former(ly)
der **Frühling** spring
das **Frühstück** breakfast

fühlen sich to feel

der **Führer (-)** guide

der **Führerschein (-e)** driving licence

der **Fünfzigmarkschein (-e)** fifty mark note

funktionieren to work, function

für for

furchtbar terrible, frightful, fearful

fürchten sich (vor) to be afraid (of)

ganz all, whole

gar nicht not at all

gar nichts nothing at all

die **Garage (-n)** garage

der **Garten (¨)** garden

der **Gast (¨e)** guest, visitor

das **Gasthaus (¨er)** inn

die **Gaststube (-n)** lounge (of inn)

geben to give

es gibt there is / are

der **Geburtstag (-e)** birthday

der **Gedanke (PO -ns)** thought

geduldig patient

geeignet suitable, suited

gefährlich dangerous

gefallen I to please

der **Gefangene (adj)** prisoner

gefroren frozen

gegen against, towards

die **Gegend (-en)** area, region, neighbourhood

das **Gegenteil** opposite

gegenüber opposite

gegenzeichnen II to countersign

gehen to go, walk

es geht um it's about

wie geht's (Ihnen)? how are you?

gehören I to belong

gekocht boiled, cooked

gelb yellow

das **Geld** money

die **Gelegenheit (-en)** opportunity

das **Gelenk (-e)** joint

gelingen I to succeed

das **Gemüse** vegetables

das **Gemüsefach (¨er)** vegetable compartment

das **Gemüsegeschäft (-e)** green-grocer's

genau exact, precise

genieren sich to be embarrassed

genießen I to enjoy

genug enough

genügend enough, suffficient

das **Gepäck** luggage

gerade just, just now

gerade erst only just

geradeaus straight ahead

immer geradeaus (gehen) to keep (going) straight ahead

das **Gerät (-e)** machine, (piece of) equipment

gern gladly

das **Geschäft (-e)** business, shop

geschehen I to happen

geschlossen closed

der **Geschmack (¨e or ¨er)** taste

die **Geschwister (plural)** brother(s) and / or sister(s)

gesellig sociable

der **Gesellschaftsraum (¨e)** lounge

gestern yesterday

das **Getränk (-e)** drink

257

gewachsen sein to be able to cope with
gewiß certainly
das **Gewitter (-)** thunderstorm
gewöhnen I **sich (an)** to get used/accustomed (to)
das **Glas ("-er)** glass, jar
der **Glaube (PO -ns)** belief
glauben to believe, think
gleich straight away, immediately, at once, same, similar
das **Glück** luck, happiness
golden gold, golden
das **Gramm (-e)** gram
gratulieren to congratulate
es graut mir (vor) I have a horror (of)
die **Grenze (-n)** frontier, border
grillen to grill
groß big, large, tall
die **Größe (-n)** size
die **Großmutter (:)** grandmother
der **Grundpreis (-e)** basic price
die **Gruppe (-n)** group
grüßen to greet, wave
grüß Gott! hello!
gucken to look, peep
gut good, well
na gut! (oh) all right!
guten Abend! good evening!
guten Morgen! good morning!
guten Tag! hello!
meine Gute! my goodness! good heavens!

haben to have
das **Hackfleisch** minced meat
das **Hähnchen (-)** chicken
halb half
die **Hälfte (-n)** half

hallo! hello!
halt just, simply
halten to hold
halten (von) to think (of/about)
die **Hand ("-e)** hand
der **Handball** handball
handeln sich um to be about
das **Handgelenk (-e)** wrist
harmlos harmless, innocuous
hart hard
hast (you) have
der **Haufen (-)** heap, pile
das **Haus ("-er)** house
nach Hause (to) home
zu Hause at home
die **Hausbesitzerin (-nen)** house owner (female)
der **Hausschlüssel (-)** house key, front door key
die **Haustür (-en)** front door
heiraten to marry
heiß hot
heißen to be called
das **heißt** that is (to say)
der **Held (PO -en)** hero
helfen to help
hell light, bright
herausnehmen II to take out
der **Herbst** autumn
der **Herr (PO -n, plural -en)** gentleman, Mr
herrlich splendid, glorious
das **Herz (PO -ens, plural -en)** heart
heute today
heute abend this evening
heutzutage nowadays, now
hier here
die **Himbeertorte (-n)** raspberry tart/flan

hin und her backwards and forwards, to and fro

hin und zurück there and back, return

hingegen on the other hand

hinlegen II sich to lie down

hinten at the back, behind

hinter behind

hinterher afterwards, later

der Hinweg (-e) outward journey

historisch historic, historical

hoch high

am höchsten highest

die Hochzeit (-en) wedding

hoffen to hope

hoffentlich hopefully

höflich polite

holen to fetch, bring

der Honig honey

hören to hear

das Hotel (-s) hotel

der Hund (-e) dog

der Hunger hunger

ich I

ihm to/for him/it

ihn him

ihnen to/for them

Ihnen to/for you

ihr her, their, to/for her

Ihr your

immer always

immerhin after all

immer wieder again and again, repeatedly

in in, into

indem by

die Inflation inflation

infolgedessen consequently

informieren to inform

inklusiv inclusive

innerhalb inside of

installieren to install

das Instrument (-e) instrument

interessant interesting

interessieren to interest

interessieren sich (für) to be interested (in)

interessiert (an) interested (in)

interviewen to interview

irgendein some or other, any

irgendwo somewhere, anywhere

ist is

ja yes, of course

das Jahr (-e) year

jahrelang for years

der Januar January

jawohl! certainly!

je each, ever

jed. . every, each, any

jedenfalls at any rate

jedoch however

jemals ever

jen. . that

jenseits on the far side (of), beyond

jetzt now

jeweils each time

der Juli July

jung young

der Junge (PO -n, plural often -ns) boy

der Juni June

der Kaffee coffee

die Kalorie (-n) calorie

kalt cold

kaputt broken (down), exhausted

die Karotte (-n) carrot

die **Kartoffel (-n)** potato
der **Käse** cheese
der **Kassenbon (-s)** till receipt, sales slip
die **Kassette** (audio) cassette
die **Katastrophe (-n)** catastrophe
die **Katze (-n)** cat
der **Kauf (-e)** purchase
   kaufen to buy
   kaum scarcely, hardly
   kein not a, no, not any
der **Kellner (-)** waiter
   kennen to know (people, things)
das **Kind (-er)** child
der **Kinderarzt (-e)** paediatrician
das **Kino (-s)** cinema
die **Kirche (-n)** church
   klagen to complain
die **Klarinette (-n)** clarinet
der **Klassenbeste** (adj) best in the class
der **Klassenkamerad (PO -en)** classmate
das **Klavier (-e)** piano
der **Klavierlehrer (-)** piano teacher
das **Kleid (-er)** dress
   klein small, little
   klingen to sound
   klopfen to knock
der **Klub (-s)** club
   klug clever
der **Koffer (-)** suitcase
der **Kohl** cabbage
der **Komfort** comfort
   kommen to come
   kommen zu to happen
die **Konferenz (-en)** conference
   können can, to be able
   kontrollieren to check

das **Konzert (-e)** concert
der **Kopf (-e)** head
der **Kopfsalat** lettuce
der **Korken (-)** cork
   kosten to cost
der **Krach** noise, racket, quarrel, row
   krank ill, sick
die **Krankheit (-en)** illness, sickness, disease
die **Kreuzung (-en)** crossroads, junction
   kriechen to creep, crawl
   kriegen to get
die **Kritik (-en)** criticism
die **Küche (-n)** kitchen
der **Kuchen (-)** cake
der **Kühlschrank (-e)** refrigerator
der **Kunde (PO -n)** customer
die **Kusine (-n)** cousin (female)
der **Kurs (-e)** course, rate of exchange
   kurz short
   kurz danach shortly afterwards
   kurz davor shortly before

   lachen to laugh
   landen to land
   lang(e) long
   langsam slow
   langweilig boring
   lassen to let, make, leave
   laufen to run, walk
   laut loud, noisy
die **Leberwurst (-e)** liver sausage
   lecker tasty, delicious
   leer empty
   legen to put, lay (flat)
die **Lehrerin (-nen)** teacher (female)

leicht easy
leiden to suffer
leider unfortunately, (to be) sorry (that)
leihen to lend, borrow
leisten to achieve, manage, accomplish
lesen to read
letztens recently, lately
die Leute (plural) people
das Licht (-er) light
die Liebe (-n) love
lieben to love
lieber rather
das Lieblingsreiseziel (-e) favourite destination
liegen to lie, recline, be (situated)
liegenlassen II to leave (lying) about/behind
die Limonade (-n) lemonade
losfahren II to set out, come out, drive off
loslassen II to set off
der Löwe (PO -n) lion
lügen to lie (fib)
der Luxus luxury

machen to make, do
machen sich nichts daraus not to worry about it
es macht nichts it doesn't matter
das Mädchen (-) girl
mager lean, thin
der Mai May
mal just
das Mal (-e) time, occasion
malen to paint
man one, you, people
manch. . quite a few, a fair number of
manchmal sometimes
der Mann (¨er) man, husband
manuell manual
die Manteltasche (-n) coat pocket
die Mark (-) mark
die Deutsche Mark (D-Mark) (-) German mark
der Markt (¨e) market
der Marktkauf (typical hyper-market name)
der Marktplatz (¨e) marketplace
der März March
die Maschine (-n) machine, plane
der Maurer (-) bricklayer
die Mayonnaise mayonnaise
das Mehl flour
mehr more
mehrer. . several
mein my
meinen to think, mean, say
meinetwegen on my account, as far as I am concerned
die Meinung (-en) opinion
am meisten most of all
der Mensch (PO -en) person, human being, (plural) people
merken to notice
messen to measure
das Messer (-) knife
der Meter (-) metre
der Metzger (-) butcher
mich me, myself
die Miete (-n) rent
der Mieter (-) tenant
die Milch milk
die Milchkanne (-n) milk jug
der Minister (-) minister
mißlingen I to fail
mit with

mitbringen II to bring (with one)
mithelfen II to assist, help, co-operate
das **Mitleid** sympathy, pity
das **Mittagessen (-)** lunch
die **Mitte (-n)** middle
das **Mittelmeer** Mediterranean
mitten in the middle
die **Mitternacht (¨e)** midnight
der **Mittwoch** Wednesday
mögen may, to like
die **Möglichkeit (-en)** possibility, opportunity
möglichst as far as possible
der **Moment (-e)** moment
im Moment at the moment
Moment mal! just a moment!
momentan at the moment
der **Monat (-e)** month
der **Montag** Monday
morgen tomorrow
müde tired
die **Musik** music
müssen must, to have to
die **Mutter (¨)** mother

nach after, to, according to
der **Nachbar (PO -n)** neighbour
nachdem after
nachher afterwards
nachholen II to catch up
der **Nachmittag (-e)** afternoon
nächst next, nearest
am nächsten nearest of all
die **Nacht (¨e)** night
der **Nachttisch (-e)** bedside table
nahe near
nähern sich to approach
nämlich for, you see
naß wet

natürlich naturally, of course
neben next to, alongside
nehmen to take
nein no
die **Nelke (-n)** carnation
nett nice, kind, good
das **Netz (-e)** net
neu new
das **Neujahr** New Year
das **Neujahrsfrühstück (-e)** New Year's (Day) breakfast
der **Neujahrstag (-e)** New Year's Day
neulich recently
nicht not
nichts nothing
nichts los nothing happening/doing
nichts mehr no more, nothing more
nie never
niedrig low
niemand no one, nobody
noch still, yet, even, nor
die **Nordsee** North Sea
der **November** November
na gut! all right (then)!
null nought, zero, nil
das **Nummernschild (-er)** number plate
nun now, well (now)
nur only

ob whether
oben upstairs, at the top
ober. . top, upper
obwohl although
oder or
offen open
offensichtlich obvious, evident, clear

öffnen to open
oft often
ohne without
ohnehin anyway, as it is
der Oktober October
das Öl oil
das Orchester (-) orchestra
die Ordnung order
der Orthopäde (PO -n) orthopaedics specialist
der Osten east
östlich east, eastern

das Paar (-e) pair, couple
ein paar a few
die Packung (-en) pack, packet
die Palette (-n) palette
das Papier (-e) paper
parken to park
passen to fit, suit
passieren to happen
der Patient (PO -en) patient
die Pause (-n) break, interval, pause
das Pech bad luck
Pech haben to be unlucky
die Person (-en) person
persönlich personal
der Pfeffer pepper
pfeifen to whistle
der Pfeifton (-̈e) whistling sound
der Pfennig (-e) pfennig
der Pflaumenkuchen (-) plum tart
das Pfund (-e) pound
das Picknick (-s) picnic
der Pinsel (-) brush
der Plan (-̈e) plan
planen to plan
der Platz (-̈e) place, room, space, seat, square

plötzlich sudden
der Politiker (-) politician
politisch political
der Polizist (PO -en) policeman
die Popmusik pop music
praktisch practical, handy
der Präsident (PO -en) president
der Preis (-e) price
preiswert reasonably priced
pro per
probieren to try
das Problem (-e) problem
das Programm (-e) programme
prüfen to test
die Prüfung (-en) test, examination
der Pullover (-) pullover

das Quintett (-e) quintet

der Rahmen (-) frame
rasen to rush
rasieren sich to shave, get shaved
raten to advise, guess
das Rathaus (-̈er) town hall
rauchen to smoke
der Raum (-̈e) room, space
recht haben to be right
rechts to/on the right
der Rechtsanwalt (-̈e) lawyer
die Rede (-n) speech, talk
reden to speak, talk
das Regal (-e) shelf
regelmäßig regular
der Regenschirm (-e) umbrella
regnen to rain
reich rich, wealthy
reichen to pass, hand, reach
reichhaltig varied, comprehensive, extensive

der Reifen (-) tyre
die Reihe (-n) row, series
reintun II to put in
der Reis rice
der Reiseleiter (-) courier
der Reisepaß (¨-sse) passport
die Reklamation (-en) complaint, refund
die Revolution (-en) revolution
das Rezept (-e) recipe, prescription
riechen to smell
richtig correct, right, proper
röntgen to X-ray
die Rose (-n) rose
der Rosenkohl brussels sprouts
rostig rusty
rot red
der Rotwein red wine
die Rückfahrt (-en) return journey
der Ruf (-e) call, reputation
rufen to call (out)
ruhig quiet, calm

die Sache (-n) thing, item
sagen to say, tell
die Sahnesoße (-n) cream sauce
die Salami salami
der Salat (-e) salad
das Salz salt
der Samstag Saturday
satt full, satisfied
sauer sour
schaffen to manage, do, make, create
schämen sich to be ashamed
der Scheibenkäse cheese in slices, sliced cheese
scheinen to seem, shine
schenken to give (as a present)
schicken to send
der Schinken (-) ham
schlafen to sleep
das Schlafzimmer (-) bedroom
schlagen to hit, beat
die Schlagsahne whipped cream, whipping cream
schlecht bad, poor
schließen to shut, close
schließlich finally, after all
das Schloß (¨-sser) lock, stately home
der Schlüssel (-) key
schmecken to taste (good)
der Schmerz (-en) pain, ache
schmutzig dirty, filthy
schneiden to cut
schnell quick, fast
schon already, even
schön nice, lovely, pretty, beautiful
schonen to spare, save
der Schrank (¨-e) cupboard, wardrobe
schrecklich terrible, awful
schreiben to write
der Schuh (-e) shoe
der Schulanfang (¨-e) start of school
die Schuld (-en) fault, debt
die Schule (-n) school
die Schüssel (-n) dish
schwach weak
der Schwager (¨-) brother-in-law
die Schwägerin (-nen) sister-in-law
schwatzen gossip, chatter
schwer heavy, serious, grave, difficult
die Schwester (-n) sister, nurse

die Schwiegertochter (") daughter-in-law
schwierig difficult, awkward
die Schwierigkeit (-en) difficulty
schwimmen to swim
sehen to see
sehnen sich (nach) to long (for)
sehr very
sein to be, his, its
seit since, for
seitdem since (then)
die Seite (-n) side, page
die Sekretärin (-nen) secretary (female)
das Sektfrühstück (-e) champagne breakfast
die Sekunde (-n) second
d. . selb. . the same
selbst -self, even
selten seldom, rarely
der Semmelknödel (-) dumpling
der September September
servieren to serve
die Show (-s) show
sicher sure, certain, reliable
sie she, her, they, them
Sie you
die Silvesterfahrt (-en) New Year('s Eve) trip
das Silvesterfestessen (-) New Year's Eve banquet
sind are
singen to sing
sinken to sink
sitzen to sit
das Skelett (-e) skeleton
das Skifahren skiing
die Skimöglichkeit (-en) opportunity for skiing, (plural) skiing facilities

so so, like this / that
so (et)was something / anything like that
so ... wie as ... as
sobald as soon
sofort immediately, straight away
der Sohn ("e) son
solch. . such
der Soldat (PO -en) soldier
sollen must, ought to, is / are to
somit therefore, thereby
der Sommer (-) summer
sondern but
der Sonderpreis (-e) special price
der Sonnabend (-e) Saturday
die Sonne sun
sonnen sich to sunbathe
der Sontag (-e) Sunday
sonst otherwise, at other times, or else
die Sorge (-n) worry, concern
sorgen (für) to see (to), take care (of)
die Sorte (-n) sort, type, kind
sowieso anyway
sparen to save
die Sparsamkeit thrift, economy
der Spaß ("e) joke, fun
viel Spaß! enjoy yourself!
(zu) spät late
später later, afterwards
spazierengehen II to go for a walk
spielen to play
der Sportler (-) sportsman
der Sportwagen (-) sports car
sprechen to speak, talk
die Sprechstundenhilfe (-n) (doctor's, receptionist, etc.)

265

springen to jump
die **Stadt (¨e)** town
der **Stadtführer (-)** town guide
stammen (von/aus) to originate (in), come (from)
stark strong
starten to start, take off
statt instead of
stattdessen instead (of that)
das **Steak (-s)** steak
stecken to be (situated), put (inside), insert
stehen to stand
stehlen to steal
steif stiff
steigen to climb
die **Stelle (-n)** place
stellen to put, place (upright)
sterben to die
im Stich lassen to leave in the lurch
stoppen to stop, halt
stören to disturb
stoßen to bump
der **Strand (¨e)** beach
die **Straße (-n)** street, road
streiten to quarrel
das **Stück (-e)** piece, item
der **Student (PO -en)** student
studieren to study
die **Stunde (-n)** hour
stundenlang for hours
suchen to look for
der **Supermarkt (¨e)** supermarket

der **Tag (-e)** day
guten Tag! hello!
die **Tageszeitung (-en)** daily (news)paper
tagsüber during the daytime

die **Tante (-n)** aunt
der **Tanz (¨e)** dance
tanzen to dance
die **Tasche (-n)** pocket
in die Tasche greifen to dip into one's pocket
das **Taschengeld** pocket money
die **Tasse (-n)** cup
der **Teilnehmer(-)** participant
das **Telefon (-e)** telephone
telefonieren to phone
die **Telefonnummer (-n)** telephone number
der **Tennis** tennis
der **Teppich (-e)** carpet
teuer dear, expensive
wie teuer? how much?
das **Theater (-)** theatre
der **Theaterplatz** Theatre Square
die **Theke (-n)** counter
die **Tiefkühltruhe (-n)** (chest) freezer
die **Tischdecke (-n)** tablecloth
die **Tochter (¨)** daughter
die **Toilette (-n)** toilet
die **Tomate (-n)** tomato
der **Ton (¨e)** sound, tone
das **Tonband (¨er)** (audio) tape
das **Tor (-e)** gate, gateway, goal
der **Tourist (PO -en)** tourist
die **Touristeninformation (-en)** tourist information office
tragen to carry, wear
treffen to meet
treiben to drive
trennen to separate
die **Treppe (-n)** stairs, staircase
treten to step, kick
trinken to drink
der **Tropfen (-)** drop
trotz in spite of

trotzdem in spite of (that), nevertheless
das **T-Shirt (-s)** T-shirt
die **Tube (-n)** tube
tun to do, put
die **Tür (-en)** door

über over, across, about
überdies besides
das **Übergewicht** excess weight
überhaupt in general, at all, altogether
überlassen I to leave
der **Überlebende** (adj) survivor
übermorgen the day after tomorrow
die **Übernachtung (-en)** overnight stay
überreden I to persuade
die **Überstunde (-n)** (plural) overtime
überweisen I to transfer
übrigens by the way, incidentally
überübermorgen the day after the day after tomorrow
die **Uhr (-en)** clock, watch, o'clock, time
um round, about, at
um . . . zu in order to, so as to
umgehen II **mit** to handle, deal with
der **Umzug** move, removal
unangenehm unpleasant, embarrassing
unbedingt absolute, really, without fail
unberechtigt unjustified
und and
die **Unruhe (-n)** disturbance, noise

uns (to/for) us
unser our
unsympathisch unpleasant, uncongenial
unten downstairs, at the bottom, below
unter under, below, beneath
unterbringen II to accommodate
die **Unterhaltung (-en)** entertainment, conversation
die **Unterkunft (-̈e)** accommodation
unterschreiben I to sign
untersuchen I to examine
unterwegs on the way
unwichtig unimportant
der **Urin** urine
der **Urlaub (-e)** holiday(s)

die **Vase (-n)** vase
der **Vater (-̈)** father
veranstalten I to arrange, put on
die **Veranstaltung (-en)** item of entertainment, event
die **Verantwortung** responsibility
der **Verbrecher (-)** criminal
verbringen I to spend (time)
die **Vereinigten Staaten** (plural) the United States
vergessen I to forget
das **Verhältnis (-se)** relationship, (plural) means, circumstances
verheiratet married
verirren I **sich** to get lost
verkaufen I to sell
verlassen I to leave
verlaufen I **sich** to get lost
verletzen I to injure, hurt
verletzen I **sich** to get hurt

verlieren I to lose
der Verlust (-e) loss
vernünftig sensible
verrückt mad, crazy
verschieden different,
various
verschulden I sich to get into
debt, go into the red
versprechen I to promise
verstehen I to understand
der Versuch (-e) attempt
versuchen I to try
vertun I sich to make a
mistake, slip up
der Verwandte (adj) relative
verzeihen I to forgive, pardon
der Vetter (-) cousin (male)
viel much, a lot
viel.. much, many
vielleicht perhaps
das Viertel (-) quarter
die Viertelstunde (-n) quarter of
an hour
voll full
vollkommen perfect
von from, of, by
vor before, in front of, ago
vorbeischauen II to look in
vorbereiten II to prepare
die Vorbereitung (-en)
preparation
vorbeugen II to avert
vorfinden II to find, discover
vorgestern the day before
yesterday
vorhaben II to intend, have
planned, have (got) on
der Vorhang (¨e) curtain
vorher before (that)
vorhin a little / short time ago
vorig.. last

vorkommen II to happen,
occur
vornehmen II to undertake
vorn at the front
vorrätig in stock, to hand
vorschießen II to advance
(money)
der Vorschlag (¨e) suggestion,
proposal
vorschlagen II to propose
der Vorschuß (¨sse) advance
vorsichtig careful, cautious
vorstellen II to introduce
vorstellen II sich to imagine

wachsen to grow
der Wagen (-) car
die Wahl (-en) choice, election
wahnsinnig crazy
während in the course of,
during, while
währenddessen during that
wahrscheinlich probably
der Wald (¨er) wood, forest
wann(?) when(?)
warm warm, hot
warten (auf) to wait (for)
warum? why?
was(?) what(?)
was = etwas
was für (ein)? what sort
of (a)?
waschen to wash
waschen sich to wash, have a
wash, get washed
das Wasser water
das Wassersystem (-e) plumbing,
water system
weg away, gone
der Weg (-e) way, path
wegen on account of,

because of
weggehen II to go away
dabei wegkommen II **(mit)** to get away (with)
wegwerfen II to throw away
weich soft
das **Weihnachten (-)** Christmas
die **Weihnachtsferien** (plural) Christmas holiday(s)
weil because
der **Wein (-e)** wine
die **Weintraube (-n)** grape
weiß white
weiß knows
das **Weißbrot (-e)** white bread / loaf
welter further
weiterdrehen II to turn on / further
welch. .(?)(!) which(?), what(?)(!)
der **Weltkrieg (-e)** world war
wem? (to / for) whom?
wen? who(m)?
wenig little
wenig. . little, few
wenigstens at least
wenn if, when, whenever
wer? who?
werden will, shall, to be going to, to become
werfen to throw
wesentlich essential, significant, substantial
wessen? whose?
der **Westen** west
das **Wetter** weather
wichtig important
widersprechen I to contradict
wie(?) how(?)

wie (bitte)? pardon?
wieder again
auf Wiedersehen! goodbye!
wieso (denn)? how's that?
wieviel? how much?
wieviele? how many?
der **Wille (PO -ns)** will
der **Winter (-)** winter
der **Winterprospekt (-e)** winter brochure
winzig tiny, minute
wir we
der **Wirt (-e)** landlord
die **Wirtin (-nen)** landlady
wissen to know (facts)
witzig funny, amusing
wo(?) where(?)
die **Woche (-n)** week
das **Wochenende (-n)** week-end
wohl well, probably, no doubt
wohnen to live, reside
die **Wohnung (-en)** flat, dwelling
der **Wohnwagen (-)** caravan
das **Wohnzimmer (-)** living room, lounge
der **Wohnzimmertisch (-e)** living-room table
wollen to want, intend
das **Wort ("er** or **-e)** word
worüber over / about which
wundern sich to be surprised
wunderschön beautiful, lovely, glorious, splendid
der **Wunsch ("e)** wish
wünschen to wish, desire
die **Wurst ("e)** sausage
der **Yoghurt (-s)** yoghurt

die **Zahl (-en)** number

zahlen to pay
zählen to count
der Zähler (-) counter
der Zahnarzt ("e) dentist
der Zehnmarkschein (-e) ten
mark note
zeigen to show
die Zeit (-en) time
vor einiger Zeit some time
ago
in letzter Zeit recently
eine Zeitlang for a time
die Zeitung (-en) newspaper
zerstören I to destroy
ziehen to pull, move
ziemlich fairly, rather, pretty
das Zimmer (-) room
zögern to hesitate
zu to, at, too
der Zucker sugar

zudem besides
zufällig by (any) chance
der Zug ("e) train, draught,
procession
zuhören II to listen
die Zündkerze (-n) spark plug
zunehmen II to put on
weight
zurück back
zusammen (al)together
der Zuschlag ("e) additional
charge, surcharge
zustehen II to be due
zwar to be sure, admittedly,
though
und zwar namely
zweimal twice
der Zwilling (-e) twin
zwischen between
das Zypern Cyprus

Index

272